STRATEGIES FOR
COMMUNICATION RESEARCH

SAGE ANNUAL REVIEWS OF COMMUNICATION RESEARCH

SERIES EDITORS

F. Gerald Kline, *University of Michigan*
Peter Clarke, *University of Michigan*

Other Books in this Series:

Volume 6

SAGE ANNUAL REVIEWS OF COMMUNICATION RESEARCH

Strategies

for

Communication

Research

PAUL M. HIRSCH,
PETER V. MILLER,
and

F. GERALD KLINE
Editors

SAGE PUBLICATIONS

Beverly Hills · London

For information address:

SAGE PUBLICATIONS, INC.
275 South Beverly Drive
Beverly Hills, California 90212

SAGE PUBLICATIONS LTD
28 Banner Street
London EC1Y 8QE

Printed in the United States of America

International Standard Book Number 0-8039-0891-1 (cloth)
International Standard Book Number 0-8039-0892-X (paper)

Library of Congress Catalog Card No. 77-088630

FIRST PRINTING

CONTENTS

To Our Families

INTRODUCTION

Paul M. Hirsch, Peter V. Miller, F. Gerald Kline

IN SELECTING THE TOPICS AND ORIGINAL ARTICLES for this sixth *Sage Annual Reviews of Communication Research,* we have chosen three areas for special attention. Each spotlights a basic concept and reviews or applies new methods for the study of social communication. Questions raised by our three topics—mass media organizations, measurement strategies, and the concept of time—are too often left unacknowledged or only implicit in research designs. This book is intended to provide each an expanded and more focused forum.

The first part, on organizational analysis, reminds us that mass communication is not produced in a vacuum. Rather, it requires the collaborative work of interdependent occupations and professions, molded into large-scale organizations. How the internal processes of these occupations and organizations operate, their relation to issues of professional autonomy and social control, and their combined impact on mass media content are among the issues discussed in this section. Paul M. Hirsch's introductory chapter sets forth an organizational perspective on mass media and considers several approaches to studying them from this standpoint. Gaye Tuchman, drawing on her field studies of newsgathering, points out the substantive and methodological payoffs of noting easily missed "exceptions" to the rule. E. Barbara Phillips contrasts social science and journalistic perspectives on objectivity in producing news, utilizing both observational and survey methods. Joseph Turow applies organizational analysis in an unusual and interesting case study of children's book publishing. William N. McPhee closes the section with an elegant mathematical model of why mass media organizations, under present conditions in the United States, may be expected to continue producing about the same types and levels of mass entertainment.

Part II emphasizes several conceptual issues inherent in decisions about data collection and modeling. Peter V. Miller proposes that new techniques, available to better analyze and interpret data, are not yet familiar enough to the communication research community. Recent advances in measurement techniques and modeling, though highly promising, still appear too complex and new to have realized their potential. His chapter reviews and describes several innovations in these areas, and urges more careful consideration of the appropriate measurement techniques for particular problems in data collection and the generation or testing of theory. Additional suggestions, and examples for obtaining more accurate answers from sample survey respondents, are provided in the article by Miller and Charles F. Cannell. The two studies which follow provide interesting applications of this line of argument by employing innovative procedures to interpret and model their data: F. Gerald Kline utilizes Coombs's theory of data in his study of cognitive communication between family members; Susan C. Greendale and, Eric S. Fredin draw on this resource also, as well as on graph theory, in their study of agenda-setting by newspapers.

The final section brings together conceptual and methodological issues concerning time as a variable. Research designs often make heroic and unstated assumptions about issues like temporal order and intervals before, after, and in between surveys or events. This has long been an issue in the philosophy of science and has clear application to nearly all communication research. Kline's introduction to this section reviews and extends several conceptualizations of time. James Danowski and Neil E. Cutler reanalyze data on political socialization by applying a model of cohort curves. Time series analysis in communication research is described and illustrated by Robert Krull and Albert S. Paulson. And last but not least, the section ends with Arundale's application and simulation of sampling methods across time for small group communication.

Each of our major topics—organizational analysis, data collection and modelling, and conceptions of time—is introduced by one of the editors at the start of its section. We believe these topics pose important issues for contemporary communication research and thank each of the contributors for helping to illuminate them.

PART I

ORGANIZATIONAL ANALYSIS AND FIELD STUDIES

OCCUPATIONAL, ORGANIZATIONAL, AND INSTITUTIONAL MODELS IN MASS MEDIA RESEARCH: TOWARD AN INTEGRATED FRAMEWORK

Paul M. Hirsch

PROLOGUE

THE STUDY OF MASS MEDIA is typically ordered around a principle of uniqueness which confuses the concepts of internal organization and institutional function. Institutionally, there are differences in the audience for (and prestige accorded) print versus broadcast journalists, and to all journalism versus (mere) entertainment. But in terms of how news and entertainment actually are produced and distributed, across media, the organizational similarities outweigh the differences. For example, both news and entertainment are forms of symbolic content created by employees to be utilized, modified, or discarded by employers whose organizations seek to earn profits or find subsidies. Under these (and other) common constraints, the creators and overseers of print and broadcast news and entertainment all share a preoccupation with organizational issues like budgets, salaries, deadlines, circulation, ratings, advertisers, and reputation. While the institutional functions served by each type differ significantly, both news and entertainment features are usually produced and distributed by the same organizations (newspapers, syndicates, broadcasting corporations) and supported by advertising (or other funding agencies). Their audiences also overlap, and both come from departments lodged in the same organizational entities. Each type of communication boasts high standards of craftsmanship, jealously guards its prerogatives against censorship, forms its own occupational community, and often complains about the same (bureaucratic)

AUTHOR'S NOTE: I wish to thank Michael Schudson for helpful comments, and the Rockefeller Foundation for supporting the research on which this chapter is based.

enemy. Interestingly, both occupational communities often accord higher honor to those members with audiences which are elite in status and small in size, such as columnists for the *New Yorker* or actors in theater rather than television. To point to these commonalities is not to suggest that either form is inherently corrupt because of its similarity to the other. Rather, it is to distinguish between the (similar) manner in which each is produced by organizations running rationally, on the one hand, and the social values placed on news versus entertainment on the other.

Against these similarities, the principle of uniqueness emphasizes distinctions between types of symbolic content. It assigns each to predesignated categories like "news" and "entertainment" and strongly asserts these are mutually exclusive, as well as internally differentiated according to which of the mass media they are created for. Generally, print is more serious; broadcasting more entertaining. These distinctions, however, derive from competing functions, interests, and professional rivalries more than from organizational differences in how each is created and distributed; and they are frequently exaggerated into ideologies and espoused by each specialty's practitioners and professional schools—of journalism versus radio and television versus theater arts, for example. Here, the categories "news," "entertainment," "print," and "broadcast" are effectively utilized to distinguish and segregate media and types of content that nevertheless remain strikingly similar in the manner that each is organized. In the university setting, analytical similarities have been downplayed, with each area more often concerned with substantive research and training students for their respective crafts and professions. In academic departments, particular slices of content or categories, across media, also are selected and predictably emphasized by researchers according to specialty—for example, election coverage by political scientists, drama and narrative form by English departments, sex role stereotypes and violence by sociologists. Studies of media audiences, economics and public policy (in marketing journals, policy institutes, and law and business schools, primarily) add useful ideas and information, though often these begin and end with very few words about the content of the particular media or industries on which they focus (see, for example, Aacker and Myers, 1975; Owen, 1975; and Noll, Peck, and McGowan, 1973).

This curious division of intellectual labor has fragmented the study of mass communication into an enormous number of fiefdoms and provinces, each with its own special interests or ideological stance. It has had the effect of inflating differences between the activities involved in producing different types of content, their meaning, and the significance of their appearance in different media. While the internal operation and institutional function of mass media organizations may be independent of each other, the ideologies of news producers and of their counterparts in entertainment have long and studiously resisted comparison, all claiming their activities are unique, in structure and mission. After a certain point, however, the respective ideologies appear short-sighted and often lead to unnecessary embarrassment, as when it is pointed out (and true but not shameful) that journalism reflects deadlines, or that much news is organizationally "manufactured," like spaghetti. Yet, perhaps because the ideology of each content group is lodged in such different settings, each continues to claim near-total uniqueness, based on those few dimensions on which it stands most apart from all the rest. What actually *is* unique about each area risks getting lost, for it is thereby merged with aspects which are not very unusual (as, for example, when the Associated Press once argued unsuccessfully for its immunity from the National Labor Relations Act, on the grounds that it had absolute and unrestricted freedom under the First Amendment to hire and fire its employees; cf. Gillmor and Barron, 1969). Such topics and issues, when improperly claimed as unique and defended as necessary for the maintenance of high standards, often become the stuff of "dirty laundry" as soon as outsiders discover and report them as such (e.g., Epstein, 1973; Altheide, 1976). The prospective loss of legitimacy, in turn, jeopardizes recognition of the important analytic distinction between the social functions served by particular symbolic content (e.g., news) and the manner in which it is produced.

This chapter is not intended to equate mass media information and entertainment content. As a field of study, however, mass communication must encompass both, and do a better job of treating the two comparatively in terms of a set of common dimensions, on some of which the two will vary. For example, utilizing recent work in industrial and organizational sociology and cutting across the different media and content categories, we can compare the administration of mass media organizations, social control of subordinates, organizational levels of authority, working conditions, organization size, uncertainty, boundary-spanning roles, and occupational communities. These and other dimensions for comparison will be incorporated in the occupational, organizational, and institutional approaches to be discussed shortly.

AN ORGANIZATIONAL PERSPECTIVE

My point of departure and basic conceptual framework is an organizational perspective on mass communication. This provides a useful counterweight to the insistence upon uniqueness asserted so often by spokesmen for particular media or types of symbolic content. It reverses the logic common to most professional schools by looking upon the people, crafts, and product as distinctive only after examining the bureaucracies in which they reside, and asking how these are similar to other organizations processing other types of tangible or intangible commodities, be they books, stock market prices, or automobilies. This perspective finds clear analytical similarities among the constraints on and organizational context in which reporters, writers, artists, actors, directors, editors, producers, publishers, executive vice presidents, and others learn and carry out activities characteristic of their respective roles, crafts and occupations. From an administrative standpoint, the symbolic content created or supervised by each is both vital to mass media organizations and produced and syndicated by many of the same entities. There also is substantial cross-ownership among the different media in which it appears. The organizational perspective thus emphasizes that since news and entertainment usually are produced and distributed through the same mass media bureaucracies, *each constitutes a mere department (or division) in large-scale organizations,* along with sales and advertising, audience and market research, printing, film processing, bookkeeping, and others. Its clear expectations are that (1) occupations and organizations engaged in the production of any symbolic content will share many characteristics in common (despite their own denials); (2) what is most distinctive about them is best understood by comparing them to occupations and organizations engaged in producing other types of products; and (3) we can learn more about how news and entertainment production differ by first inquiring into areas in which they are, in fact, similar.

As an example of the direction in which this approach leads, consider the economic concept of oligopoly. Firms in oligopolistic markets (regardless of the products or services they provide) are predicted by economists to act in similar ways regarding strategies in such areas as pricing policies, product differentiation, innovation, and wage rates. Today, the television industry, with three dominant firms (networks) acts remarkably like an oligopoly (Dominick and Pierce, 1976; Noll, Peck, and McGowan, 1973), as did the motion picture industry before it was divested of movie theaters by antitrust action and had to adapt to the advent of television (Hirsch, 1972). Like radio, it has since become more diverse in the subjects (or formats) treated, and more economically competitive. A similar relation between competition and innovation has been found in the recording industry (Peterson and Berger, 1975), and it is widely suggested that television content would become more diverse if the number of networks and channels available were to increase. Most newspapers, on the other hand, are best characterized as local monopolies, and tend to behave in the directions predicted by that economic model (Roose, 1967). As will be emphasized throughout, it is important for mass media researchers to keep in mind such nonmedia-based economic models, conditions, and contexts. The behavior of mass media organizations toward their product, mission, employees, regulatory agents, and audience cannot be explained solely by the type(s) of symbolic content (news, entertainment) which they provide, or by the personal desires of their owners and managers.

When taking the entire organization, rather than specific roles, units, or departments within it as a unit of analysis, this general perspective also offers a means of examining how professions and mass media organizations interact with audiences and agencies in their political and economic environments. It seeks to take account, for example, of the peculiar fact that significant portions of the mass media audience make few distinctions between informational, editorial, and entertainment content (Goodhardt, Ehrenberg and Collins, 1975). Nor, apparently do: political representatives conducting hearings about mass communication; mass media trade papers; many executives in media organizations; some citizens' groups in the United States; and many governments seeking to regulate print and broadcast content. When violence on television is deplored by respondents to surveys, it is violence on news broadcasts to which a majority objects (Robinson, 1972); and when American news programs seek to improve ratings, it is to more entertaining features, pacing, and attractive anchorpersons that television organizations have turned increasingly—as did many newspapers earlier, analogously, when there was greater competition in the cities where the survivors are located (Hirsch, forthcoming). Obviously, the distinction between news and entertainment content has become more complex during the last decade. As Tuchman points out (in this volume), such common distinctions as hard and soft news may derive more from internal organizational needs and bureaucratic convenience than from the nature or institutional functions of "news" itself. These types of questions, in turn, raise others about the general role of mass media in society, and the pros and cons of whatever degree of consensus is achieved by blanketing a nation with the same information and images. They call for the articulation of organizational and institutional models, in which mass media organizations *qua* organizations play a far larger role than they are usually accorded in case studies of single newsrooms, entertainment production units, or occupational communities. The intellectual roots of these questions trace back to a series of earlier, pioneering studies in precisely these latter areas, however. One of our major concerns is to explore ways to incorporate, draw on, and further develop their insights.

THREE MODELS OF MASS MEDIA ORGANIZATIONS

Three distinct models, or levels of analysis, characterize nearly all social science research on the operation of mass media. The *first* focuses on occupational roles, careers, and the interaction of mass media organizations with the individuals fulfilling them. The classic studies of gatekeeping, social control, and occupational socialization in journalism, or of conflicts between the ideals expressed by professional actors, directors, or reporters versus constraints found in the newsroom or other organizations exemplify this model. The *second* model takes the organization as a whole, and its administration, as the main object of analysis. Here, the task of coordinating the newsgathering activities of reporters and editors, or defining production requirements that affect filmmakers' decisions about scripts, casting, and the amount of running time for a finished work are more typical subjects for study. The *third* level, interorganizational and institutional analysis, examines relationships between organizations or professions and the larger societal environment in which they operate. Cross-ownership of media properties, postal rates' impact on magazine publishers' cost structures, and the derivation of news categories and journalistic traditions from the economic requirements of putting out a daily newspaper exemplify the types of issues taken up in interorganizational and institutional analyses. Like industrial sociology and social science more generally, mass communication research traditionally has focused on the individual creator/worker and his or her occupational experience. Studies taking the second or third approach have appeared more recently.

When these models are ranged on a continuum from "closed" to "open" systems, the earliest studies—of individuals and roles at the bottom of organizational hierarchies (actors, reporters)—come closest to utilizing the theoretical framework of a closed system. These take the organization in which people work as their surrounding environment. More recent examinations taking the organizations themselves, or sets of organizations as their units of analysis, encompass broader aspects of mass media environments—such as advertisers, government regulatory agencies, and audience demand factors. In so doing, they conform more to the theoretical tenets of open systems analysis by emphasizing larger units of analysis, activities on the boundaries of organizations, and external variables as primary agents of organizational change (Katz and Kahn, 1966; Hirsch, 1975a). These models, while analytically distinct, are not mutually exclusive. Rather, they work best when taken together, with each helping the others present alternative interpretations of findings or raise new questions for investigation. They are further interrelated in that the first examines how individuals work to create mass media content, while the second focuses on the organizational arrangements within which this occurs, and which corporately produce and distribute the finished product. The third is most useful for studying the cultural, economic, and political environments in which mass media and the professions comprising them act as a major social institution (albeit one among others). [1]

We will discuss and elaborate on each model in the order just presented. The attendant literature review is more illustrative than exhaustive in intent.

OCCUPATIONAL ROLES AND CAREERS

Occupational sociology, in theory, is concerned with the roles and careers of all organization members. In practice, surveys and field studies of people in occupational roles usually are confined to organizational participants of relatively low rank and status. Studies of professionals in the mass media, for example, cast light on the everyday routines and constraints felt by reporters or screenwriters far more frequently than on publishers or movie studio executives. For this reason, research about occupations, crafts, and professions—including those in journalism and entertainment—has come to be associated with the study of lower-level participants across many organizational hierarchies. This sample bias is due only in part to the personal tastes of scholarly investigators. For lower-level subordinates are typically more accessible to outsiders than their superiors (by rank). There are more of them, with fewer secrets to hide, less stake in their organizations, and possibly more interest in and time for an interviewer. In addition, however, university researchers often seem to prefer focusing studies on lower participants. For some, they are easier to control and pose fewer potential problems for the project; for others, they are simply more attractive and glamorous subjects.

Over time, an implicit difference between "occupational" and "organizational" sociology has thus developed. Each studies and "explains" its findings from the standpoint of different vertical levels in the same organization. What one subfield interprets as arbitrary or politically inspired interference and censorship, the other sees as perfectly reasonable in terms of the rationales and logic followed at the higher level of organization with which it is familiar. News media organizations' policies toward free-lance reporters provide an excellent example. News organizations are reluctant to accept controversial stories by nonstaff reporters (such as reports of the My Lai massacre in Vietnam, originally brought to the *New York Times* and other papers by Seymour Hersh, and rejected). Occupational analysts are likely to interpret this as unwarranted discrimination and editorial censorship, while the organizational analyst would more likely assert that where stories are particularly controversial, the reporters' reliability is a crucial element in the decision to print them. In such cases, staff members' credibility is generally higher than free-lancers', so the organization's policy of restricting investigative reporting to staff members and established wire or syndication services is seen as organizationally prudent, fair, and legitimate. (After his stories proved factually correct, Hersh was hired as a staff investigative reporter by the *New York Times*.). To a significant degree, occupational and organizational analyses have come to represent and argue for the contrasting standards and viewpoints embodied in their respective sets of respondents. Although there has been too little dialogue between them historically, research on mass media-based occupations and organizations has started to combine models, recently presenting a more integrated and sophisticated set of findings and interpretations.

THE GATEKEEPER TRADITION

With the publication of his classic study, "The Gatekeeper: A Case Study in the Selection of News," David Manning White (1950) began one of the most important traditions in communication research. The questions he posed include: By what criteria do editors select a small minority of stories from a far larger available universe for presentation to their publics? Are there hard and fast decision rules and, if so, are these universal? Or are individual decisions based more on subjective biases, idiosyncratic preferences, and questionable value judgments?

These questions have inspired studies in such disparate areas as journalism, entertainment, political elections, fine art, and popular culture—all of which are linked by an awareness of the surplus of potential items (news stories, screenplays, candidates for office, paintings, pop records, television series pilots) for adoption by mass media decision-makers. These share a common interest in learning what characteristics, if any, separate the losing candidates from those which make the front page, the best galleries, the academy awards, the top 40, or high Nielson ratings. As suggested in Table 1, the mass-media gatekeeper's mandate to filter out items for which there is not available space or air time occurs at several organizational levels, for virtually all types of content printed, filmed, or broadcast by the mass media. Occupational roles comparable to White's wire service editor include disc jockeys and radio station program directors, book publishers' readers and editors (discussed in Turow's article in this volume), and television network programming executives.[2] Analytically, the gatekeeping *process* is very similar across these media and occupations. Interpretations of its meaning, legitimacy, and inner workings vary substantially, however.

TABLE 1
GATEKEEPING ROLES IN THE FIELDS OF
MASS ENTERTAINMENT AND POLITICS

1. *The Artist*—provides the creative input. He is in constant demand because of the rapid turnover of product. The novelist, the politician, the playwright, and the clothing designer all exemplify the "artist."

2. *The Agent*—in service of a "producer." Agents operate in the field, linking the artist and producer. They serve as talent scouts for the book publisher. as political clubs in service of a party, as scouts for the Broadway producer, and for the clothing manufacturer.

3. *The Producer*—in the form of an entrepreneur or a corporation, supplies the capital and organization required to manufacture and/or promote the artist's product; e.g., the book publisher, political party influentials, the Broadway producer, the clothing manufacturer.

4. *The Promoters*—within the industry, are employed by the producer to create, plan for, and manage anticipated demand. Not all products at this level can be promoted with equal success. Promoters would: arrange for the book publisher's promotional parties, for the nomination of a candidate by party delegates, for the theater producer's "angels," and for fashion trade paper endorsements.

5. *The Gatekeepers*—linked by promoter to producer, they mediate between an industry and its consumers. Gatekeepers perform the crucial final filtering function of screening and selectively choosing from among the available products those which are to be publicized. The gatekeepers are mass media, e.g., book reviews, election editorials, theater reviews, coverage of new styles by fashion magazines.

6. *The Public*—votes upon and rank-orders those candidates who have successfully passed through all the previous stages of the filter, having thereby been pre-selected for the consumer to choose.

SOURCE: P. HIRSCH, "The structure of the popular music industry" (1969:7).
NOTES: 1. For authors and entertainers, the mass media often do not enter the picture until stage 5, when their performances, records or books receive (or are denied) publicity and reviews.
2. In this model, the "artist" is also the product to be processed. In terms of a comparison to journalism, the product would become the individual news story; the reporter would be the "agent" and the newspaper the "producer."

Gatekeeping by journalists has been researched more extensively and taken somewhat more seriously than gatekeeping by professionals with comparable tasks in other media fields. This reflects the larger role and institutional function of journalism in a democratic society more than it signals differences between constant categories at the production level, for a discovery that news editors' selection criteria are subject to personal bias and political pressure suggests more significant implications for public policy. Initial interpretations of editorial bias relied almost entirely on psychological explanations. As these have been supplemented by more sociological interpretations and hypotheses, the study of gatekeeping as a process has expanded to include organizational and institutional levels of analysis, in addition to the original emphases on individual traits and occupational roles. Taken together these provide complementary perspectives on the selection of mass media content.

One of the central issues raised by the gatekeeping tradition has been: How do decision-makers narrow down the glut of items competing for attention to a size manageable for the amount of space, time, or airplay available? A simple and attractive design for locating and interpreting variations in outcome and in the rationales employed is to search for individual differences among the decision-makers. Why does a news story run as a lead item in one newspaper but get buried in the back pages of a second? Or why have so many book publishers and record companies refused to sign artists whose works shortly became best-sellers for their competitors? If luck, intuition, probability theory, and, occasionally, politics leave too many unanswered questions, a search for personality differences between the individuals involved may yield additional information. Pool and Shulman (1959:156), for example, suggest that "accuracy of reporting is low on good and bad news alike when the news is incongruent with the tone of the reporter's [own] fantasies," predispositions, and stereotypes. By close analogy the same conclusion holds true for editors' selection and assignment of news stories, and comparable decisions by people in gatekeeping positions elsewhere.

Pool and Shulman also recognize, however, that professionals socialized into the norms of their occupation have learned to "distance" themselves from purely personal reactions and stereotypes. Personal tastes aside, they know how "this type" of story, or record, is supposed to read or sound. This is because mass media professionals do not work in isolation, but must meet the expectations of their organizations, occupation, and (to a less obvious extent) ultimate audience. The "subjective bias" of selection decisions can be individual, organizational, or both. Thus, the issue of accounting for decisions taken by lower-level and other gatekeepers becomes an analysis of variance—both statistical and conceptual. To what extent an employee gatekeeper can base decisions on personal rather than organizational criteria is a major question for additional research. What conditions are particularly conducive or detrimental to the exercise of personal discretion?

"Organizational logic," or the study of constraints imposed on an individual's selection decisions, enters the genre of gatekeeping studies through the work of Gieber (1956, 1964), Gans (1974), and Tuchman (in this volume), among others. The individual, occupational, and organizational components of gate-keeping are well illustrated by an analysis of White's original study of decisions by a wire service editor ("Mr. Gates"). White compared all stories from the major wire services which were rejected with those selected to appear in the newspaper, and also obtained a brief explanation for each decision from his respondent. One major result was a graphic demonstration of the extent to which gatekeeping occurs as an organizational necessity: White's "Mr. Gates" had to reject eight items for every one story there was space for in his paper's next edition.

White also coded all the items accepted or rejected into a set of common story types. Table 2 reproduces his comparison of the types and percentages of news stories received with those selected by the editor. We see that the types and proportions of news stories supplied by the wire services and the types and proportions chosen for the subscribing paper were *virtually identical.* In only three instances do the editor's choices, by category, differ more than two percentage points from the proportions sent by the wire services. From an

TABLE 2
AMOUNTS OF PRESS ASSOCIATION NEWS MR. GATES RECEIVED
AND USED DURING SEVEN-DAY PERIOD

Category	Wire Copy Received		Wire Copy Used	
	Col. In.*	*% of Total*	*Col. In.**	*% of Total*
Crime	527	4.4	41	3.2
Disaster	405	3.4	44	3.4
Political				
State	565	4.7	88	6.8
National	1,722	14.5	205	15.8
Human Interest	4,171	35.0	301	23.2
International				
Political	1,804	15.1	176	13.6
Economic	405	3.4	59	4.5
War	480	4.0	72	5.6
Labor	650	5.5	71	5.5
National				
Farm	301	2.5	78	6.0
Economic	294	2.5	43	3.3
Education	381	3.2	56	4.3
Science	205	1.7	63	4.9
Total	11,910	99.9	1,297	100.1

SOURCE: D.M. White, "The Gatekeeper: A Case Study in the Selection of News." Journalism Quarterly, 27, 4(fall, 1950).
*Counting five lines of wire copy as one column inch.

organizational standpoint, this is the important finding and invites a reinterpretation of the more general conclusion that Mr. Gates's judgments (which later proved to be representative of most wire service editors) were strongly affected by his own personal and idiosyncratic biases. More likely, this editor was exercising discretion only within the latitude permitted for selecting particular stories to fit standard, widely agreed-upon categories, in the usual (expected) proportions that characterize a medium-sized, midwestern daily with a predominantly conservative readership.

The conclusion that editors are personally "subjective" in their decisions most often receives support when choices over individual news items are studied, rather than the aggregate totals of which types of stories consistently appear across papers over long time periods. White found, for example, that some individual stories were denied space because, as Pool and Shulman suggest, they violated the editor's own sense of reality. Reasons provided for rejection in these cases included: sheer "propaganda," "don't care for suicide stories," and "b.s." But even here, White's data show that out of 1,333 explanations for why a piece was rejected, almost 800 cited lack of space and about 300 cited overlap with stories already selected, or criticized the item for poor writing or absence of journalistic interest. Another 76 rejections dealt with events in areas too far from the paper's locale to expect reader interest. As a matter of interpretative emphasis, such craft-oriented norms and criteria statistically overwhelm personal bias in terms of the explanations provided by the editor and reported by White.

My reinterpretation of White's data—suggesting that occupational, craft, and organizational norms concerning news and story categories explain more of the variance in story selection than personal bias—represents a position forcefully argued in connection with other studies by Gieber (1964), Tuchman (1972), Wright (1975), Donahue et al. (1972), and Gans (1970), among others. An important intellectual bridge between these explanatory levels and interpretations was Warren Breed's (1955) classic analysis of the occupational socialization of newspaper reporters as a study in social control.

SOCIAL CONTROL IN THE NEWSROOM AND ON THE CUTTING ROOM FLOOR

For journalism more than for any other mass-media profession, charges of subjectivity and bias raise sensitive institutional and political issues. One can discount the importance of gatekeeping for pop records or pulp novels more easily by positing their functional or aesthetic equivalence. This is a less credible perspective in the area of news reporting, however. The issue becomes especially complex when we seek to take into account the phenomenological argument that all decisions by newspeople are *inherently* subjective and political, for "objectivity" is both a fictional construction and a defensive ploy (see Phillips's chapter in this volume, and Schudson, forthcoming). The model of mass media professionals and gatekeepers as socially controlled by the subtle reward systems and political preferences of their employers is closely associated with Warren Breed's (1955) early work, and receives more recent support from studies of news and entertainment organizations and producers by Cantor (1971), Sigal (1973), Sigalman (1973), Dreier (1977), and Metz (1975), among others. This model of social control also analyzes how the apprenticeships served by mass media professionals shape their later decisions. In so doing, it is closely related to the general study of occupational recruitment and socialization for all fields, and not restricted to research on the everyday actions of mass media organizations and personnel.

Breed's study yielded several interesting findings about journalists, which should also apply to professionals creating entertainment content. First was the observation that overt confrontations hardly ever occur. This is because most news stories do not raise issues of editorial policy. Rather, they fall into preset categories (see Tuchman in this volume) and follow established writing styles and routines. In addition to their statistical rarity, Breed pointed to the interpersonal dynamics of the newsroom as containing mechanisms to reduce the reporter's dissonance between the real and ideal: the neophyte's respect for his editor's superior news judgment, authority, and technical competence; a desire to advance as a constraint against dissent; sociability and the desire for friendly informal relations; a lack of intense feelings about the issue; and time pressures imposed by tomorrow's deadlines to seek "new" stories rather than agonize over those already located.

Breed's finding that both "policy" stories and disputes over them rarely arise has been replicated often enough to become an established proposition. In fact, his original formulation—which inquired into the reasons for their rarity—led to a reposing of the question to ask: Under what organizational conditions do such conflicts arise, and why *do* newspapers vary in the number of disputes which occur over policy stories, or concerning reporters' writing in general? These, in turn, encourage an examination of mass media organizations as a whole, leading away from the study of interpersonal relations between reporters and editors, and toward the study of administration and management of the larger corporate entities for which journalists work.

THE ORGANIZATION QUA ORGANIZATION

Historically, much of the best writing about the fields of journalism and entertainment has, in effect, discovered and addressed the occasional conflicts which follow from the necessary, if forced, subordination of individuals to the organizations they work for. As Breed (1955) also noted, this leaves unexamined the "normal," more harmonious, everyday routines which constitute the rule to which dissension over policy issues is the exception. The analytical perspective taking the entire organization as its object of analysis incorporates a broader interest in (1) the roles assigned and played by its managers and executives, and

(2) the importance of organization structure as the immediate context in which mass media content is produced and role relations are played out.

Within the broader framework of an entire organization, what may look like the "absolute" power of an editor or television producer over his reporters, writers, or directors loses some of its luster. Cantor (1971) points out, for example, that while television producers exercise full authority over writers, directors, and actors concerning story lines and their execution, their decisions are all subject to veto by the television networks for which the programs are being produced. (Network representatives, in turn, will explain their decisions in terms of having to meet sponsors' wishes and a need for high ratings.) In his own eyes, the producer becomes a mere "middle man," negotiating with both his staff and client for a product acceptable to all. Elite newspaper editors are described similarly by Sigal (1973). Whereas the reporter is aware mostly of what has been blue-penciled, desk editors must seek visibility for their staffs' reporting, argue its merits, and defend it against criticism from their colleagues and superiors. Their position is analogous to the factory foreman, who must frequently mediate between the demands of superiors and reactions of subordinates. Where the occupational analyst will focus on the reporter's potential frustrations at the hands of an editor, Sigal observes that changes in management or ownership affect reporters and content far more than a change in who occupies the desk of city editor. (For an interesting illustration of this point, see Whelton's [1977] personal description of "getting bought," as the *Village Voice* changed owners twice in a four-year period.) Knowledge of such varying perspectives by role occupants at different points in the hierarchy is best tapped through studies of the entire organization.

Sigal's study (1973:18) also illustrates how organization structure alone may affect the probability of reporters' copy being heavily edited or second-guessed:

> Geography complicates action channels at the *Times* by adding a bureaucratic layer between the national desk and the Washington bureau.... In the case of national news, the intervening layer ... insulates the national desk in New York from the pressure of reporters covering Washington. This insulation probably gives rise to newsmen's perceptions of the *Times* as an "editor's paper," in contrast to the *Post,* which is seen as a "reporter's paper," When reporters work in the newsroom, as most Washington correspondents at the *Post* do, they can follow their story as it is edited. ... New York is too remote to allow this feedback at the *Times.*

Here, the variable of physical proximity overrides individuals' predispositions or personalities as explanatory of differences between two otherwise similar media organizations. Organizational analysts also look to variations in technology, goals, and market opportunities and constraints in seeking to account for potential variations in how they operate and what is produced (Perrow, 1970; Roshco, 1975).

Lawrence and Lorsch (1967) report that where manufacturing firms face uncertain and changing markets, the most successful exhibit many competing departments (e.g., sales, promotion, quality control, research, manufacturing), each cherishing its autonomy and placing little value on the contribution of the others toward realizing organizational goals. At the same time, these departments require coordination, supervision and liaison staffs in order to function smoothly together. Successful organizations in simpler market environments exhibit simpler, more centralized structures. These guidelines might well apply to the mass media, where newspapers and television stations in major cities appear more complex in structure and subject to more rapid changes than their counterparts in smaller towns.[3]

Whereas the goal of business enterprises is usually profits, news media owners and publishers often are quoted and described as pursuing other values as well, e.g., personal prestige and influence. Searching for "norms of rationality" (Thompson, 1967), the organizational analyst refuses to rule out the balance sheet as a prime motive in frequent publishers' decisions to forego "quality" journalism and investigative reporting. Circulation studies repeatedly show these do not affect sales. As more local papers become absentee-owned, the owner's continued absence leads organizational researchers to propose the profit motive and a respect for the mass readership's actual preferences (sports, comics, advertisements, and human interest pieces) as significant and sufficient explanations of the most typical newspaper formats.[4] In this view, overt political bias on the part of publishers need not be presumed as the (only) cause of editors' discouraging expensive or investigative reporting. It is likely a frequently misplaced attribution in the current climate of chain ownership. A more realistic, of sadder reason, is a combination of cost accounting and disinterest.

These considerations are important in interpreting studies of mass media organizations from the standpoint of their lower participants. During the 1976-1977 television season, for example, the commercial networks responded to advertiser pressure and scheduled virtually no new series with on-screen violence for 1977-1978. The advertisers' main reason for vetoing this type of program content was, as usual, an unwillingness to associate their products with anything "controversial." An identical reluctance has long characterized the virtual absence of sponsors (with few exceptions, and then at discounted prices) for network-prepared documentaries. These advertisers' reasons are business-based: fear of boycotts, ill will, publicity from a subset of angered viewers (Metz, 1975). At the level of organization where program ideas and story lines are conceived, however, taboos are experienced as censorship and frequently seen as politically motivated. (This example is similar to the experience of free-lance journalists seeking to place controversial news stories with major newspapers, described earlier in this chapter.) From the standpoints of management and students of these broadcasters' and advertisers' behavior, the basis appears far more related to simple economics. In fact, government-sponsored public television has been more clearly responsive than commercial networks to direct political pressure. Organizational analysis reminds us that the issue here is not whether social control exists (for it is a constant), but rather who exercises power and for what reasons.

ORGANIZATIONAL PERSPECTIVES ON THE NEWSROOM

Newspapers' newsroom operations have been studied by Gieber (1964), Sigal (1973), and Bagdikian (1971) from the standpoints of the reporter and the organizations' management as a whole. Gieber both replicated White's study of gatekeeping by a wire service editor, and confirmed Breed's observation that disputes over policy issues seldom arise. He further noted that reporters are caught up in the machinery of newsgathering and writing to such a degree that it seldom if ever occurs to many that how individual stories are covered and "played" represents and carries out earlier policy decisions. Gieber presents the newsroom as an occupational culture, with standards of professionalism that derive from the organizational machinery of deadlines, beats, and accepted writing style. In his judgment, however, the resulting standards of reporting fail to qualify as truly professional, for they have confused means with ends by abandoning the goals of telling the reader what s/he really "needs" to know and of "critically evaluating" incoming (wire service) news stories.

Sigal (1973) and Phillips (1975 and in this volume) also have studied the organization structure of newspapers, and replicated Gieber's finding of little dissatisfaction among journalists with the demands it has placed on the craft. Sigal also conceives the newspaper as a set of structural arrangements consisting of hierarchy, goals, technology, roles, and individuals. Analytically, the resultant occupational constraints, opportunities, subculture, individual failures, and superstars are derived from the organizational context in which they function. Sigal (perhaps because his elite papers were what academic researchers consider the best) arrives at conclusions far less evaluative than Gieber's, however.[5] The idea that craft traditions and occupational norms interact with and follow from the organization's bureaucratic needs is a major contribution of Gieber, Bagdikian, Sigal, Tuchman and, more recently, Phillips and Dreier.

The organization *qua* organizational model focuses attention on the whole entity as the coordinator of, and environment surrounding, mass media occupations. It seeks to predict and explain variations in internal structure, administration, and individual roles, and lies midway between our first model of occupations (primarily of lower participants) in organizations and our final model inquiring into relations among mass media organizations and their larger role as a social institution.

THE INTERORGANIZATIONAL AND INSTITUTIONAL PERSPECTIVE ON MASS MEDIA

Interorganizational and institutional analysis both call attention to the single mass media organization as but one of many competitors, suppliers, distributors, and regulators which shape, and are shaped by, a broader and complex industry system. This larger system also constitutes an important social institution, that is, a large-scale organizational complex which collectively performs an important function for the surrounding society.[6] Mass media do this by collectively producing and disseminating the symbolic content of myths, fantasy, and hard information to entire populations.

All social institutions are influenced by the political and cultural values of their societies, and also play an important part in reinforcing and, less frequently, revising them. Institutional analyses of mass media focus on (a) the (reciprocal) influence of the content transmitted on the surrounding political and cultural environment, and vice versa; and (b) economic and organizational interrelationships among the elites of mass media corporations and those at the top in other institutional sectors. While interorganizational and institutional approaches often begin by studying the structure and operations of an entire industry, the former tends to focus on describing economic and managerial relationships, while the latter places more emphasis on interpreting their political ramifications.

INTERORGANIZATIONAL RELATIONS

When mass media are viewed as organizational complexes (tentatively holding aside differences in the types of content they produce), we find that all share a common set of needs and relationships. To reach its intended audience, for example, symbolic content must be not only created in (or for) production organizations; it also must obtain distribution and arrive at some form of retail outlet (Hirsch, 1972). Historically, the most successful organizations and media have combined each of these functions, but these also often become unbundled and embodied in entirely separate organizations. Today, as Table 3 suggests, virtually no mass media organization is entirely self-sufficient in all of these areas. While newspapers combine news-gathering, writing, and manufacturing facilities, for example, most are dependent on wire and syndication services for much of the copy in every edition. Magazines depend on autonomous distributors to get each issue onto the newsstand; television networks (as distributors) require station affiliates to "retail" their product to consumers; and movie production companies, distributors, and theaters share few common organizational boundaries or ties. Each medium thus contains an aggregation of organizations whose actions affect one another, and which have developed a variety of stable traditions, understandings, and pressure points. These customs and organizational interdependencies at different processing stages form the topic area researched by students of interorganizational relations.[7]

That mass media *content* is a product of interorganizational webs and relationships often seems clearer in retrospect than at a single point in time. Earlier models of mass culture and mass society, for example, equated the magazine medium with large circulation giants like *Life* and *Look,* and defined the radio and movie media as entertainment media dominated by a few major networks and production companies, respectively (see, for example, Rosenberg and White, 1957). While this was certainly the case in the 1940s, it hardly characterized the same media twenty years later. And as their market structures and forms of interorganizational relations radically changed, so did their content. The mass journalism or entertainment produced by these media was rooted in an environment comprised of a heterogeneous audience, few competitors, and close ties between organizations in the production and distribution sectors. As all of these attributes came to characterize commercial television, the others came to resemble "class" more than "mass" media, with more segmented and homogeneous audiences, more competition, and fewer ties between producer and distributor organizations. Their editorial and entertainment content was adapted accordingly, and the greater diversity they now offer, combined with more demographically homogeneous audiences, also accounts for the decline in political and cultural controversy surrounding these media. (It, too, has followed the mass audience to television.)[8]

Some organizational and content characteristics are less sensitive to changes in market structure than others, however. News organizations or departments remain more tightly integrated than their counterparts in entertainment. Here, as we have seen, source credibility and producers' reliability are weighed carefully due to the greater institutional importance of news in American society. At the major television networks, for example, all news must be developed in-house, whereas entertainment programs are generally purchased from outside production companies.[9] Where news stories and columns are taken by newspapers from wire services and syndicators, these "outside" sources are usually acknowledged in the text, and are not even subscribed to unless most journalists have reached a consensus about their general reliability.

In terms of combining separate production and distribution operations within one or a few organizations, newspapers and news are now the most tightly integrated content and media. In the U.S., power relations are more evenly distributed among wire services, syndicators, and subscribers than among television networks, program producers, and station affiliates. The latter two, while more formally autonomous, are less free in reality to expand their client roster (for programs) or locate alternative sources of popular program fare. Where many operations occur within the same formal organization, as with newspapers, the interorganizational conflicts experienced in other media appear in the guise of interdepartmental disputes.

The syndication of newspaper copy (opinion and advice columns, comics) and broadcasts (popular show reruns, movies, some documentaries) highlights a way in which interorganizational needs and relationships transform producers' categories into distributors' commodities, or "product." Here, form comes to take precedence over content, as "liberal" and "conservative" viewpoints (in separate columns) are distributed by the same syndicates, and often appear side by side in the same newspapers. The product (a "column") is the important currency exchanged by the organizations, irrespective of its particular orientation. In this way, newspaper syndication differs little from the independent distribution of broadcast talk programs, game shows, or series reruns. A major

TABLE 3
SCHEMATIC OUTLINE OF ROLES AND ORGANIZATIONS PROCESSING SYMBOLIC CONTENT

Medium	Supply Function (Input)	Processing Function (Throughput)	Distribution and Retailing (Output)	General Description (c. 1977)
Newspapers	Wire services Syndicators Correspondents	Newsroom reporters, editors, executives; manufacturing plant, printers; distribution facilities (truck drivers)	At retail: newsstands, coin boxes, subscriptions. Distribution handled directly by processing organization	Tightly coordinated; strong in-house control over content but responsibilities delegated to trusted supplier organizations; controls its own local distribution
Television	Entertainment production companies; Independent syndicators	TV Networks; Leased telephone lines (transmission)	At retail: local affiliates; independent stations	Dominated by the major networks. Suppliers and station affiliates vulnerable to nonrenewal of lucrative contracts. Where independent stations buy programs directly, there is no processing organization.
Movies	Production companies; Independent producers; directors; actors	Movie studios and distributors	Movie theaters, television, and cable television	Highly fragmented in re locus of control; many aspects negotiated on a case-by-case basis. Strong mutual distrust between sectors. (At earlier period, resembled television's current structure.)

Radio	Phonograph records; Syndicated features	Small staff, mainly for programming and local sales	None; local stations all received directly by consumers	Simplest organization system included here. Few national (network) interconnections; national formats tailored to local markets. Present organization of radio and newspapers makes them the most accessible and locally responsive mass media.
Magazines	Free-lance writers	Staff writers; editors; management	Mail subscriptions; distributors	National magazines highly dependent on distributor organizations; access to newsstands growing in importance as postal rates increase.
Book publishers	Authors	Editors; management	Distributors; retail stores; book clubs	Dependent on editors (for books), distributors (for placement at retail), and mass media for reviews and publicity. Promotion and distribution are key factors for trade book divisions.

reason for both is the reduction in costs permitted by the economies of scale involved. The resulting standardization of content—most localities receive the same programs and columns—is peculiarly democratic: the most "popular" columns or programs are featured, more so because to do so is economically rational than because they reflect the political or cultural preferences of media owners.

That this all occurs within legally sanctioned monopolistic (for newspapers) and oligopolistic (for television) market structures is also important to recall. It is in this economic context, for example, rather than because it broadcasts television programs, that the ABC network's introduction of new programming concepts like Monday-night sports, Olympics coverage, more youth-oriented and violent entertainment, and some tough investigative reporting, is best interpreted. In economic terms, it was as the poorest performer with the most to gain in a tight oligopoly that it undertook innovative documentaries and programming risks. That its product was communication and not widgets loses significance insofar as economic theory would expect firms in a comparable position in any industry to follow the same course (Scherer, 1970; Stigler, 1968).

One area in which interorganizational relations in mass media industries are distinctive is the extent to which formal vertical integration is considered unethical, or has been made formally illegal. Movie studios are barred from owning movie theaters; television networks forbidden to own cable television operations, program syndication services, or more than seven television stations; program producers are required to announce donations or payments from businessmen for using or naming their products on the air; and so forth. Much as newspaper editors filter the output of wire services, the legal separation of mass media production from distribution creates a large class of *organizational gatekeepers*. Radio station program directors, book review editors, talk show staffs, and other professionals who select the copy and programming for their organizations act as gatekeepers who filter the output of production organizations like record companies, book publishers, and filmmakers (Hirsch, 1969, 1972, 1975b). The latter seek to coopt them to feature their productions, for they cannot legally control which ones will be selected for coverage. Their inability to control this aspect of the distribution process provides mass media gatekeepers with substantial power over them, and sets up a situation in which periodic scandals over the latter's efforts to buy influence through forms of "payola" should be expected.[10] One reason for their persistence is the frequent inability of gatekeepers of both news and entertainment to pinpoint exactly which, if any, aspects of most individual news stories, popular records, or television shows account for their appeal to large audiences. And to the extent that "one is as good as another," there is added incentive for public relations departments and promoters to seek influence over decisions taken in gatekeeping organizations.

INSTITUTIONAL ANALYSIS

Interorganizational relations remain basically stable and avoid serious disruption so long as the external environment they share also cooperates. To maintain favorable conditions, or seek changes in those viewed as harmful, industry-wide trade associations lobby in Washington and keep a watchful eye on political developments relevant to their members' financial health or internal operation. The institutional role and relation of the mass media to other sectors of American society are well illustrated by the topics on which officials of the American Newspaper Publishers Association, National Association of Broadcasters, National Cable Television Association, and other groups testify before congressional committees, work to have legislation passed, or take to the courts on appeal.

Consider the issues of postal rates, mergers, copyright and tax law, television programming, and cable television. Each has the power to restructure the mass media industries it affects, even though it may seem (and is) far removed from the media organization's day-to-day operations. As a general rule, in fact, the farther away they are from the activities of its lower level participants, the more likely these issues are to be studied by lawyers and economists than by social scientists, for whose research they also have important implications. Mergers among newspapers, and their chain ownership, for example, often are attributed to American tax law, which makes it extraordinarily costly for families which own a newspaper to maintain outright control beyond two generations. Additionally, without the successful passage of the Failing Newspaper Act in the late 1960s, many recent newspaper mergers would probably be in violation of antitrust laws. For the magazine industry, the societal decision to trade off postal subsidies for a more balanced budget has meant sharp rises in costs for those with a small percentage of newsstand sales, and hastened the demise of several with the largest general circulation. An additional potential effect is a decline in the number of prospective small magazines of opinion, such as the *Nation* or *National Review,* and smaller circulations for those remaining, as subscription costs rise to meet postal rate increases.

Copyright law involves major stakes for authors and publishers, composers, television broadcasters, and cable TV operators. The transcript of speakers before congressional committees on this topic consistently reads like a *Who's Who* in the arts and mass media. It is on the topics of television violence and advertising that interest groups *outside* the industries affected directly are most likely to appear and be heard. (Earlier, when protesters were not awarded legal standing before the Federal Communications Commission, they were of far less political significance. It is not that protests of broadcast content are new, but rather the FCC's recent reaction which has made them a significant factor for the major networks to take into account.) Once the commerical networks agreed to institute a "family hour" featuring less sex and violence during the early evening hours, some television writers and producers litigated against the resultant restrictions on story lines and won a court ruling against their acceptability (as a matter of law rather than on the basis of the networks' own business or professional judgment).

Government policy towards mass media technologies—ranging from telecommunications satellites and cable TV networks, to allocating the broadcast spectrum for VHF and UHF television channels, citizens' band radio, and other uses—also impacts on the content produced for and distributed by these media channels and agencies. If all television stations had been assigned UHF frequencies during the early 1950s, for example, most major cities would have had more channels in operation earlier, sets could have been equipped to receive UHF signals better, and the amount and diversity of available programs might have been greater (Bagdikian, 1971; Kittross, 1960; Metz, 1975). Such "procedural" decisions by the Federal Communications Commission often exert indirect effects on content. A 1966 ruling forbidding AM and FM radio stations to broadcast the same programs throughout the day in cities of over 100,000 led to a search for successful new FM formats and audiences. One genre developed was the progressive rock music format, which featured recordings with music and lyrics previously passed over by AM radio "Top 40" stations (Hirsch, 1969; Denisoff, 1975). Within a short time, the FCC—apparently unaware of the correlation between its own ruling (to promote greater diversity) and the rise of a radical new format—issued a reminder to licensees to pay stricter attention to the content of records selected for air-play. Similarly, government regulatory policies toward cable television, regarding its legal status, access to programs, and public access to it, have long been affecting its growth rate and efforts to promote the new technology in urban and rural markets.[11]

Government agencies are not the only organizations whose policies have a substantial, albeit indirect, impact on mass media content. American movie scripts, for example, are commissioned and cast with an eye on financing and on distribution far beyond domestic movie theater box offices. Up to 50% of their gross receipts come from international sales; hence some producers seek to create films which will appeal to a worldwide audience, rather than "just" to the largest possible cross-section of Americans. Additionally, many films attain their largest audiences only after being rented or sold to television. Some movies are therefore produced in several versions: for distribution to American theaters, to television stations or networks, and to the world market. When producers seek financing, all of these are considered by both parties to any agreements signed.

Relations between advertisers and newspapers have affected not only editorial policies (this is studied quite often at the local level), but also the number of newspapers in a single city. Bagdikian (1971) notes that advertisters frown on the economic inefficiency entailed in having to place the same ad in several newspapers competing in the same city. A newspaper losing circulation may find advertising linage disappearing faster than the percentage drop in readers alone would warrant. If it ceases publication or merges, the advertisers' cost for reaching about the same number of readers decreases, even if the sole survivor raises (but does not double) its rates. Just as columns of opinion may be syndicated irrespective of the opinion contained, such advertising decisions, even though they determine the fate of newspapers, are usually based on circulation figures alone. This obviously has both direct and indirect effects on newspapers' availability and content.[12]

DIVERGENT INTERPRETATIONS

What are some of the other cultural and political consequences of these interorganizational relations, and their importance for our understanding of mass media as a social institution? On several points, there is a broad consensus among diverse sociologists (and others) employing functional analysis. For example, Breed (1958), Warner (1959), Phillips (1975), and Marcuse (1964) all conceive mass media as providing standardized, patterned rituals, with whose forms audiences are familiar and for which there are common expectations. Also, for mass newspapers and commercial television especially, mass media provide news, advertising, and entertainment content carefully designed so that every member of society can understand and participate in it. To the extent that certain media no longer fit this description, being "targeted" to segmented, homogeneous audiences (radio formats, special-interest magazines), then they no longer fulfill the functions classically attributed to mass media.

However, after agreeing that mass media function in this way in modern, capitalist, industrial societies, institutional analysts offer divergent interpretations of the social value of having these functions performed at all. Historically, the entertainment content of mass culture has been more widely debated than news or advertising, although the issues raised in connection with any one usually apply to the others as well. Debates over popular books, movies and broadcasting have been sparked by critics and advocates of catering to or manipulating mass taste, "engineering" a cultural consensus, or maintaining local diversity versus endorsing our technological capacity to create national markets for all types of products, including information and entertainment (Hirsch, 1977; Gans, 1974). More recently, the cultural politics surrounding mass entertainment have intensified, with large-scale exchanges and concern arising over the growth of pornography, violence in films and on television, and television's effects on children. (See McPhee's interesting model of mass entertainment producers in this volume.)

These have inspired more research on, and discussion of the very categories and aesthetic elements employed by entertainment producers but long taken for granted and, hence, seldom examined (see especially Gerbner, 1972; and Gerbner and Gross, 1976). Quantitative content analysis of slices of content (e.g., how many violent acts, or racial stereotypes) challenge and spotlight previously unarticulated assumptions about audiences, fantasy, and meaning held at the production level of entertainment-creating organizations. While many producers protest these analyses as misguided or out of context, they afford a rare opportunity for researchers to link occupational, organizational and institutional nexes and cross-pressures. Additional and related research opportunities abound for analysts of the prospective "deep" versus surface content of news and entertainment, and for considerations of whether popular culture is a meaningful cultural activity, merely a leisure time pursuit, or both.[13]

These developments in research on entertainment content and producers are closely paralleled in the fields of print and broadcast news. Much as Cantor's (1971) organizational analysis of television entertainment producers is related to the studies by Sigal (1973), Diamond (1975), and Breed (1955) of social control in the newsroom, Gerbner's strategy of interpreting television entertainment in terms of social science rather than producers' categories is paralleled by Tuchman's analysis (in this book) of newswriting and newsgathering. More than for producers of entertainment, the study of news categories touches on the legitimacy claims of the profession employing them. Modern journalism bases much of its claim to rewards and special privileges from society on the fairness and accuracy of its reporting. Earlier I noted that while news differs little from entertainment in how it is organized and coordinated at the production level, its institutional function and the attendant expectations differ markedly. Since news is defined by its practitioners and audience both as the more serious of the two, public awareness of the "tricks of the trade," and varying interpretations of their potential meaning by politicians or social scientists, pose a far greater potential threat to journalism's claims to legitimacy (cf. Phillip's chapter). As with the functions of mass media in general, sociological and cultural interpretations of objective journalism often agree as to its social role, but not on its social value. Phillips, Warner, and Breed contend it contributes by helping to set out and define a nation's common culture; Tuchman, Marcuse, Schiller, and others propose it (like all mass media) only distracts audiences from a truer reality; James W. Carey (1969) and Michael Robinson (1975) believe much of the institutional impact of objective journalism has been to disrupt and threaten widespread consensus.

These agreements and divergent interpretations of the very categories taken for granted by mass media professionals can promote increasing linkages between researchers employing the occupational model reviewed earlier and those engaged in institutional and content analysis. Research combining the levels of analysis each represents can better decompose the idea of biased reporting into the "professional bias" of the norms of journalism (cf. Gieber, 1964, on the use of denotive rather than evaluative symbols), and the personal bias of reporters or editors. The "personal bias" component of any analysis should now consist of the residual of what is left after accounting for the limits set by professional norms on how stories might best be covered. These norms, in turn, are seen by the organizational analyst as largely molded by the organizational constraints on, and bureaucratic convenience mandated by, mass media organizations (Molotch and Lester, 1974).

SUMMARY

In comparing occupational, organizational, and institutional models of mass media, I have suggested several commonalities among them, and proposed that they be linked more closely in empirical studies as well as in theories of mass communication. The organizational perspective underlying each analytical approach rejects the principle of uniqueness commonly held by practitioners. It sees clear similarities between news and entertainment forms, across media and in the manner they are organizationally produced.

We began by focusing attention on similarities in the roles and bureaucratic constraints found at the production level, across categories. This decreases the number of surface differences, and treats only the remaining "unexplained variance" as casting light on characteristics and attributes distinguishing the categories news, entertainment, print, and broadcast from each other. In presenting the three models side by side, I have noted places where each complements the others and thus increases our confidence in causal attributions when they appear in empirical studies. For example, before occupational analysts conclude that editors exercise near-absolute power over reporters' copy, the organization *qua* organization model insists they inquire to see how much discretion the editor is accorded by his or her *own* superiors in the organizational hierarchy. In relating studies of lower-level mass media participants to interorganizational and institutional research, and in linking the media content they produce and the corporations they work for to the surrounding societal environment, I have suggested these topics and levels of analysis are interdependent and will profit from further steps toward conceptual integration.

Occupational, organizational, and institutional models treat, in rough order, individuals in roles, occupational careers, organizational contexts, hierarchies, technologies and markets, interorganizational relations, and institutional roles and ramifications. In social science terms, these perspectives follow a continuum from closed to open systems analysis, and encompass substantive studies across specific topic areas and categories. Each model also was discussed (and sometimes evaluated) from the standpoint of the others. While each has an intellectual history of its own, all share a strong and common interest in linking the study of mass media occupations, organizations, and the societal conditions in which they operate. This chapter represents an effort to delineate their similarities and differences, dismantle unnecessary barriers between them, and point out frontier problems for organizational research.

NOTES

1. For an application of these categories to arts organizations, see DiMaggio and Hirsch, 1976.

2. In addition to the research on occupations in organizations discussed shortly, studies of importance also include: Alley (1977) and Miller and Rhodes (1964), on television

entertainment; Argyris (1974), Cater (1959), Cohen (1963), Donahue (1967), Eliot (1972), Johnstone et al. (1976), Rivers (1965), Rosten (1973), Tunstall (1974), and Warner (1971), on print or broadcast journalism; Peterson and Berger (1971) and Rosenblum (in press), on record producers and photographers, respectively; and Eliot (1977) and Riley and Riley (1959), on all mass media occupations at the production level.

3. American radio stations require few staff members and exhibit less variance by size of city. Newspapers and television stations in major cities may also be more complex organizationally simply because they are larger than the typical media organization in smaller cities. In addition to the organizational analyses discussed shortly, studies of importance also include: Johnstone (1976) and Talese (1969), on newspapers; and Brown (1971) and Lourenco and Glidewell (1975), on television.

4. A long-standing enmity between editorial and advertising or market research departments stems from the former's desire to give readers what they *need,* versus the latter's commitment to finding out what they actually *want.* Occupational studies' application of reference group theory to journalists and actors suggests that they see their "real" audiences as colleagues and peers rather than a mass audience of readers or viewers. However, these often stop short of also noting the limits to which creators may be permitted to actually "play" to these intended audiences. For small-town newspapers, Bowers (1967) reported direct interference by publishers in the decisions made by the editorial staff.

5. As a matter of logic, if all editors arrived at identical decisions—even the "right" ones—it is far from clear that this would be desirable from a public policy standpoint. As Pool and Shulman (1959) also suggest, such a prospect provides small likelihood of resolving the issue of biased reporting. Presently, where divergence is found, researchers infer distortion of the "true" account by one or more of the reports published; yet, if they were all the same, the resulting uniformity would very likely be experienced and described as oppressive. In the belief that divergence in opinion and reporting generally operates to the common good, American courts have chosen to permit high variance in editorial decisions and discretion, thus electing to take the good with the bad.

6. For example, business organizations collectively produce material goods and services, and educational organizations transmit knowledge, inculcate skills, and prepare young people for future jobs.

7. The division of activities into production, distribution, and retailing is further elaborated by Owen (1975). An excellent introduction to interorganizational relations is Evan (1976). Studies of the mass media which incorporate this perspective include: Brown (1968), DeFleur and Ball-Rokeach (1975), Hirsch (1969 and 1971), and Peterson and Berger (1972).

8. It is for this reason, for example, that the Nixon administration was so disturbed by CBS News' broadcasts about the Watergate scandal, which it was then trying to contain (Porter, 1976; Halberstam, 1976; Agnew, 1969). For until then, only the geographically and politically isolated *Washington Post* was according the story serious attention. CBS, however, was broadcasting it to a heterogeneous, nationwide audience. For further discussions of changes in magazines and radio, see Welles (1971) and Peterson (1964), on magazines; and Honan (1967) and Hirsch (1969), on radio.

9. Even for entertainment programs, however, a "track record" of earlier successes is sought. This provides networks more confidence that programs will be brought in on time, produced well, and appeal to their audiences.

10. This behavior would be subject to less scandal (and at one time was considered far more legitimate) if public opinion was not offended by practices like reporters' sources also buying them gifts and paying travel expenses, or record companies' artificially determining which songs were selected for radio station air-play.

11. These issues have been covered extensively by the press and in professional journals. See, for example, Schorr (1976), MacAvoy (1977), and Crandall (1974).

12. Such developments, in turn, affect the communities in whose geographical boundaries newspapers and broadcast media operate. On the relation between mass media and local communities, see Donahue, et al. (forthcoming), Tichenor, et al. (1976), and Janowitz (1967).

13. Several interesting volumes touching on this topic are Newcomb (1974), Cawelti (1976), Newcomb (1976), Sahlins (1976), and Arens and Montague (1976). See also Carey (1977).

REFERENCES

AACKER, D., and MYERS, J. (1975). Advertising management. Englewood Cliffs, N.J.: Prentice-Hall.

AGNEW, S. (1969). "Speech on television news bias." Pp. 195-204 in W. Hammel (ed.), The popular arts in America. New York: Harcourt Brace Jovanovich.

ALLEY, R. (1977). Television: Ethics for hire? Nashville: Abington.

ALTHEIDE, D. (1976). Creating Reality: How TV news distorts events. Beverly Hills, Calif. Sage.

ARENS, W., and MONTAGUE, S. (eds., 1976). The American dimension. Port Washington, N.Y.: Alfred Publishing.

ARGYRIS, C. (1974). Behind the front page. San Francisco: Jossey-Bass.

BAGDIKIAN, B. (1971). The information machines. New York: Harper and Row.

BLUMLER, J. (1969). "Producers' attitudes towards television coverage of an election campaign: A case study." Sociological Review, 13:85-116.

BOWERS, D.R. (1967). "A report on activity by publishers in directing newsroom decisions." Journalism Quarterly, 44(spring):43-52.

BREED, W. (1958). "Mass communication and social integration." Social Forces, 37:109-116.

——— (1955). "Social control in the newsroom." Social Forces, 33:326-335.

BROWN, L. (1971). Television: The Business behind the box. New York: Harcourt Brace Jovanovich.

BROWN, R. (1968). "The creative process in the popular arts." International Social Science Journal, 20(4):613-624.

CANTOR, M. (1971). The Hollywood television producer. New York: Basic Books.

CAREY, J.W. (1977). "Mass communication research and cultural studies." In J. Curran, M. Gurevitch, and H. Woollacott (eds.), Mass communication and society. London: Edward Arnold Ltd.

——— (1969). "The communications revolution and the professional communicator." Sociological Review, 13:23-38.

CATER, D. (1959). The fourth branch of government. Boston: Houghton Mifflin.

CAWELTI, J. (1976). Adventure, mystery, and romance. Chicago: University of Chicago Press.

COHEN, B. (1963). The press and foreign policy. Princeton, N.J.: Princeton University Press.

CRANDALL, R. (1974). "The profitability of cable television: An examiniation of acquisition prices." Journal of Business, 47, 4(October):543-563.

CROUSE, T. (1973). The boys on the bus. New York: Random House.

DeFLEUR, M., and BALL-ROKEACH, S. (1975). Theories of mass communication (3rd ed.). New York: David McKay.

DENISOFF, R.S. (1975). Solid gold: The popular record industry. New Brunswick, N.J.: Transaction Books.

DIAMOND, E. (1975). The tin kazoo. Cambridge, Mass.: MIT Press.

DIMAGGIO, P., and HIRSCH, P. (1976). "Production organizations in the arts." American Behavioral Scientist, 19, 6(August):735-752.

DOMINICK, J., and PIERCE, M. (1976). "Trends in network prime-time programming, 1953-1974." Journal of Communication, 26(winter): 70-80.

DONAHUE, G., TICHENOR, P., and OLIEN, C. (1972). "Gatekeeping: Mass Media systems and information control." Pp. 41-69 in F.G. Kline and P.J. Tichenor (eds.), Current perspectives in mass communication research. Beverly Hills, Calif.: Sage.

––– (forthcoming). Communication, policy and community decisions. Beverly Hills, Calif.: Sage.

DONAHUE, L. (1967). "Newspaper gatekeepers and forces in the news channel." Public Opinion Quarterly, 31(spring):61-68.

DREIER, P. (1977). The urban press in transition: The political economy of newswork. Unpublished doctoral dissertation. University of Chicago, Department of Sociology.

ELIOT, P. (1977). "Media organizations and occupations: An overview." In J. Curran, M. Gurevitch, and J. Woollacott (eds.), Mass communication and society. London: Edward Arnold Ltd.

––– (1972). "The making of a television series: A case study in the sociology of culture. London: Constable.

EPSTEIN, E.J. (1973). News from nowhere. New York: Random House.

EVAN, W. (ed., 1976). Interorganizational relations. Baltimore: Penguin.

GANS, H. (1974). Popular culture and high culture. New York: Basic Books.

––– (1970). "How well does television cover the news?" New York Times Magazine, January 11:30-45.

––– (1957). "The creator-audience relationship in movie-making." In B. Rosenberg and D.M. White (eds.), Mass culture. Glencoe, Ill.: Free Press.

GERBNER, G. (1972). "Violence in television drama: trends and symbolic functions. In E. Rubinstein, G. Comstock and J. Murray (eds.) Television and social behavior, vol. 1. Rockville, Md.: National Institute of Mental Health.

GERBNER, G., and GROSS, L. (1976). "Living with television: The violence profiles." Journal of Communication, 26: 172-199.

GIEBER, W. (1964). "News is what newspapermen make it." In L. Dexter and D.M. White (eds.), People, society, and mass communication. Glencoe, Ill.: Free Press.

––– (1956). "Across the desk: A Study of 16 telegraph editors." Journalism Quarterly, 43(fall): 423-432.

GILLMOR, D., and BARRON, J. (1969). Mass communication law: Cases and comment. St. Paul, Minn.: West.

GOODHARDT, G.J., EHRENBERG, A.S.C., and COLLINS, M.A. (1975). The television audience. Lexington, Mass.: Lexington Books.

HALBERSTAM, D. (1976). "CBS: The power and the profits" (parts 1 and 2). Atlantic, (January and February):33-71 and 52-91.

HIRSCH, P. (forthcoming). "Television as a national medium: Its cultural and political role in American society." In D. Street (ed.), Handbook of urban life. San Francisco: Jossey-Bass.

––– (1977). "Public policy toward television: Mass media and education in American society. School Review, 85, 4(August).

––– (1975a). "Organizational analysis and industrial sociology: An instance of cultural lag." American Sociologist, 10, 1(February): 1-10.

––– (1975b). "Organizational effectiveness and the institutional environment." Administrative Science Quarterly, 20, 4(September): 327-344.

––– (1972). "Processing fads and fashions: An organization-set analysis of cultural industry systems." American Journal of Sociology, 77, 4(January):639-659.

––– (1971). "Sociological approaches to the pop music phenomenon." American Behavioral Scientist, 14, 3(January): 371-388.

––– (1969). The structure of the popular music industry. Ann Arbor: University of Michigan Survey Research Center.

HONAN, W. (1967). "The new sound of radio." New York Times Magazine, December 3:56-76.

JANOWITZ, M. (1967). The community press in an urban setting (2nd ed.). Chicago: University of Chicago Press.

JOHNSTONE, J. (1976). "Organizational constraints on newswork." Journalism Quarterly, 53(1):5-13.

––– SLAWSKI, E., and BOWMAN, W. (1976). The news people: A sociological portrait of American journalists and their work. Urbana: University of Illinois Press.

KATZ, D., and KAHN, R. (1966). The social psychology of organizations. New York: John Wiley.

KITTROSS, J. (1960). Television frequency allocation policy in the United States. Unpublished doctoral dissertation. University of Illinois.

LAWRENCE, P., and LORSCH, J. (1967). Organization and environment. Cambridge, Mass.: Harvard University Graduate School of Business Administration.

LEUBSDORF, C. (1976). "Comment on campaign coverage." Columbia Journalism Review, (March-April):6-8.

LOURENCO, S., and GLIDEWELL, J. (1975). "A dialectical analysis of organizational conflict." Administrative Science Quarterly, 20:489-508.

MacAVOY, P. (ed., 1977). Deregulation of cable television. Washington, D.C.. American Enterprise Institute.

MARCUSE, H. (1964). One dimensional man. Boston: Beacon.

METZ, R. (1975). CBS: Reflections in a bloodshot eye. New York: Playboy Press.

MILLER, M., and RHODES, E. (1964). Only you Dick Darling. New York: William Sloane Associates.

MOLOTCH, H., and LESTER, M. (1974). "News as purposive behavior." American Sociological Review, 39:101-112.

NEWCOMB, H. (ed., 1976). Television: The critical view. New York: Oxford University Press.

––– (1974). TV: The most popular art. New York: Doubleday Anchor.

NOLL, R., PECK, M. and McGOWAN, J. (1973). Economic aspects of television regulation. Washington, D.C.: Brookings Institution.

OWEN, B. (1975). Economics and freedom of expression. Cambridge: Ballinger.

PERROW, C. (1970). Organizational analysis: A sociological view. Belmont, Calif.: Brooks/Cole.

PETERSON, R., and BERGER, D. (1975). "Cycles in symbol production: The case of popular music." American Sociological Review, 40:158-173.

––– (1972). "Three eras in the manufacture of popular music lyrics." In R. Peterson and R. Denisoff (eds.), The sounds of social change. Chicago: Rand-McNally.

––– (1971). "Entrepreneurship in organizations: Evidence from the popular music industry." Administrative Science Quarterly, 16:97-106.

PETERSON, T. (1964). Magazines in the 20th century. Urbana: University of Illinois Press.

PHILLIPS, E.B. (1975). The artists of everyday life: Journalists, their craft, and their consciousness. Unpublished doctoral dissertation. Syracuse University.

POOL, I., and SHULMAN, I. (1959). "Newsmen's fantasies, audiences, and newswriting." Public Opinion Quarterly, 23:145-158.

RILEY, J., and RILEY, M. (1959). "Mass communication and the social system." In R. Merton, L. Broom, and L. Cottrell, Jr. (eds.), Sociology today. New York: Harper and Row.

RIVERS, W. (1965). The opinion makers. Boston: Beacon.

ROBINSON, J. (1972). "Mass communication and information diffusion." In F.G. Kline and P. Tichenor (eds.), Current perspectives in mass communication research. Beverly Hills, Calif.: Sage.

ROBINSON, M. (1975). "American political legitimacy in an era of electronic journalism: Reflections on the evening news." In D. Cater and R. Alder (eds.), Television as a social force: new approaches to TV criticism. New York: Praeger.

ROOSE, J. (1967). "Daily newspapers, monopolistic competition, and economies of scale." American Economic Review, 57, 2(May):522-533.

ROSENBERG, B., and WHITE, D.M. (eds., 1957). Mass culture. Glencoe, Ill.: Free Press.

ROSENBLUM, B. (forthcoming). "Style as social process." American Sociological Review.

ROSHCO, B. (1975). Newsmaking. Chicago: University of Chicago Press.

ROSTEN, L. (1937). The Washington correspondents. New York: Harcourt Brace.

SAHLINS, M. (1976). Culture and practical reason. Chicago: University of Chicago Press.

SCHERER, F.M. (1970). Industrial market structure and economic performance. Chicago: Rand McNally.

SCHORR, B. (1976). "Television's scrambled signals." Wall Street Journal (June 29).

SCHUDSON, M. (forthcoming). A social history of American journalism. New York: Basic Books.

SIGAL, L. (1973). Reporters and officials. Lexington, Mass.: D.C. Heath.

SIGALMAN, L. (1973). "Reporting the news: An organizational analysis." American Journal of Sociology, 79(July):132-151.

STIGLER, G. (1968). The organization of industry. Homewood, Ill.: Irwin.

TALESE, G. (1969). The kingdom and the power. Cleveland: World.

THOMPSON, J. (1967). Organizations in action. New York: McGraw-Hill.

TICHENOR, P., NNAEMEKA, T., and DONAHUE, G. (1976). "Community pluralism and perceptions of television content." Paper presented at Association for Education in Journalism annual meetings.

TUCHMAN, G. (1972). "Objectivity as strategic ritual: An examination of newsmen's notions of objectivity." American Journal of Sociology, 77(January):660-679.

TUNSTALL, J. (1974). Journalists at work. Beverly Hills, Calif.: Sage.

WARNER, L. (1959). The living and the dead. New Haven: Yale University Press.

WARNER, M. (1971). "Organizational context and control of policy in the television newsroom: A participant observation study." British Journal of Sociology, 22, 3(September):283-294.

WELLES, C. (1977). "Can mass magazines survive?" Columbia Journalism Review, (July-August):7-14.

WHELTON, C. (1977). "Getting bought: Notes from the overground." Village Voice, (May 2):51.

WHITE, D.M. (1950). "The gatekeeper: A case study in the selection of news." Journalism Quarterly 27, 4(fall):383-390.

WRIGHT, C. (1975). Mass communication: A sociological perspective (2nd ed.). New York: Random House.

Chapter 2

THE EXCEPTION PROVES THE RULE:
THE STUDY OF ROUTINE NEWS PRACTICES

Gaye Tuchman

FOLK WISDOM PROCLAIMS, "The exception proves the rule." This common saying may be understood to have both popular and scientific meanings. An unusual circumstance highlights the ordinary and expected by providing a contrast. Read as a statement about methods in the social sciences, the folk saying stresses the importance of variation to the generation of social science laws. Especially for those using statistical methods, only the examination of variegated or contrasting categories can lead to generalizations about social order. Validating folk wisdom, Lipset, Trow and Coleman (1956) suggest a use of exceptions by qualitatively inclined researchers. By examining the structure and processes of an exceptional case, one may learn about the customary situation: Lipset et al. study a democratic union to learn why most unions are not democratic.

This article offers an additional use of the rule-proving exception. It assumes that important components of organizational routines are necessarily hidden from the sociological observer. For routines are built upon understood and frequently unexpressed knowledge of organizational structure, ideologies and power. Sometimes that knowledge is ineluctable. Participants in an organization may take that knowledge so much for granted they cannot express it succinctly. Or, knowledge may be so embedded in routines that it is hidden from their view. Exceptions enable the observer to perceive and so to examine hidden structures, ideologies, and powers.

AUTHOR'S NOTE: This paper was prepared through a planning grant, "Making News: An Exploratory Study," from the Russell Sage Foundation. I benefited from the editorial comments of Paul Hirsch and Robert Kapsis.

For the past few decades, this fundamental insight has been important to the sociological study of mistakes at work (cf. Hughes,1964, Light,1972, Stelling and Bucher,1973). Recently, Molotch and Lester (1974) have expanded this idea to the study of political power. They suggest that news routinely promotes occurrences that those with institutionalized power define as public events. It structurally blocks occurrences and information inimicable to those with power. "Only by the accident and the scandal"—the exceptions—"is that political work transcended, allowing access to other information and thus to a basis for practical action . . . directly hostile to those groups who typically manage the political state."[1] By studying how accidents and scandals are made into routine events, Molotch and Lester (1975) suggest, one may study the processes of political power. To take an example still unfolding when they published these articles, the Watergate scandal was transformed from an accidentally uncovered and illegal occurrence to a lesson in democracy. First viewed as an illustration of corruption and the abuse of power, it was later interpreted as proof that the news media, courts, and Congress protect the integrity of the American system of government.

Molotch and Lester's work emphasizes the importance of routines in constituting the everyday world, including the world called "news." Incorporating Garfinkel's (1967) analysis of a clinic's accounts of suicides as a "bad record" and Tuchman's (1972) analysis of news as a routinely constructed account, they stress that events are formed by the way they are processed. The rest of this article will develop that insight. First, I will describe how the everyday activities of professionals working in organizations make news. Second, I will apply the use of exceptions to portrayals of power. Throughout both sections, I will discuss the use of exceptions to the rule by engaging in sociological analysis, rather than by making explicit comments about methods. The third section of this paper is explicitly methodological, raising questions derived from the use of exceptions as an analytic tool.

Throughout this article, I draw upon examples gathered at three news organizations at which I was a participant observer and upon a set of extended interviews at other news organizations. These are (1) a television station in a major market observed from 1966-1968; (2) a daily newspaper with a circulation of over 200,000 observed from 1967-1968; (3) the press room at New York's City Hall, with emphasis upon the city hall bureau of a major New York daily, observed in the fall of 1975 and winter of 1976; (4) interviews with reporters covering the women's movement for major New York City daily newspapers undertaken in summer of 1975.[2]

Throughout the discussion I will distinguish between occurrences and events. Following Molotch and Lester (1974), "occurrences" are amorphous happenings in the everyday world. "Events" are occurrences given meaningful structure as news or potential news.

HOW ROUTINES MAKE NEWS

The professed goal of any news organization is to provide accounts of significant and interesting events. Although apparently a straightforward aim, like many other seemingly simple phenomena, this goal is inextricably complex. The everyday world—the source of news accounts—is composed of a "glut of occurrences," many identifying themselves as significant news events for some individual or group. News organizations must sort these claims of occurrences. Minimally, sorting entails recognizing that an occurrence is an event, and a not a random happenstance whose shape and character eludes capture. The task of sorting is made more difficult by an added demand of occurrences.

Each occurrence can claim to be idiosyncratic—a particular conjunction of social, economic, political, and psychological forces that formed an occurrence into "this particular occurrence" and not into any other existing or having existed in the everyday world. Accepting this claim for all occurrences is an organizational impossibility. Like any other complex organization, a news medium cannot process idiosyncratic phenomena. It must reduce all phenomena to constructed classifications, much as hospitals "reduce" each patient to sets of symptoms and diseases, and teachers view individual students in terms of categories pertinent to learning. Any organization that sought to process each and every phenomenon as a thing in itself would be so flexible that it would be unrecognizable as a formal organization. Some mean between flexibility and rigidity must be attained (see March and Simon, 1958).

Together, these demands of the glut of occurrences suggest that news organizations must fulfill three tasks (among others) in order to provide news accounts:

(1) they must enable recognition that an occurrence (including an exceptional one) is a news event;

(2) they must facilitate modes of reporting events that discount each occurrence's demand for idiosyncratic treatment and processing; and

(3) work must be scheduled in time and space so that recognizable news events can be routinely encountered and processed.

These tasks are interrelated. Modes of reporting are tools for revealing an occurrence to be a viable news event. Conventions arising from the scheduling of work call forth different modes of reporting. Accordingly, by enabling the second and third tasks to be accomplished, routines simultaneously recognize and reconstitute everyday occurrences in the everyday world as news. They make news.

Scheduling Work: The news organization's scheduling of work in time and space is an institutionalized news-net (see Tuchman, 1976a; cf. Fishman, 1975). It scatters reporters at civic, state, national, and (sometimes) international sites where legitimated institutions are expected to generate news events. For instance, even small papers have a police and criminal justice beat and assign a specific reporter to attend to the activities of local government.

Spreading a news-net accomplishes several things. First, the arrangement insures that events generated by the covered institutions will be caught by the net's grid. Second, since beat reporters take their task to be filing a daily story, reporters will promote some occurrences as events in order to have story to write. To be sure, not all such stories will be disseminated. But, generating and writing them provides fodder with which to fill a newspaper's columns or a television station's air time. Furthermore, the stories are an economic investment. A news editor may be loath to discard a suitable story for which the news organization has essentially prepaid (by paying the reporter's salary or investing in film), when the alternative is searching for an occurrence that might not pan out as recognizable news. Each inch of space (or second of time) occupied by news of an event located at at institutional beat represents an inch or second that will not be allocated to news happenings at an uncovered location. Since the news-net uses a finite number of reporters, its mesh necessarily contains gaps. Some occurrences, particularly those generated by social movements and grass-roots organizations, will escape through these gaps. They will not be defined as news.

The news-net also has temporal gaps. Just as definable news events are expected to occur at some institutional locations, but not at other sites, so too news events are expected to cluster during normal business hours, 9 a.m. to 6 p.m. weekdays. During these hours, news organizations have the bulk of their reporters and photographers available to cover stories. An occurrence happening before or after these hours must present a clear claim to characterization as a news event in order to justify allocating a reporter to cover it. Sending a reporter to an occurrence whose definition as news is marginal may seriously deplete the supply of reporters on hand should a more readily identifiable news event emerge from the glut of occurrences. The consequences of temporal scheduling are similar to those generated by the news organization's use of space. Some occurrences cannot become news.

However, concentrating reporters' working hours cannot ensure a temporal anchoring of the news-net. A comparison makes this clearer. Providing more doctors than usual in a hospital's emergency room on weekend and holiday nights does not guarantee that the seriously ill or wounded will receive adequate medical treatment. To facilitate such treatment, hospitals institute special routines. For instance, they may schedule all elective surgery[3] before 5 p.m. on weekdays. Schedules also take into account the amount of time customarily required by the expected surgical procedures. What appears to be a personal medical emergency to a patient is thus rendered as routine by the hospital so it may plan the use of both personnel and physical resources and so control the flow of work. When allocating resources each week, some hospitals even check the list of critical patients to estimate the kind and amount of work to be expected by the morgue's personnel (Sudnow, 1967).

Just as hospital personnel differentiate among diseases according to their demands for organizational resources, news personnel must anticipate the claims events may make of their resources. To control work, news organizations have developed typifications of events as news stories. Their most important distinction is between hard and soft news (see Tuchman, 1973b).

Most hard news stories concern prescheduled events (e.g., a debate on a legislative bill) or unscheduled events (e.g., a fire). Reporters and editors do not decide when stories about prescheduled and unscheduled events are to be disseminated. But they do decide when to gather and disseminate information about nonscheduled events. (A nonscheduled event is one whose date of dissemination as news is determined by news personnel.) Most soft news stories concern nonscheduled events. Members of the news enterprise almost always control the timing and flow of work required to process them. For instance, a reporter may be assigned to a story about Valentine's Day several days in advance, and the specific information to be included in the story may be gathered, written, and edited well before its eventual dissemination.

Clearly, decisions to carry items about prescheduled and nonscheduled events facilitate the organization's control of work. Knowing that a reporter will be attending a trial on next Tuesday helps both reporter and editors to plan what next Wednesday's news coverage will be. The ability to predict also has personal and professional components for the reporter: He/she may plan which reportorial techniques to draw upon to cover the story and still accomplish such mundane but necessary tasks as chatting with potential sources. Most important, anticipating what will happen next week—using prediction to control the flow of work—has two important consequencs. First, it has a direct influence on the assessment of individual occurrences as news. Second, it influences the mode or tone of the eventual news report.

Scheduling's Impact on the Assessment of Events: One impact of the scheduling of work upon the assessment of routines has already been considered. The anchoring of the news-net in time and space prevents some occurrences from being noticed. Having escaped the grid used to predict the flow of work, they cannot become news.

Additionally, events that have defied the predictions of news experts are valued more than those which are expected. Termed "what-a-stories" for the gleeful expressions with which they are greeted, events both defying news predictions and the staff's common stock of taken-for-granted knowledge generate "emergency-routines." The term "emergency-routine" appears to be internally contradictory. Yet, when a what-a-story occurs, everyone knows what is to be done. That a what-a-story is routine is forcefully indicated by the reaction of a TV anchorman reporting to work in the midafternoon of the day Robert Kennedy died. (Other staff members were called in at 6 a.m.; the anchorman arrived late so he would still look fresh on the 11 p.m. newscast. Entering the newsroom, he asked "Did we gather the usual reaction?" An apt comparison is the hospital's emergency-routine for cases of cardiac arrest.

Scheduling's Impact on Modes of Reporting: Modes of reporting are associated with scheduling. Designated important because it defied prediction, a what-a-story receives larger headlines and more intensive coverage than other news events of comparable historic urgency. Size of headline and extensiveness of coverage may be said to represent the mode in which a what-a-story is routinely handled. Their headlines scream. But screams may meld into everyday routines, just as the urgent appeal of a newscaster interrupting an entertainment program to announce a plane crash sounds less urgent every time it is experienced.

Again, a comparison with hospitals helps. Sudnow (1967) reports that hospital drivers were instructed to sound their ambulance sirens when approaching the emergency room with an expected "dead-on-arrival." Supposedly, medical staff would scurry to revive the technically dead and near-dead. Instead, recognizing the driver's skill at assigning death, doctors lingered over coffee, requiring a particularly long siren before they would meet the ambulance's patient. Modes of reacting to the expected and unexpected become routine; they decrease any individual's or event's claim to idiosyncratic processing.

The tendency to discount claims to idiosyncratic treatment is even clearer in the case of hard news and soft news. Although both sorts of accounts may be factual (in the sense that observers could agree that a certain phenomenon did happen in a certain way at a certain time in a certain place), both need not be treated with reportorial conventions associated with objectivity. Rather, reporters and editors use one set of reportorial techniques on hard news stories and routinely abandon those conventions when processing soft news. For instance, writing a hard news story, the reporter will lead with the most important "facts"; writing a soft news story, he/she may not do this (see Tuchman, 1972). Filming a hard news story (see Tuchman, 1973a), a TV cameraman[4] will avoid tampering with the time-rhythm of the phenomenon being filmed. At least he will not film in slow motion.[5] But slow motion and fast motion are frequently used to achieve special effects when filming soft news stories.

Ultimately, knowledge of routine modes of processing different kinds of news stories enables reporters to work more efficiently. Significantly, reporters and editors identify this knowledge with professionalism. For them, professionalism—a method of controlling work—consists of mastering techniques of writing appropriate to hard and soft news stories. Mastery also includes knowing what questions must be asked of what sources to elicit "facts" that should appear in the eventual story. In so doing, professionalism also limits the occurrences that may come to be defined as news events.

Knowing what questions to ask promotes trained incapacity. Assuming certain facts will be associated with certain kinds of stories means other "facts" delineating a different or even contradictory reality will be ignored. What are held to be "the facts" differentiate this occurrence from all other occurrences inasmuch as "facts" are associated with definitions of reality. By training reporters to search for some "facts," news organizations and the news profession may make reporters incapable of seeing "what's really going on."

Two contrasting examples may help to clarify this point. Mastery of techniques used to cover occurrences in political institutions may hamper reporters faced with occurrences promoted by social movements. Political institutions generate scheduled events whose actors are frequently familiars of reporters. When reporters witness or learn of such events, they can assess their eventual ramifications and attribute a "plot" to the events as stories. Sometimes the same plot will be given to seemingly different events. For instance, New York City Hall reporters commented that the "story" of New York's fiscal crisis remained the same as it marched from City Hall to Albany and eventually to Washington, D.C. In each case, it was the story of impending disaster, like the threat of an earthquake or tornado. A city hall bureau chief told me that the day New York City was expected to default, reporters were scattered in the pattern used for natural disasters.

Another example of the attribution of a plot was provided by a *New York Times* reporter's discussion of political coverage. She felt that male political reporters cover the conventions of the National Women's Political Caucus the same way they cover men's conventions, "only they talk about the women in front [on the podium] instead of talking about men." By applying this plot rather than exploring other possibilities, the reporters force the story into a possibly inapplicable mold.[6]

Concentrating on familiar stories in new forms makes it difficult for reporters and possibly readers to deal with issues. As Phillips puts it (1976:92),

> Craft-related habits of mind, such as dependence upon [professional] "instinct," the logic of the concrete, a present time orientation, and an emphasis on contingent events rather than structural necessities, serve to bias[7] the presentation of news. Externally imposed constraints (e.g., regularly scheduled telecasts) and organizational pressures to routinize work combine with the journalist's tendency to view the day's events as discrete, unrelated facts to produce the news mosaic of surface reality. . . . Linkages between events are not suggested . . . the news gives the feeling that there is novelty without change.

Covering an issue, such as the emergence of the Women's Political Caucus and the interaction among problem-oriented factions, requires more digging for information by a reporter and goes against the grain of externally imposed constraints and organizational pressures. It also relegates issues to soft news.

Equally important, proponents of an issue may make their case by offering a world-view alien to reporters' event-orientation. Halloren et al. (1970) report that London peace marchers protesting British support of the American-Vietnamese war carried signs about inflation and higher taxes, problems they associated with British foreign policy. Rather than understand those pickets as components of a sophisticated analysis, reporters read them as indications of a haphazard (nonevent oriented) approach.

A *New York Times* reporter provided another example of this trained incapacity. She was assigned to keep track of the women's movement during the early 1970s—a period of turmoil involving squabbles about such issues as lesbianism, broadening minority participation, methods of converging conscious-ness-raising into political action, and defining the movement's next arena of assault on sexism. Speaking of this period, the reporter said,

> There were a lot of interesting things going on, but I couldn't nail them down. There was formless kind of talk. I could see things changing, but it was hard to put my finger on it and say to the metropolitan desk, "This is what's happening."[8]

In both cases, the event-orientation implicit in routine reportorial techniques blinded reporters to issues (see Tuchman, forthcoming). In the second case, professionalism prevented the reporter from realizing that an amorphous happening may be viewed as a defined event and so may yield a viable news story.

In sum, routines intended to control work help define what may be seen as news. Through the anchoring of the news-net, through typifications associated with modes of reporting, and through professional techniques, routines enable some occurrences to emerge as news, but banish others from public consideration.

EXCEPTIONS AND POWER

Throughout the previous discussion, I have had to refer to some exceptions to routine in order to clarify customary news practices. For each instance, I spoke of occurrences that escape the news-net, those that challenge the reporter's understanding of previous events, and those promoted by agents with world views alien to those of newsworkers, such as the British march against the American-Vietnamese war. In and of themselves, such references indicate that learning of exceptions to customary practices elucidates the rules of newswork: by temporarily suspending agreements about how work is to be done, exceptions may reveal the taken-for-granted basis of decision-making as the researcher observes everyday practices.[9]

Technical Skills and Understandings of Power: Informants' discussions of exceptions and mistakes in techniques used to gather and write stories may reveal aspects of power within the news organization and simultaneously demonstrate ways that the news organization, as a societal force, is allied with other powerful institutions. The following three examples illustrate how accepted professional techniques also serve to mask understandings of organiza-tional and political power. Each example involves the same basic technical skill, the choice of a lead or first sentence for a story. Leads are central to the definition of an occurrence as an event. In the first two examples, an ambitious young black reporter with weak alliances within his news organization bucks authority. In the third, a powerful senior reporter goes against dominant interpretations of an occurrence.

Case One:

A City Hall reporter, assigned to tour a city prison with a committee of the city council, chose not to write a story about the prisoners' complaints (see also Tuchman, 1976a). As he tortured over his typewriter to produce a lead before abandoning the attempt, he explained that the event he witnessed violated his editors' preconceptions of the story. He wished to write about the prisoners' view that judicial practices of setting bail violate the Bill of Rights. The reporter stressed that city council members and other reporters could not "even hear" the constitutional complaints skillfully articulated by the prisoners.[10] Furthermore, he reasoned, his editors would demand an article about prison conditions, because a powerful reporter, popular with the editors, had previously penned and published a lengthy news analysis blaming conditions at the prison for a recent riot there. Once a police reporter, this powerful reporter had drawn upon his contact with those institutional sources to gather his information and so turn a riot from an occurrence into a news event.[11] Turning in the story he wished to write would also be problematic, the city hall reporter reasoned, because another article he had written recently, on violations of teachers' civil rights, had prompted an editorial dispute. The editor who opposed it has since received a promotion.

The reporter decided it was more judicious for him not to file the story he wished to write than to buck authority once more; he could not bring himself to file the expected story.

It is possible that this refusal to file contributed to the following dispute about a lead sentence in which the same reporter's technical skill was questioned.

Case Two:

The reporter was assigned to rewrite a press release into a short news item. (Such a task is frequently reserved for inexperienced reporters, not those who, like this man, could boast several years'experience.) Editing the copy, the bureau chief instructed the reporter to convert his lead into a second-day lead, a generalizing sentence that frames an occurrence in terms of an ongoing event.[12] Lead sentences of experienced reporters are rarely challenged, yet the reporter made the change without voicing his objection. When the city editor received the revised copy, he telephoned the reporter to request a first-day lead. At this point, the reporter explained he had originally written a first-day lead and the bureau chief had challenged his judgment. After learning of the city editor's phone call (the copy boy gossiped about it), the bureau chief apologized to his reporter for getting him in dutch with the city editor.

The apparently felt need for an apology suggests that the attribution of basic technical skills depends upon status in the organizational hierarchy. To be sure, to equate reputation for technical skills with status in an organization seems tautological. Yet, the reporter claimed he had not been subject to such basic critiques before filing his story on teachers' civil rights and bucking the hierarchy. He appeared to feel that the critique arose from the melding of office politics with disputes about civil liberties.[13]

An incident about a lead sentence involving the top political reporter at a different newspaper affirms that framing a lead depends upon taken-for-granted professional views, such views drawing upon news personnel's ongoing familiarity with official sources.[14]

Case Three:

Covering the 1968 New Hampshire primary, the top political reporter had led a story with the statement President Johnson "is running scared" in his contest with Eugene McCarthy. Despite this reporter's reputation as a specialist, editors challenged and changed the lead. They argued that a President—not even officially on the ballot—could not "run scared" because of the institutional resources at his command.

In this instance, professional news judgment seemed to also reinforce the interests of the more powerful.

That the lead sentence of a high-status reporter was changed enables tentative but more specific formulations about connections between news routines and societal power. It suggests, as Molotch and Lester (1975) put it, that professional practices defining occurrences are practices permitted to survive by those with societal power. Historical proof of this assessment is difficult, if not impossible, to locate. However, exceptions to the rule provide evidence of a derivative generalization: *Organizational and professional practices entail the stratification of access to the news as a social resource.* Those with the most economic and political power in the society have the most access to news processes and the most power over reporters. Those with the least economic and political power in the society are subject to the power of reporters. Although implied and captured by the distinction between event-orientation of institutions and reporters and the issue-orientation of social movements and reformers, this generalization is directly experienced when exceptions to news practices are uncovered.

Exceptions and Access to News: Reporters are themselves quick to point to several sorts of exceptions to professional practices. Foremost among these is the business-office or front-office must. Such stories must be carried because they have been requested by an advertiser or a friend of someone well-placed in the news organization's managerial hierarchy.

Critics of news practices cite the obverse phenomenon.[15] News organizations are more apt to report about public institutions than powerful private ones. For instance, the New York City media criticize spending at units of the City University, but not at Columbia University or New York University. They discuss waste at the municipal hospitals, but not at Columbia University's Presbyterian Hospital or Cornell's New York Medical Center. This practice is pertinent, because the news' distinction between public and private institutions is at best weak and, at worst, fallacious. The "private institutions" receive federal grants; the private hospitals are heavily financed by Medicaid and Medicare funds. A portion of New York state's budget for higher education is earmarked for the so-called private institutions.[16] By maintaining the distinction between private and public, the news media mask the actual economic organization of significant services. They enable "private institutions" not to make news, much as in an earlier day, members of the upper class sought to keep their names *out* of the papers except for birth, marriage, and death announcements.

The ability *not* to make news has also been accredited to the politically powerful. For example, federal officials may proclaim that a specific topic involves national security and they can normally expect that definition to be honored (cf. Porter, 1976). Breed (1958) discusses several community controversies not reported, because coverage would exacerbate class conflict by revealing the power of a community's social and economic elite. Trying to locate what does not get reported clarifies what does get reported and so clarifies hidden alliances between news organizations and other institutions: *The power to keep an occurrence out of the news is power over the news.*[17]

Unfortunately, the observer of news routines does not frequently encounter the unreported. The reason is simple: the observer is accompanying a reporter to an assigned event and so sees what the reporter sees. Like the reporter, the observer may be seduced by the anchoring of the news-net. Yet, through memoirs or reporters' accounts of their experiences, the researcher may learn of unreported events, revealing the structure of power. Wise (1973) cites Bernstein and Woodward's account (1974) of information about Nixon deleted from their story about one of his news conferences: Nixon's hands shook throughout the hour, giving the impression of a man not fully in control of himself. Their *Washington Post* editors deleted that information, judging it to be in bad taste because they were already attacking Nixon about Watergate.

Would the nonpowerful be extended the same courtesy? The *Washington Post's* handling of Watergate provides some evidence. Bernstein and Woodward (1974) made it clear that their articles were carefully examined by Ben Bradlee, their executive editor, and that the editors established stricter rules than usual for verification of information. Bradlee does not customarily check reporter's copy; a rule that two sources must verify a fact is not applied to stories about the powerless. Most statements presented as facts by informants are taken as facts by reporters (see Tuchman, 1972).

The news' proclivity to protect the powerful and protect themselves from the powerful may sometimes run against the direct wishes of an individual with actual or symbolic power. One such case I witnessed resulted in the burial of a newsworthy statement. The example is pertinent, because reporters were protecting a revered spokesman from siding with the powerless.

Case One:

The evening Martin Luther King was assassinated, a reporter phoned Richard Cardinal Cushing to ask his reaction to King's murder. Cushing was known to be in bad health and, on occasion, heavy medication interfered with his usual articulateness, information routinely withheld by the Boston newspapers. Possibly awakened to be told of King's death, Cardinal Cushing informed the reporter that if King had been Catholic, Cushing would consider him a candidate for canonization. Reporters and editors argued ferociously about the statement. An Irish Catholic assistant city editor felt that Cushing's statement harmed the church. A senior editor credited this man with claiming that if King were canonized, he would leave the church. Ultimately, a Protestant assistant managing editor deleted the sentence from the published account of Cushing's reaction. The editorial justification was: Cushing had probably been awakened to speak to the reporter, may have been medicated, and might not have been aware of what he was saying.

Given a choice between angering some white Catholics and some powerful individuals and leaving blacks in ignorance of a statement supportive of their drive for their rights, the editors chose the powerful.

The disbanding of a beat (a piece of the news-net) seems to confirm that reportorial techniques (based on professional judgments) support the powerful. Disbanding a beat qualifies as an exception to the rule, since this was the only elimination of a beat reported to me in my year of observation at that newspaper.

Case Two:

The beat was the local civil rights beat, established at the behest of the front office during a period when the news media were being attacked for "biased coverage" of civil rights. The assigned reporter developed contacts with a variety of established and grass-roots civil rights groups and routinely filed copy on their activities. Most of those stories were discarded by the city editor and the assistant managing editor, who argued they were not as newsworthy as other articles filed the same day.

Although items generated at a beat may be discarded, it is rare for most of them to be thrown out, as those were. Furthermore, a greater proportion of stories generated by this reporter were rejected than was true of items submitted from other beats. The editorial judgments were interpreted as proof that "nothing much" was going on locally in civil rights and that earlier criticisms of the news media had been unjustified. Reportorial staff did not interpret the pattern as indicating that the editors opposed or disliked news about the civil rights movement. Nor did the publisher suspect the news judgment of his editors. The possibility was not raised that news judgments based upon professional practices might routinely slight news of social movements or blind editors to the importance of movement activities.[18]

Three considerations supported my interpretation that professional judgments routinely slight the powerless. First, disbanding a beat was a rare occurrence. Second, a reporter on the police beat identified for me the following mistake of a young reporter whom he had helped to train. Covering a fire, the apprentice had gone to gather the names of those driven from their homes, as is customary. The experienced reporter stopped the reporter, those losing their homes were lower-class blacks and inevitably, the reporter explained to me, everyone has a different surname. The affinitive relationships are entangled, difficult to sort out, and take too much space to explain while keeping an article brief. Therefore, standard practice need not be followed.

A third item (that was not a mistake) also seemed to validate my interpretation. That item was linguistic misunderstanding in a brief conversation with an assistant city editor. (It may be considered "exceptional" inasmuch as disputes about the meanings of terms clarify opposing world views of discussants.) The week preceding the conversation, the newspaper had published several stories about civil rights demonstrations. I commented that there had been a lot of "black news" recently. The assistant city editor asked me to specify what I meant; I answered, "news about blacks." The editor replied that the paper had not carried much news about crime that week. As in the case of those driven from the fire, newsworkers associated specific types of stories and story-plots with powerless social groups; they used past professional experience to interpret stories of the moment.

A qualification is in order: The last two examples may reveal more about the individual prejudices of two men than they do about routine news practices. Other news organizations, including one competitor, maintained a civil rights beat through the middle and late 1960s. However, other editorial identification of reportorial mistakes buttress the general argument that the media's allegiances are with the powerful and are constituted in news routines.

The following two mistakes indicate that the media may set about to redress wrongs to a specific individual, but are slow to address the institutional arrangements and procedures generating the grievances of the poor. Reporting about institutional arrangements requires extensive work over a period of time and undermines the rhythm of producing daily hard news.

Case One:

A reporter was sent to a building owned by an absentee landlord; the tenement had been without heat for several days in the midst of a cold spell (see also Tuchman, 1972). (The story fell into the news-net when the teacher of a child made homeless by the lack of heat telephoned the city desk.) After the initial editing, a reporter was sent to gather more facts for the story so that the paper would not appear to be editorializing on its news pages and could not be accused of libeling the landlord.

But the editors did not take this opportunity to gather still more facts about the problems arising from the pattern of absentee ownership in certain areas of the city. Nor did they order a reportorial investigation of the relationship between housing inspectors and slum landlords. Doing so would have entailed much work (digging up facts) and committing the paper to run the story some time in the future.[19]

The second and more explicit case involved a discarded story about a man accused of child-neglect (Tuchman, 1972).

Case Two:

According to the politically liberal local editor, the suburban editor had made a mistake by passing the story on to him. The local editor explained, "The story is similar to one about a man whose wife had been murdered, and the man has not been arrested, but he has been told not to leave town. The man goes to the newspapers and tries to clear himself of accusations not yet made. If a week later, the man is indicted for murder and we have printed the story, how do we, the newspapers, look?" The local editor emphasized the need to appreciate an institution's procedures and expertise: "Newspapers have to follow the legal steps as they appear in a normal arrest-indictment-trial sequence, unless they are convinced there has been a miscarriage of justice."

Reporters and editors assume that normal police practices justify indictments. However, as indicated by this example, those practices also assume that the accused is guilty until proven innocent. This interpretation is strengthened by the local editor's sympathy for this not-yet-accused man. Sorrowfully, the editor stated, "The man is living under a cloud." Personal views of editors and reporters thus did not determine the fate of the story. On the contrary, newsworkers like to see themselves as defenders of the underdog and persons keeping the powerful honest; reportorial and editorial sympathy had pushed the story to higher levels of editorial authority. There, judgments based on routine considerations prevailed. The nature of newswork (not of newsworkers) determined the fate of the story.

THEORETICAL IMPLICATIONS OF EXCEPTIONS

That media reports favor the powerful is not news to the communications researcher. The use of exceptions to study the routine identification and processing of events as news does, though, provide new theoretical insights. In the past, researchers echoed the judgments of reporters and editors: The powerful frequently generate newsworthy events; the powerless rarely do so. This summary statement assumes that there is either a match or a high correlation between the importance of events in the everyday world and their rendition as news. To paraphrase a reporter's statement of this common theory: the media report reality; they do not make it. Unfortunately, this view does not examine the derivation of the standards by which newsworthiness and importance are assessed. It assumes those standards may be taken for granted as absolute, as being as clear as day.

Other researchers have departed somewhat from the idea that "newsworthiness" is an absolute, as measurable as the frequencies of discernible light. Roshco (1975) put it this way: Definitions of what is newsworthy depend upon people's attitudes; those attitudes in turn are formed by a society's institutional arrangements. Although this theoretical rendition specifies that standards of newsworthiness are socially determined and may change, it too is blind to the way identifications of newsworthiness are themselves a function of reportorial and editorial routines incorporating allegiances to the powerful. Roshco's rendition deflects criticisms of the media. Rather than seeking to introduce social change by studying the activities of media organizations and so locating the media as potential loci of social change, he turns to individual and collective attitudes.

The following passage places the responsibility for changing the media upon the consumers of news.

> The American daily press has a constant potential for social subversion. Its institutional bias as a merchant of the novel and unexpected makes it an instrument for popularizing new attitudes and behaviors. If these deviant ways of thinking and acting are taken up by sizeable segments of the mass-media audience, the consequences are institutional change, revised social values, the restructuring of newsmen's [sic] frame of references, and the redefinition of who and what is newsworthy (Roshco, 1975).

In this quotation, those seeking to introduce change are "deviant." Identified as unusual (like that old reportorial hacksaw, the man who bit the dog, and who or what is the stuff and substance of soft news) they may sneak into the news. But, genuine social change is not to be dismissed as the result of novelty. Pushed by human actors, social change runs its inexorable course as conflicts are introduced by contradictions in social institutions. Identifying seekers of change as novelties and thus relegating them to occasional soft news stories is therefore problematic. It is an extension of newsworkers' professional ideology inasmuch as it directs newsworkers to identify important happenings with established institutions and unusual happenings with deviants.

To be sure, that this statement is an extension of newsworkers' professional ideology is implied, not stated. But it is an uncritical adoption of news-workers' evaluations including their refusal to draw connections between events (Phillips, 1976). Without reflecting upon the use of such important distinctions as hard and soft news to simplify the everyday world for organizational processing, it incorporates them in communications theory. Also, like newsworkers, it locates ultimate responsibility for the nature of newswork with institutions other than the news media. Under the Nixon administration, the news media certainly needed to be defended against coordinated government assault (Porter, 1976). But, there is a difference between defending the First Amendment and launching an apologia, especially if theorists are to understand the role of the media in contemporary society.

It is not sufficient to cite the much-validated theory that the communications media of any society support those in power. To implement changes, one must understand how that support is accomplished by specifying the workings of the media. To this end, I have suggested that exceptions to the rule uncovered through participant observation facilitate an understanding of how news routines make news. Identification of organizational and professional routines and exceptions reveals that an occurrence is not necessarily newsworthy, for there is no objective standard of newsworthiness against which events may be assessed. Instead, the anchoring of the news-net, typifications and professionally sanctioned skills merge to make news.

EXCEPTIONS AND THE RULE

Although observational studies of the media are becoming increasingly common (e.g., Altheide, 1976, Fishman, 1975; Lester, 1975; Engwall, 1976; Gelles and Faulkner, 1976; Halloren et al., 1970), much communication research is still based upon content analysis. A research method may be used to explore and test different theories, but historically one assumption often accompanies content analysis: the content of the media reflect social values and changing social structures.

The previous discussion poses several problems for the use of content analysis. First, one may only code material that has been disseminated. Cardinal Cushing's complete remarks on Martin Luther King's death are not available to the coder (although the importance of its omission depends on the research topic). Second, each item is coded by the same standards and according to the same set of categories. Any datum is not and cannot be considered in and of itself. Third, if one wishes to comment on kinds of content that are either omitted or underrepresented, one must have some standard against which to compare the published (or televised) material—such as earlier content analyses or some set of independent "facts" about the present.

A variety of solutions have been offered to the problem of finding a standard of comparison. Janowitz (1976) commends the use of trend data, particularly when coupled with economic indices. Together, he suggests, a cultural index and an economic index enables substantive statements about emerging social problems. Gerbner and Gross (1976) view content analyses as "cultural indicators" when teamed with survey data about audience response to televised content. Both sets of data enable comments about social values. Molotch and Lester (1975) locate a standard internal to the media,[20] comparing local news reports and national reports to discuss the dispersion of information. Yet, despite the ingenuity used in finding a standard, most researchers still agree that jumping from content analyses to statements about either the structure or the effects of the media is a very tricky business (see Janowitz, 1968-1969; 1976). That trickiness is clarified by the problem of omission and the problem of standardization. Whether these are serious issues is, of course, dependent upon the research topic and the theories being tested.

The Problem of Omission: If one uses the content of the mass media to document the path of social movements, this problem is severe. Access to the mass media is stratified and least open to those often involved in the early stages of a social movement—the powerless.[21] If a social movement increasingly recruits middle-class and upper-class participants, access will increase (see Tuchman, 1976b, forthcoming; Goldenberg, 1975; Jenkins and Perrow, 1977). Furthermore, when the activities of wealthy individuals run counter to the interests of corporations, corporations are better equipped politically to promote their events as news (Molotch and Lester, 1975).

Does the alteration in the pattern of media reports about a social movement indicate change in the quantity of movement activities or in the characteristics of participants, or is it anchored in news practices? Are all three of these factors compounded? If so, how? The last and most likely alternative clearly indicates the dangers of using content analysis alone to study past and present events.

The Problem of Standardization: Kraus, Davis, Lang, and Lang (1976) have argued that studying key events, such as the first Kennedy assassination, a presidential election, or the Watergate scandal, reveals more about media coverage and American values than content analysis of usual events. Paralleling the psychological theory that key events may foster change (by helping an individual to change the course of his life or reconstituting his personality in some new way), they suggest that certain public events prompt new public behaviors and activities. Unfortunately, standardized content analysis may obscure key events by submerging them in the pattern of qualitatively dissimilar coverage. Standardization obscures exceptions to the rule, whether or not they would have been recognized as exceptions by newsworkers or observers. And, exceptions to the rule may ultimately reveal how the rule operates.

Identifying problems associated with content analysis does not mean that the technique should be abandoned. But it does call for increased sophistication in the use of that method as well as increased awareness of the dangers of generalization. It also suggests the wisdom of using additional methods to validate statements based upon content analysis.

Both theoretically and methodologically, the story that does not get disseminated or that requires special handling may tell more about news processes and American society than published and broadcast stories can. The event that prompts emergency routines may elucidate everyday routines more than other happenings do. Exceptions are a necessary tool in the collection and analysis of observational data. They prove the rule.

NOTES

1. According to Molotch and Lester (1974:109-110), "Accidents are unplanned occurrences which are promoted by a party other than the agent who inadvertently caused the underlying occurrence. . . . A scandal involves a deliberately planned occurrence which is promoted by a party different from the occurrence's agent."

2. The collection of data at site (3) above, and analysis of data at sites (3) and (4) were funded by the Russell Sage Foundation. Some of the data presented here have been published elsewhere, as indicated by references where appropriate. Their present use represents a conceptual extension and integration of my previous work.

3. An important empirical question is, How do medical personnel distinguish between elective and non-elective surgery?

4. The term "cameraman" is used because occupants of this job are overwhelmingly male. The supposed justification is the weight of sound cameras; however, appreciably more men than women are being trained to use the new lightweight portable minipack cameras.

5. Some exceptions that prove this rule are cited in Tuchman, 1973a.

6. This example is discussed further in Tuchman (forthcoming).

7. The term "bias" must be understood in the loosest possible sense. See Tuchman, 1972. [See also Phillips's discussion of objectivity in this volume. *Eds.*]

8. Another possible interpretation is that reportorial professionalism could only view this story as either soft news requiring digging or as nonnews. To quote Phillips (1976:92) "Ambiguities, developments in flux, and contradictions tend to be non-news." Tuchman (1976a, 1976c, and forthcoming) uses this example to argue that professionalism prevents reporters from viewing "developments in flux" as news because such developments do not fit into reportorial frames designed to convert occurrences into stories.

9. Theoretically, the term "decision-making" is inappropriate. My data suggest that routines are so encompassing that formal decisions are not made. Newsworkers "merely" do what is "natural." By refusing to reflect upon their practical activities (cf. Phillips, 1976; Tuchman, 1972) they eschew formal decisions between alternative outcomes. An analogy makes this clearer. The newsworkers are in the position of a man in a shoe store deciding among extra pairs of black shoes and brown shoes. He may not question why he needs to buy extra shoes at all.

10. Those complaints were in the last paragraphs of stories written for two other daily newspapers.

11. The reporter transforms *a* riot into *the* riot: a happening is publicly defined as *the* or *this* riot having specific particulars or characteristics.

12. The reporter was told to speak of a possible hike in taxi fares in terms of added expenses for citizens already beset by New York's fiscal crisis.

13. The reporter's close colleagues tended to affirm his view.

14. I am using the term "familiarity" in two senses. Reporters and editors have knowledge of institutions through their experiences on beats. Also, institutional sources are their "familiars"; because of ongoing contacts, reporters may trust sources' evaluation of occurrences if the sources have a record of success at predicting shifts of power within their own institutions. Thus, the police sources used to write the original story about prison conditions as the cause of the riot were familiars of that reporter.

15. Fred Goldner reminded me of this phenomenon.

16. In the mid-1970s, their share of monies increased, while funding of the City University decreased.

17. Everett C. Hughes pointed this out to me in 1968. (cf. Molotch and Lester, 1974 and 1975.)

18. This beat is also discussed in Tuchman, 1976c. Phillips's (1976) observation that developments in flux tend to be nonnews may also apply here.

19. Nonetheless, the news repertoire includes stories like this one would have been. They are frequently run on Sundays when the large number of advertisements and Saturday's dearth of hard news require stories to be fillers. Phillips (1976) points out that newsworkers are committed to "facts," not "truth."

20. Analyses comparing the content of one medium (magazine or newspaper) to another are relatively common. Generally the contrasts are based upon demographic characteristics of each medium's audience.

21. Of course, many social movements have their own media. But, these may develop after the movement has gained many recruits.

REFERENCES

ALTHEIDE, D. (1976). Creating reality: How TV news distorts events. Beverly Hills, Calif.: Sage.

BERNSTEIN, C., and WOODWARD, B. (1974). All the president's men. New York: Simon and Schuster.

BREED, W. (1958). "Mass communication and socio-cultural integration." Social Forces, 37:109-116.

ENGWALL, L. (1976). Travels in newspaper country. Unpublished manuscript. Uppsala, Sweden: University of Uppsala, Department of Business Administration.

FISHMAN, M. (1975). News of the world: What happened and why. Ph.D. dissertation, University of California, Santa Barbara.

GARFINKEL, H. (1967). Studies in ethnomethodology. Englewood Cliffs, N.J.: Prentice-Hall.

GELLES, R. and FAULKNER, R. (1976). "Time and television newswork." Unpublished manuscript.

GERBNER, G. and GROSS, L. (1976). "The scary world of TV's heavy viewer." Psychology Today, (April):41-45, 89.

GOLDENBERG, E. (1975). Making the papers. Lexington, Mass.: D.C. Heath.

HALLOREN, H., ELLIOTT, P. and MURDOCH, J. (1970). Demonstrations and communication: A case study. London: Penguin.

HUGHES, E.C. (1964). Men and their work. Glencoe, Ill.: Free Press.

JANOWITZ, M. (1968-1969). "Harold Lasswell's contribution to content analysis." Public Opinion Quarterly 32:643-653.

——— (1976). "Content analysis and the study of sociopolitical change." Journal of Communication, 26(4):10-21.

JENKINS, C. and PERROW, C. (1977). "Insurgency of the powerless: Farm worker's movement." American Sociological Review.

KRAUS, S., DAVIS, D., LANG, G.E. and LANG, K. (1976). "Critical events analysis." In S. Chaffee (ed.), Political Communication: Issues and strategies for research (Vol. IV, Sage Annual Review of Communication Research). Beverly Hills, Calif.: Sage.

LESTER, M. (1975). News as a practical accomplishment: A conceptual and empirical analysis of newswork. Unpublished doctoral dissertation. University of California, Santa Barbara.

LIGHT, D. Jr. (1972). "Psychiatry and suicide: The management of a mistake." American Journal of Sociology, 77(5):821-838.

LIPSET, S.M., TROW, M. and COLEMAN, J.A. (1956). Union democracy. Glencoe, Ill.: Free Press.

MARCH, J. and SIMON, H. (1958). Organizations. New York: John Wiley.

MOLOTCH, H., and LESTER, M. (1974). "News as purposive behavior: On the strategic use of routine events, accidents and scandals." American Sociological Review, 39:101-112.

--- (1975). "Accidental news: The great oil spill." American Journal of Sociology, 81:235-260.

PHILLIPS, E.B. (1976). "Novelty without change." Journal of Communication, 26(4):87-92.

PORTER, W. (1976). The assualt on the media: The Nixon years. Ann Arbor: University of Michigan Press.

ROSHCO, B. (1975). Newsmaking. Chicago: University of Chicago Press.

STELLING, J. and BUCHER, R. (1973). "Vocabularies of realism in professional socialization." Social Science and Medicine, 7:661-673.

SUDNOW, D. (1967). Passing on: The social organization of death and dying. Englewood Cliffs, N.J.: Prentice-Hall.

TUCHMAN, G. (1972). "Objectivity as strategic ritual: An examination of newsmen's notions of objectivity." American Journal of Sociology, 77:(4)660-679.

--- (1973a). "The technology of objectivity: Doing objective television news." Urban Life and Culture, 2:3-26.

--- (1973b). "Making news by doing work: Routinizing the unexpected." American Journal of Sociology, 79(1):110-131.

--- (1976a). "Telling stories." Journal of Communication, 26(4):93-97.

--- (1976b). "Beating around city hall: Professionalism, flexibility and the professional prerogatives of reporter." Delivered at the meetings of the American Association of Public Opinion Research.

--- (1976c). "Ridicule, advocacy and professionalism: A newspaper's reporting of a social movement." Delivered at the meetings of the American Sociological Association.

--- (forthcoming). "The newspaper as a social movement's resource." In G. Tuchman, A.K. Daniels, and J. Benet (eds.), Home and hearth: Images of women in the mass media. New York: Oxford University Press.

WISE, D. (1973). The politics of lying. New York: Vintage.

Chapter 3

APPROACHES TO OBJECTIVITY: JOURNALISTIC VERSUS SOCIAL SCIENCE PERSPECTIVES

E. Barbara Phillips

THIS PAPER EXPLORES the organizational and occupational structuring of objectivity, setting out an interpretation of the clash in views between much of social science and journalism. This clash over the meaning and operation of objectivity has long been latent, but, judging from the spate of recent studies, has now exploded at the surface. Fieldwork and a survey of journalists conducted by the author will be drawn on and compared in a discussion of the results obtained in studying the structuring of objectivity.

Watergate dramatized a truism of mass society; namely, that journalism is the most important institutional mode of communication impacting on the public domain. Performing political roles on a stage of fact, journalists are now America's chief knowledge-linkers, translating and interpreting what politicians, philosophers, and scientists conceive. That is, knowledge—in its most elementary form—is mass-media-created and disseminated.

Interestingly, although they are the key links in the chain between government action and citizen information, journalists make no claim to expert knowledge as a way of legitimating their social role. Nor do they point to shared standards of competence; unlike doctors, lawyers, real estate agents, or beauticians, journalists do not need a license to practice their craft. In the absence of competency criteria and claims to a monopoly of specialized knowledge or technical skills, how do journalists justify their position as mass society's unofficial experts in interpretation? How do they shield themselves from challenges to their legitimacy? For many years, a set of conventions or canons of "objectivity" has served as a protective device. These canons, based on vague notions of balance, fairness, lack of bias, accuracy, and neutrality in newsgathering and editing, acted as safeguards to the newsperson's legitimate authority.

Recently, however, the professional norm—or ideology—of objectivity has been attacked on a number of grounds. To begin with, some journalists themselves declare the norm inoperative. Former feature-writers-turned-New-Journalists, like Jimmy Breslin, state that the major media's dependence on elites as authoritative sources renders the news less than objective. Others reject the commitment to the norm, stating that reportage should go beyond the "facts" and a neutral presentation to provide analysis and interpretation (see Johnstone et al., 1974). And advocacy journalism, which makes no pretense of being balanced or neutral, is apparently gaining supporters within the journalistic community (see Phillips, 1975:Ch.4).

From a political perspective, critics on both left and right argue that news media offer a highly partisan view of social reality, not an unbiased presentation. To name just a few, Aronson (1972) and Cirino (1971) decry the established media's rightward slant while Efron (1972) and Keeley (1971) bemoan what Spiro Agnew used to call the news' liberal "ideological plugola." Others (e.g., Phillips, 1973) note that objectivity is usually narrowly defined as a problem in two-party politics and bias viewed as partisan favoritism; this definition obfuscates the larger picture, that is, that the news media may indeed be biased, but in a direction which benefits the interests of political and economic elites, whether Democratic or Republican. For example, a recent study by the Glasgow University Media Group (1976) suggests that British television's labor news reportage, including the BBC (known for its "reliability" and "objectivity"), is biased in terms of acceping too many taken-for-granted assumptions about the causes of industrial strife: "strike-prone workers who, despite high wages, are not content" (203).

Increasingly, scholars, working from a variety of disciplines and theoretical perspectives, have joined in holding the professional norm of objectivity to be problematic. "Gatekeeper" studies (e.g., White, 1964) and social control research (e.g., Breed, 1955) suggest that news selection and treatment are more often based on expectations of the newsroom, including what the boss will think, than any concept of what the public needs to know. Students of reference group behavior (e.g., Bauer, 1964; Hilton, 1966) indicate that journalists address themselves not to the manifest audience but rather to key reference groups (including news sources) who may "often exert the determining influence in the organization . . . as well as in the flow of communication" (Bauer, 1964:138).

Other research (e.g., Gerbner, 1964) notes that messages produced by any institutional source carry some ideological freight. One study of newsroom decision-making (Bowers, 1967) discovered that three out of four publishers actively direct news decisions, most especially concerning issues that affect the newspaper's bottom line—revenue.

From the standpoint of organizational theory, Sigal (1973), Argyris (1974), Tuchman (1972), and Epstein (1973; 1975) point out that news is not an objective, mirror image of sociopolitical reality. Rather, they argue, news is a reflection of the organizational processes which generate it. After examining substantive and procedural processes in news production, Tuchman (1972) concluded that the newsperson's notion of objectivity is a "strategic ritual." Though it may mitigate deadline pressures and help avoid libel suits and bosses' expected reprimands, it has little relation to the manifest goal, that is, objective reporting.

Finally, at the philosophical level, some (e.g., Molotch and Lester,(1974) suggest that objectivity vis-à-vis the social world is illusionary, that no objective world exists out there to be reflected. Others (e.g., Novak, 1971:125, 130) hold that the very style of objectivity used by journalists is a symbolic strategy which is—in itself—politically and ideologically loaded, presenting the world as it appears to educated, cosmopolitan elites. From another view, reportorial objectivity is seen as fostering the neutralization of opposites, obliterating "the difference between true and false, information and indoctrination, right and wrong" (Marcuse, 1964:98).

In sum, then, the professional norm or ideology of objectivity is increasingly suspect to social theorists in both theory and practice; it may not be an attainable ideal, and it may not uphold the journalist's legitimate authority. Some thoughtful journalists, confronted by these arguments, agree. But most journalists argue that all they can do is to try harder—to be as fair and balanced (i.e., objective) as humanly possible. So, a stand-off occurs, with social scientists denying that objectivity is even possible while many journalists insist that the notion of objectivity informs their work. Indeed, in a survey of daily journalists I conducted in 1974, 98% of the newsgathers and editors polled virtually defined journalism as adherence to the norm of objectivity. From this and other studies, it is clear that the norm of objectivity forms the core of the defining logic and mission of news creation. Further, my research suggests that the daily journalists observed had habits of mind, attitudes, and personal characteristics which depend on and are structured around, the ideal of objective reporting.

RESEARCH METHODS

To investigate questions concerning how daily journalists use and negotiate the canons of objectivity, as well as related issues, a combination of research techniques was employed: (1) participant observation and interviewing—13 months of accompanying reporters to their "stories" and sitting in the newsrooms of a daily newspaper, two commercial radio stations, and a commercial television affiliate located in a medium-sized American metropolitan area; interviewing news sources and journalists in several Northeastern cities; (2) survey research—a regional survey of (a) 165 radio, TV, and newspaper newsgatherers and processors (this was a nonrandom sample whose characteristics were consistent with the larger random sample of U.S. journalists drawn by

Johnstone et al., 1974) and (b) four comparison groups of graduate students in social science, college journalism students, nurses, and high school editors; and (3) unobtrusive measures, including analyses of reporters' notes, staff memos, bulletin board notices. This multimethods, integrated approach led to mutual benefits, sometimes unexpected, in terms of data collection, analysis, and redesign.

In some cases, qualitative data and unobtrusive measures helped to reinterpret survey findings, placing the contextless questions into a broader context. For example, there was a great discrepancy between my fieldwork observations and the survey data concerning journalists' views of their job autonomy. At the daily newspaper research site, the *Morning Beacon* (a pseudonym), editors, copy-readers, and reporters constantly complained about the lack of control over their work. One beat reporter told the city editor,

> I play for pay. Whatever you tell me to do, I'll do. But I can't say I agree with it.

A copy editor bemoaned, "We're like assembly-line workers here, turning out Camaros." The poem encased under the city editor's desk provided a measure of his perceived lack of autonomy:

MY JOB

I'm not allowed to run the train
Nor see how fast 'twill go.
I'm not allowed to let off steam
Or make the whistle blow.
I cannot exercise control
Or even ring the bell.
But let the damn thing run off the track
And see who catches hell!

Yet, when asked the forced-choice question, "I have a great deal of autonomy in my job," over 60% of the *Morning Beacon* respondents agreed. How can this discrepancy between survey responses and fieldwork observations be explained? By referring back to other fieldwork observations. Here I noted that despite their bitter complaints over lack of job autonomy, journalists at the *Beacon* (and other research sites) did not perceive themselves to be bureaucrats or organization men and women in comparison to other occupational groups. They did not feel a sense of relative deprivation. The *Beacon* journalists, in particular, disassociated the nature of their work, which they regarded as nonroutine, from the organizational context in which they worked.

In other cases, survey data shed new light on field observations. Concerning their sense of political efficacy, for instance, it was not a startling revelation that journalists observed for this study felt less alienated from government than most Americans. After all, journalists are participants or pseudo-participants in the political process. While many journalists say that they are aloof from politics and play no active role in local political parties or groups, journalists *qua* journalists do political work. In the main, they recognize this. For instance, 85% of the journalists (N = 157) polled believed they had written or supervised at least one story which had public policy impact. Further, 83% (N = 162) agreed that "the news media are a powerful force in this community." As a TV news director said, "I get my biggest thrill out of getting the electorate turned on to some guy," adding that, "I don't want to be [so] powerful that we [the mass media] tell government what to do."

Despite these indications of political efficacy gained from fieldwork observations, I was unprepared for the journalists' comparative lack of alienation from government and politics which the questionnaire data revealed. During Watergate, when 86% of a national random sample felt estranged from government and unable to understand what was going on (U.S. Congress, 1973), only 23% of the journalists polled felt similarly.[1] Moreover, the journalists observed did not seem to suffer from rootlessness or anomie, a condition characterized by a context of mutual distrust.[2] Objectively speaking, journalists may operate under conditions of widespread distrust—afraid of being used by news sources. But the questionnaire data confirm that, at least as measured by the Srole anomie scale (1956), journalists are far more trusting of the larger social context than national random samples, the four comparison groups, and the police force in "Selville" (the hometown of the *Morning Beacon*).[3]

These findings suggest that trust—both of the political process and the larger social context—is related to the craft of journalism itself. Other findings from the survey data (e.g., that 75% of the journalists polled believe that "journalists, more than most people, help to shape the course of government"; that a majority of journalists polled agree that "I am a member of the establishment") also indicate that daily journalists working for nonelite news organizations[4] see themselves as less than neutral observers of the scenes they describe. The implications here go beyond cracking the public image of the journalist: a cynical, hard-boiled character out of Ben Hecht and Charlie MacArthur's "The Front Page," who distrusts colleagues as well as politics. These data, combined with fieldwork observations (e.g., that often reporters and news sources share basic assumptions), deal directly with the question of objectivity. That is, trust in the political process and the larger social context combined with the subjective realization of being a major actor in political events militates against the social scientist's notion of objectivity. To a social scientist, objectivity demands some degree of detachment, sufficient detachment to permit her or him to play the role of independent critic. While Weber's (1958) ideal of "value-freeness" in scientific work may now be viewed as an unattainable ideal, social science does encourage its practitioners to recognize—and explicitly state—their values, personal preferences, and ideologies which make their work less than value-free and neutral (see Denzin, 1970:4). In contrast, daily journalism discourages its practitioners from recognizing that taken-for-granted assumptions and personal predilections cast their unreflective shadows on reportage. Indeed, by defining objectivity as equivalent to "fairness" and "balance" (which 98% of the journalists polled did), the problems of detachment, neutrality, and evidence are sidestepped. By definition, then, journalists are turned into copying machines who simply record the world rather than evaluate it. This stance toward objectivity has many payoffs which we will now explore.

OBJECTIVITY AND NEWS JUDGMENT

Historically, objective reporting is relatively young, growing up after the Civil War with the rise of the wire services whose copy had to be acceptable to either Democratic or Republican newspaper subscribers. It developed mainly for commercial reasons: "the need of the mass newspaper to serve politically heterogeneous audiences without alienating any significant segment of the audience" (Carey, 1969:32).

At the local level, objective reporting still serves this function, for, by definition, mass media serve mass audiences. Unlike the social scientist, who typically communicates via the learned journal article, the daily journalist does not address her/himself to particular groups in society with special interests and needs. Instead, the journalist directs words or images to any adult or, some say, teenaged member of the audience, whatever that person's educational, occupational, political, or socioeconomic background which might distinguish her or him from others in the mass. Modern journalism is rooted in this need to communicate across wide barriers in a heterogeneous population.

Given this need to reach people of diverse backgrounds, interests, and stocks of knowledge, objective reporting is a sensible strategy for media managers as well as journalists. Historically, its value to the publisher has received far more attention from media analysts than its usefulness to reporters and editors. For example, the "news business" is, first of all, a business—and a big business. Letting "the facts speak for themselves" instead of offering an interpretation of events avoids controversy which, in turn, avoids offending news (and advertising) consumers who may reject the news (and advertised) product along with the unwanted interpretation. By "sticking to the facts" and eschewing explicit explanation, journalism in the objective mode skirts the problem that one person's truth is another's propaganda.

Objective reporting is economically sound in yet another way. To delve into the "news behind the news," that is, the patterns, developing trends, and the whys of events, costs media managers significantly more in terms of staff resources than having their employees cover regular "beats" (and depending upon "official" sources), "spot news," or "features." Providing in-depth analysis, translated, means doing research, and the overhead is high while the perceived payoffs—other than prestige within the journalistic community—are few. It is unclear whether or not news publics reward interpretive efforts in terms of higher TV ratings or increased newspaper circulation. Indeed, audience feedback for both electronic and print media is astoundingly minimal, both to specific news stories or news presentation in general.[5] Further, there is little incentive to change the format, since 97% of all U.S. newspapers find themselves in a local monopoly position, and TV/radio news tends toward sameness. In brief, consumers have little sovereignty in the news marketplace. Thus, economic logic is on the side of objective reporting as much or more so today than it was a hundred years ago.

Aside from economic considerations, objective reporting also makes sense in terms of organizational needs. First, the news media are set up to produce on a strict time schedule; the 6 p.m. newscast or home delivery edition cannot wait for a research team to polish its findings. While social scientists may refuse to publish their findings until they are satisfied with the data analysis, journalists must meet deadlines, whether the "story" is "complete" or not. Objective reporting helps to routinize work, permitting editors to count on five inches of copy or 30 seconds of air-time to fill space or time. Moreover, when the "newshole" at the local paper is limited (about 117 columns on the average at the *Beacon,* of which 19-25 columns were devoted to local news) and air-time is short (typically about 16 minutes on a 30-minute local telecast), there is not much room, in editors' minds, for "think pieces."

Also, objective reporting is usually one-person reporting while analytical pieces, like social science research, often entail team efforts. Elite news organizations may be willing to invest in such enterprises, but at the *Beacon*, for instance, writing obituaries demanded more staff time than any interpretive effort. Not only does team reporting tie up scarce resources (reporters) when editors are crying for "more copy" rather than "different" or "better" copy, it goes against the grain of many reporters who were trained to produce individual efforts in journalism schools. "Journalism ain't join-alism," one reporter told me, referring both to his anti-organizational mentality and his dislike of team reporting.

Another organizational factor which tends to promote objective reporting concerns the news format. In both print and electronic news, the unit of analysis is the news item, a self-contained particle of "reality." Making connections between news items, say between a story on high unemployment among black youth and another story on a "racial disturbance" at a local high school, is difficult under this format, a kaleidoscope of unconnected bits and pieces. But this format does have the organizational advantage over sequencing stories that form a larger whole, for bits can be added or removed according to space-time considerations.

There are a host of other reasons for objective reporting. Some deal with the writing style of newspaper journalism which is structured around the inverted pyramid, a format which orders information bits in the descending order of their presumed importance. Or, in TV news accounts, stories are structured around a beginning, middle, and end. These fixed formats may make contradictions difficult to acknowledge, but they do allow newsworkers to plan their work and judge their output by shared criteria (e.g., did the "story" include the five Ws and one H—Who, What, When, Where, How, and [rarely] Why?).

Additional reasons for not straying from what a source actually said (whether the statement was demonstrably false or not) and similar "factual" reportage, instead of attempting to report with what Park (1973:259) called "philosophic insight," concern standards of evidence. Objective reporting obviates the need for journalists to choose between conflicting truth claims. Most journalists are generalists, not specialists or "experts" in a particular subject area. Because reporters cannot or will not use either their own feelings about external evidence, their judgment of the source's expertise on complex matters, or scientific criteria for judging truth claims, they tend to avoid making statements whose truth cannot be easily proved or disproved (e.g., did the mayor actually say that the city was broke, not, is the city actually broke?).

To recapitulate, four craft-related explanations can be offered for the mass media's dependence on objective reporting as opposed to reporting with philosophic insight: (1) the lack of human resources, money, and time; (2) the desire to avoid offending segments of the mass audience by raising ideological or socially divisive issues; (3) the difficulty of sifting evidence and judging truth claims, and (4) the journalists' lack of expertise in substantive fields of knowledge.

In addition to these, however, my fieldwork and survey data suggest another craft-related explanation: journalists themselves do not conceptualize their own experience or place particular, concrete facts into broader theoretical frameworks. This failure to cast discrete bits of information into a more general perspective is related both to the style and format of "journalese" and to the practical nature of journalism as a discipline (see Phillips, 1976). Journalists are nontheoretic knowers who depend upon instinctive, concrete, first-hand "acquaintance with" events, not formal, systematic "knowledge about" events. Just as news as a form of knowledge is concrete and based on sense data, so is the journalist's understanding of the world based on direct sense experience, not abstract, systematic reflection. Like anthropologist Claude Levi-Strauss's (1968) primitive empiricist, the *bricoleur* (roughly translated as a do-it-yourselfer adept at performing many tasks with a finite set of tools), the journalist uses a logic of the concrete, a logic of the hand and the eye. Unlike the social scientist or engineer who looks at a discrete event or fact through concepts derived from a theory, the journalist qua bricoleur apprehends "reality" by noting concrete signs.

While a social scientist may indeed begin the process of research with a hunch or instinct, she or he does not depend upon that instinct as proof. Yet, reporters, explaining their own techniques of establishing truth claims, often allude to "instinct." For instance, then *New York Times* reporter Tom Wicker relates that during the Kennedy assassination, he had none of the "ordinary means" of checking out his facts. So, he took a few isolated facts, added them up, and relied on what "he felt in his bones," for, according to Wicker (1970:6),

> In a crisis if a reporter can't trust his instinct for truth, he can't trust anything.

This instinct, or what some call the "nose for news," appears to be based on first-hand acquaintance with how a particular social system works. Like Garfinkel's (1967:21) coders of information, however, reporters treating evidence as representations of the socially ordered ways of the system make assumptions about the way in which a system works although their coding procedures were intended to produce descriptions of those processes at work.

The dependence on instinct, a logic of the concrete, and signs as opposed to concepts are linked to a romantic vision (wherein reality is tested by experiencing Life rather than structuring the experience of life systematically). Taken as a whole, this epistemological stance, which stands in contrast to that taken by the social scientist, has a direct bearing on how the news is reported. The upshot of the journalists' nontheoretic way to knowledge is that they cannot transmit "philosophic insight" to the public because they themselves do not approach the world from a reflective, theoretical mental attitude.

That this mental attitude is related to practicing the craft of journalism, not the product of early childhood socialization, finds some support from sociolinguistics. Researcher Basil Bernstein (1960) argues that analytical cognitive processes and perception are class-linked. Journalists, who tend to be of middle- and upper-middle class origins, could be expected to employ the middle-class model where a "theoretical attitude" is encouraged. Lower-class persons are expected to be more concrete and less theoretic in their cognitive processes. That journalists are more concrete and less theoretic suggests that the craft of journalism may impose certain shared habits of mind and expression. Thus, objective reporting, with its attention to concrete particulars, and notions of objectivity, with their stress on "facts" (instead of "truths") are well-suited to the daily journalist's own habits of mind.

Additionally, there are legal and career considerations for using the norm of objectivity. Objectivity may often be a "strategic ritual," as Tuchman (1972) points out, but it is not always an empty one. For example, Watergate journalist Bob Woodward, his publishers, and some colleagues at the *Montgomery County Sentinel* lost a $356,000 libel suit in 1973 brought by a high school principal after the paper called him unsuitable for his post. Norms of objectivity can also serve to protect journalists from arbitrary bosses or publishers of differing political beliefs.

Briefly, then, the style of objective reporting and the norm of objectivity appear to be the cement holding together the journalistic enterprise. Both professionally, organizationally, and personally, the norm best captures the spirit of the craft and the journalist-bricoleur's mental habits. And, the norm appears to be shared by mass, heterogeneous audiences. While a 1977 *Indianapolis News* poll suggests that news readers and news editors have widely divergent views on which news stories are "most important," audience members are not demanding or lobbying for a different style of reporting. Operationally, this means that reporters and editors are free to select stories according to their own professional and personal standards,[6] while pointing to textbook rules for news judgment: timeliness, significance, human interest, and personal benefit. In areas exhibiting an absence of shared standards for what is timely, significant, interesting, and of personal benefit to people (see Sasser and Russell, 1970; Lyle, 1967), journalists can at least rely upon the norm of objectivity in the execution of news stories to evaluate their own efforts. The shared commitment to objectivity serves as an agreed-upon measure of performance.

As an occupational group, journalists appear to be much more satisfied in their jobs,[7] less alienated from the political process, and more optimistic about the way American society is headed than other occupational groups. They also feel that they have more control over their work than most other salaried employees. This contented disposition, relative to other occupational groups, may be related to the norm of objectivity, for it permits autonomy in news judgment, personal integrity, and provides a reference point for performance. Even the so-called New Journalists are "professional" journalists, and their quarrel with the norm of objectivity should not be misconstrued as an objection to norms of objectivity as the standard. The New Journalists, who, by and large, do not write for mass audiences, seem to want to expand the notion of what objectivity means, including using "the people of the street" as authoritative sources and getting at the essence of an event via masses of descriptively rich journalese detail; they are not providing a well-ordered, conceptual framework in which to put all the details any more than "Old Journalists."

Along these same lines, there is no reason to believe that the entry of nonmale, nonpale faces into the newsroom will influence news definitions, journalistic style, or the context in which events are placed. Journalists reject the doctrine of knowledge which holds that "you've got to be one to understand one," what Merton (1972) calls the "Insider as Insighter" doctrine. The journalists polled for this study reject this doctrine in its more forceful form (i.e., certain groups in a society have sole access to certain forms of knowledge) and its weaker form (i.e., some groups have privileged access to knowledge but outsiders can learn to share in that knowledge). At first glance, this may seem illogical, given the journalists' dependence on first-hand "acquaintance with" social reality as a knowledge base. But, in the journalists' view, being marginal to a situation does not preclude the capacity for empathy or *Verstehen.* As a TV reporter told me, "You've got to get involved. If you're doing a story on prostitution, you've gotta see what the prostitutes look like, live like, feel like."

Getting involved, at least as an empathic observer, is still the journalist's path to knowledge. Here the journalist resembles the social scientist doing fieldwork, but with one major difference: the social scientist as social reporter collects information to build or verify theory, fitting concrete facts into theoretical frameworks or developing new frameworks to better explain the data. In contrast, the journalist adduces facts for their own sake. As Curt MacDougall, author of a widely used text in *interpretive* reporting, stated:

> The truth-seeking reporter . . . if he is operating correctly, has no predetermined ends to seek, no hypothesis to prove—just the truth to be determined. [1968:12]

But what is the test of "truthfulness" in the absence of conceptual frameworks and scientific methods? One journalism professor recently suggested that "comparing the content of the news and the objective reality by means of extra media data is one approach" (Hemanus, 1976:106). Yet, the "important truths" such as the hidden structures of society, abstractions which must be inferred because they cannot be seen by the eyes, are not amenable to testing by (unspecified) extra media data.

At the base of canons of journalistic objectivity is the belief that "truth is imminent in the facts, and information can tell us what has happened or is happening." (Goodwin, 1974:5) This attitude does not allow for the notion that facts are, as Molotov said after World War II, nothing but propaganda. That is, the framework of belief as well as the choice of symbols used to evoke particular facts imposes an implicit point of view on facts (see Phillips, 1975). To some critics, like Goodwin (1974), this is the irredeemable flaw of objective journalism, for the facts can mask the truth while simultaneously putting the mark of truth on an event or situation.

THE CLASH RECONSIDERED

If the very definition of daily, mass journalism today implies a norm of objectivity that differs widely from the social scientist's understanding of that norm, how is the clash between the two fields to be resolved—or at least better understood? First, by acknowledging the different goals of the two disciplines, Journalism is a practical discipline; its end or *telos* is action, not theoretical knowledge. As a craft, it stands midway between theory and action, encouraging practitioners to depend upon first-hand "acquaintance with" knowledge of events. Occupational members tend to feel a sense of participation in events. On the contrary, social scientists look for regularities, patterns among events, and universals which stem from theoretical reflection rather than personal participation. While journalists are attracted to the unusual and contingent, social scientists search for structural necessities. Interestingly, these differences among the two groups showed up in a questionnaire item, an open-ended question asking respondents to name what four or five persons who've lived within the past 150 years are essential to understanding our times?" The students of social science and the journalists both listed U.S. presidents as their top choice, but the social science students ranked social theorists (e.g., John Maynard Keynes, Sigmund Freud) as the second most-named category while the journalists ranked foreign political figures as their second most-named category. Also, cultural/ literary figures (e.g., Kurt Vonnegut, Pablo Picasso, Bob Dylan) figured about three times more prominently in the journalists' responses than in the social science students' responses. This finding may reflect the notion that knowledge about the world is gained more through literary, artistic, and creative imagination and intuition than through theoretical knowledge.

In terms of social epistemology, Kazin (1973) has called attention to the difference between the journalist and the novelist:

> The world as our common experience is one that only the journalist feels entirely able to set down. It is a confidence that those who stick to fiction do not feel, for the "world" is not an experience in common, still less is it a concept on which we all agree.

If, as Kazin claims, journalists view the world as a common experience, they should reject special claims to knowledge on the basis of ascribed statuses such as sex, race, or class, that is, the "Insider as Insighter" doctrine (Merton, 1972). Two survey questions ("Can only a black truly understand black history?" and "Who would do a better job of reporting a story about discrimination against women—a female reporter, a male reporter, or it doesn't make any difference if the reporter is male or female?)" were designed to test Kazin's assertion. Upon tabulation, the data show that Kazin is correct, at least as far as journalists are concerned, for they soundly reject the notion that an Insider has special claims to knowledge. (Interestingly, 61% of the female journalists (N = 31) state that "it doesn't make any difference" whether a story about discrimination against women is reported by a male or female.) These data, together with responses to other survey questions concerning political knowledge (e.g., "Political theories are not very helpful in understanding politics"—strongly agree to strongly disagree) indicate that the journalist's path to knowledge stems from personal "acquaintance with" events (not "knowledge about" events) and that they perceive, via "acquaintance with" knowledge, the world as "common experience."

Another difference between journalists and social scientists re the norm of objectivity concerns the social location of their disciplines. Social scientists qua social scientists tend to remain on the periphery of social action, maintaining a sense of detachment and marginality whereas journalists feel that their products have public impact. It is also noteworthy that journalists, by and large, are not "marginal" in terms of their personal characteristics. According to the national random sample of Johnstone et al., (1974), journalists tend to be white, male, youthful, and middle- or upper-middle class in background; the sample of journalists polled and observed for this study was consistent with this profile.

Roshco (1975:56) points out that objective reporting "values impartiality above validity." (It could be added that social science highly values validity and reliability.) As he rightly notes, a great deal of confusion results from using the term "objectivity" to refer to the two different modes of data verification and knowledge: personal or instinctive acquaintance with versus abstract knowledge about. That the journalist's way to knowledge—both personally, professionally, and organizationally—is structured in one direction and the social scientist's is structured in another is an important factor underlying their frequently mutual incomprehension and distrust about which is the more useful for learning about and interpreting everyday life. Yet, ironically, the issue has erupted at a time when social science is also debating the notion of objectivity. For there is a revival of what is often referred to as "the interpretive approach." That is, an approach which "accepts a wider range of 'facts' " [than the positivist or behaviorist approach] and "rejects therefore the strictly scientific criteria of explanation." (Steinberger, 1977:97) The interpretive approach, which invokes such theorists as Alfred Schutz, George Herbert Mead, and Max Weber, presents a significantly different alternative to doing social science in an "objective" manner from the positivist mode where personal knowledge is eschewed. This approach, with its attention to personal knowledge, may later come to bridge the seemingly unresolvable distance between social scientific and journalistic notions of objectivity.

NOTES

1. The questionnaire was distributed in spring and summer, 1974, less than a year after the Louis Harris firm found that "a new majority of disaffected Americans has been found in this country . . ." (U.S. Congress, 1973:29). The journalists polled felt a higher degree of political efficacy than all four comparison groups as measured on a 4-item scale developed by the University of Michigan Survey Research Center (see Robinson et al., 1968:459) as well as the national random sample. It is often maintained that persons of high social status report higher levels of political efficacy than persons of lower status. However, this generalization does not account for the journalists' greater tendency to feel politically efficacious, for when compared to the "Selville" police department (N = 396)—members of an occupation ranked above radio announcers and equal to daily newspaper reporters in occupational prestige ratings—journalists tend to feel almost twice as politically efficacious.

2. According to Scott (1965:245), anomie is a social condition typified by lack of or too little conformity to social norms: "From the viewpoint of the individual this means he [sic] distrusts the motives of those around him. He regards others as determined to use him for their own ends. In short, he lives in a 'context of mutual distrust.' "

3. To protect the anonymity of "Selville," the police study will not be revealed.

4. This study focused on journalists working at nonelite news organizations, that is, local mass media serving local markets which do not enjoy national reputations. Network

TV or radio news organizations and papers such as the *New York Times* and the *Washington Post* exemplify elite news organizations and were not included.

5. In the main, journalists must guess or anticipate audience reaction. Feedback from the public, during my fieldwork of 13 months, was minimal. Few "Letters to the Editor" were addressed to either the newspaper or TV station in Selville. The greatest number of phone calls received at the TV station had nothing to do with their newscasts: irate viewers, angered at misprints in local TV guides concerning the feature movie following the news, accounted for the majority of phone calls. However, news sources—a reference group for journalists—often phoned reporters after a telecast.

6. Above all, journalists use their own personal standards to determine what is interesting and important to the public. Both my fieldwork, probing journalists' definitions of reader or listener interest, and the survey question, probing prime loyalties (to the public, own standards, news organization, boss, co-workers, or profession), suggest that the journalistic rule of thumb is "If I like it, so will the public" (see Phillips. 1975:Ch.4).

7. Data reported in *Work in America* (1973) show that out of a cross-section of white-collar and blue-collar workers, respectively 43% and 24% would choose to do similar work again. Urban university professors scored the highest in their sample: 93% would choose the same work over again. By contrast, the journalists in my sample are 99.4% satisfied with their careers. Only .06% state that, given a chance to start over, they would not choose journalism. The authors of *Work in America* state that responses to the question concerning re-choosing the same work has been one of the most reliable single indicators of job dissatisfaction over the last 20 years (1973:15).

REFERENCES

ARGYRIS, C. (1974). Behind the front page. San Francisco: Jossey-Bass.

ARONSON, J. (1972). Deadline for the media: Today's challenges to press, TV, and radio. Indianapolis: Bobbs-Merrill.

BAUER, R. (1964). "The communicator and the audience." Pp. 125-139 in L.A. Dexter and D.M. White (eds.), People, society, and mass communications. New York: Free Press.

BERNSTEIN, B. (1960). "Language and social class." British Journal of Sociology, 11:271-276.

BOWERS, D.R. (1967). "A report on activity by publishers in directing newsroom decisions." Journalism Quarterly, 44, 1(spring):43-52.

BREED, W. (1955). "Social control in the newsroom." Social Forces, 33:326-335.

CAREY, J. (1969). "The communications revolution and the professional communicator." Sociological Review, 13:23-38.

CIRINO, R. (1971). Don't blame the people. New York: Vintage.

DENZIN, N.K. (1970). "Introduction." Pp. 1-11 in N.K. Denzin (ed.), Sociological methods. Chicago: Aldine.

EFRON, E. (1972). The news twisters. Los Angeles: Nash.

EPSTEIN, E.J. (1973). News from nowhere. New York: Random House.

——— (1975). Between fact and fiction: The problem of journalism. New York: Vintage.

GARFINKEL, H. (1967). Studies in ethnomethodology. Englewood Cliffs, N.J.: Prentice-Hall.

GERBNER, G. (1964). "Ideological perspectives and political tendencies in news reporting." Journalism Quarterly, 41, 4(autumn):495-508, 516.

Glasgow University Media Group (1976). Bad news. London: Routledge and Kegal Paul.

GOODWIN, R. (1974). Review of Mary McCarthy's "The mask of state." New York Times Book Review, June 30:5.

HEMANUS, P. (1976). "Objectivity in news transmission." Journal of Communication, 26, 4(autumn):102-107.

HILTON, C.S. (1966). "Reporting the legislature: A study of newsmen and their sources." Unpublished M.A. thesis, University of Washington.

JOHNSTONE, J.W.C. et al. (1974). "Newsmen and newswork." Unpublished manuscript. (Published in 1976 as The news people: A sociological portrait of American journalists and their work. Urbana, Ill.: University of Illinois Press.

KAZIN, A. (1973). Bright book of life. Boston: Atlantic-Little, Brown.

KEELEY, J. (1971). The left-leaning antenna: Political bias in television. New Rochelle, N.Y.: Arlington House.

LEVI-STRAUSS, C. (1968). The savage mind. Chicago: University of Chicago Press.

LYLE, J. (1967). The news in megalopolis. San Francisco: Chandler.

MacDOUGALL, C.D. (1968). Interpretative reporting. New York: Macmillan.

MARCUSE, H. (1964). One-dimensional man. London: Routledge and Kegan Paul.

MERTON, R. (1972). "Insiders and outsiders: A chapter in the sociology of knowledge." American Journal of Sociology, 78, 1(July):9-47.

MOLOTCH, H. and LESTER, M. (1974). "News as purposive behavior: On the strategic use of routine events, accidents, and scandals." American Sociological Review, 39:101-112.

NOVAK, M. (1971). "The inevitable bias of television." Pp. 121-132 in M. Barrett (ed.), Survey of broadcast journalism 1970-1971. New York: Grosset & Dunlap.

PARK, R.E. (1973). "Life history." American Journal of Sociology, 79, 2(September): 243-260.

––– (1973). "Beyond 'ideological plugola': The public interpretation of reality." Maxwell Review, 9, 2(spring):1-34.

PHILLIPS, E.B. (1975). "The artists of everyday life: Journalists, their craft, and their consciousness." Unpublished Ph.D. dissertation, Syracuse University (University Microfilms no. 76-18,550).

––– (1976). "Novelty without change." Journal of Communication, 26, 4(autumn):87-92.

ROBINSON, J.P., and SHAVER, P. (1968). Measures of political attitudes. Ann Arbor, Mich.: Institute for Social Research.

ROSHCO, B. (1975). Newsmaking. Chicago: University of Chicago Press.

SASSER, E.L., and RUSSELL, J.T. (1972). "The fallacy of news judgment." Journalism Quarterly, 49, 3(summer):280-284.

SCOTT, M. (1965). "The social sources of alienation." Pp. 239-252 in I.L. Horowitz (ed.), The new sociology. New York: Oxford University Press.

SIGAL, L.V. (1973). Reporters and officials. Lexington, Mass.: D.C. Heath.

SROLE, L. (1956). "Social integration and certain corollaries." American Sociological Review, 21:709-716.

STEINBERGER, P.J. (1977). "Hegel as a social scientist." American Political Science Review, 71, 1(March):95-110.

TUCHMAN, G. (1972). "Objectivity as stratetic ritual: An examination of newsmen's notions of objectivity." American Journal of Sociology, 77, 4(January):660-679.

U.S. Congress, Senate Committee on Government Operations (1973). Confidence and concern: Citizens view American government (Hearings). 93rd Congress, 1st session, December 3.

WEBER, M. (1958). "Science as a vocation." Pp. 129-156 in H.H. Gerth and C.W. Mills (eds.), From Max Weber: Essays in sociology. New York: Oxford University Press.

WHITE, D.M. (1964). "The gatekeeper: A case study in the selection of news." Pp. 160-171 in L.A. Dexter and D.M. White (eds.), People, society and mass communications. New York: Free Press.

WICKER, T. (1970). "The assassination." Pp. 3-14 in R. Adler (ed.), The working press: Special to the New York Times. New York: Bantam.

Work in America (1973). Report of a special task force to the Secretary of Health, Education, and Welfare. Cambridge, Mass.: MIT Press.

Chapter 4

CLIENT RELATIONSHIP AND CHILDREN'S BOOK PUBLISHING: A COMPARATIVE STUDY OF MASS MEDIA POLICY IN TWO MARKETPLACES

Joseph Turow

ONE OF THE HALLMARKS OF MASS COMMUNICATION—perhaps even one of its defining characteristics—is the framework in which it takes place. Mass communication is the industrialized ("mass") production of messages. As such, it is process which typically occurs within a mass media complex—an informal conglomeration of organizations that consistently interact in the process of producing and distributing mass media content.

Scholars have been increasingly recognizing the importance of investigating the organizations which produce patterns of messages which the large, dispersed groups in a society share as a significant part of their symbolic environment. Research has shown that factors other than the purported ultimate audience are often most immediately important to those within mass media organizations who are responsible for the selection of content, though audience images do sometimes play a significant background role (see, for example, Breed, 1955; Cantor, 1971; Epstein, 1973; Gieber, 1964; Tuchman, 1972; and White, 1950). Organizational goals and requirements; colleague and coworker rapport and pressures; the need to routinize tasks; technological constraints—these have been called more salient than the audience.

While such studies are quite important for the light they shed on some determinants of content, their frameworks for analysis are often too narrow to focus on certain types of questions regarding influences. For example, even when a researcher has gone beyond the study of a single role to investigate the interactions of several positions and learn how organizational structure and processes affect content selection, the investigator has still not addressed (and, by the nature of the research design, cannot address) the larger question of how that organization's structure and decision-making processes are themselves shaped. Studies which have scrutinized extra-organizational influences upon mass media production organizations to some degree (e.g., Powdermaker, 1951, and Denisoff, 1975) tend to lack a theoretical base from which to generalize the findings to other mass media complexes. Also missing from the literature are comparative analyses of mass media *complexes* which examine how different characteristics within otherwise similar complexes influence the production of content, its distribution, and the final choices presented to the consumer.

Conceptual frameworks for such systemic, comparative analyses are not totally lacking. Hirsch (1969, 1972), for example, proposes an "industry system" perspective to be used to examine relations among mass media organizations and to "trace the flow of new products and ideas as they are filtered at each level of organization" (1972:657). Gerbner (1969), in reviewing "institutional pressures on mass communicators," focuses attention on the continual interactions between different types of organizations that participate in the production and distribution of content. "Client relationship" is his term to describe the continual interaction between "media management" organizations (those which produce mass media content) and "patron" organizations (which advertise in or subsidize material—p. 243). Because the producers are dependent upon their patrons for solvency, the "client relationship" may be seen as the most important relationship within a mass media complex.

This paper draws on these frameworks to examine the consequences of different client relationships in the children's book publishing market for the production and distribution of mass media content directed to the same audience. General children's (nontext) book publishing contains two separate segments with distinct, usually nonoverlapping, production and distribution outlet organizations (Lanes, 1971). The *library* market consists mostly of nonprofit institutions whose selectors purchase books from library-oriented publishing firms. The commercially oriented *mass* market for children's books is dominated by department, chain, and book stores, which purchase the overwhelming majority of their titles from a different group of publishing firms. In both client relationships, the patron organizations (libraries or stores) are the most important distributors of publishers' books to the children and/or their parents.

METHOD OF STUDY

To explore the influence of the client relationship within these two publishing industry segments, I conducted a comparative case study. One important publishing organization in each market, one patron organization from the library market, and two patron organizations from the mass market were examined. The goal was to trace the factors guiding selectors of content within each publishing organization and, in the process, gauge the influence of client relationships on the decisions of editors, and buyers for stores and libraries. At the production end, the firms studied were large publishing houses whose children's book divisions have strong sales records and good reputations. At the distribution level, the nationally prominent juvenile division of a metropolitan public library system was examined, as were two mass market distribution outlets—a bookstore chain and a department store chain in the same city.

Two types of "selectors" in each organization were defined. A "direct" selector decides on the selection, timing, withholding, or repetition of particular content. An "indirect" selector is one who controls the resources needed by direct selectors to carry out their duties. For example, children's book editors are usually direct selectors while company finance directors are usually indirect selectors. An attempt was made to reach all direct selectors in each organization. In addition, key indirect selectors mentioned during interviews with direct selectors were contacted. Interviews were conducted with 62 people connected to the five focal organizations; a questionnaire survey was administered to 50 librarians; and the new titles released by the two publishers and purchased by the outlet organizations during approximately the same time period were categorized. The results strongly suggest that differences between the mass and library market client relationships have produced systemic and deeply rooted organizational differences. Those differences, in turn, appear to guide very different editorial, marketing, and buying choices within the two publishing segments, even though the purported audience of the segments (children) is the same.

THE CLIENT RELATIONSHIPS AND
THE PUBLISHING FIRMS

The division of the children's book industry into firms which produce books for retail sale and others which produce for libraries is long-standing and traces back to the development of those markets during the late 19th century (Turow, 1976). Client relationships have been shaped by three major considerations—the tradition of the publishing house and proclivities of its editors; the environment of selection in, and economic nature of, the marketplace; and the feedback and promotional environment. Both the interviews and a first-hand examination of organizational activities suggest that different conceptions of client relationship are major influences in bringing about and perpetuating differences in (1) the *structure of decision-making* (the channels and direction of communication) regarding the books to be published; (2) the *process* of selecting books to be published; (3) the *guidelines* which editors have about content characteristics; (4) their *images* of the people who read their books; and (5) the *types* of titles that are actually published in the two publishing markets.

THE LIBRARY MARKET PUBLISHING FIRM

The "bottom line" economic significance of libraries and librarians was well understood by respondents in the publishing firm producing for this market. The children's division's publisher, for example, noted that "librarians are very important to us because they are the ones who bring books to children." Interviewees also were quick to suggest that to simply imitate past successes is a sure way to failure in this market, because librarians shun formulaic material, despite its original appeal. The general consensus was that librarians are professionals who have been trained to select what people in this industry segment characterized consistently as "good books." An editor and a promotional director agreed that even in times of budgetary crises with limited book-buying funds, a librarian's first priority is "quality," not price.

These respondents' views of the library market's requirement that they publish "good books" is consonant with their own publishing interests and their division's award-winning tradition in the library market segment. Experience with the promotional and feedback environment in which they operate makes them quite confident of their ability to successfully publish "innovative" children's literature falling in the category, "good books." The library market environment encompasses direct and indirect avenues of contact with the library world. Indirect avenues include the effective utilization of trade journals and book review media and the circulation of "review copies" to important librarians. Direct avenues include the interactions of this publisher's editors, promotion director, and seven-person promotion team with librarians and library school teachers (who influence the opinions of future librarians), where they work, and at conferences. The firm's marketing director and an editor both stated that acquaintances with librarians and knowledge about them are most frequently and forcefully used for the promotion of books rather than for guidance prior to selection of publication. Stories told by several interviewees of the firm's success in promoting unusual or avant-garde books highlighted their belief that the publishing community can initiate new trends and, within limits, shape the views of the library community as to what is "good."

Selecting Books for the Library Market. Client relationships in the library market affect the organization structure of publishing houses producing for it. For example, the publisher studied employs several "readers" to conduct a preliminary examination of every manuscript submitted and suggest to the editors whether any warrant more serious consideration. One of the aims of this review (the greatest portion of which covers unsolicited manuscripts from "unknowns") is promotional—to show librarians that the firm is indeed actively searching for the best in children's literature wherever it can be found. One editor pointed to somewhat more concrete demands from the marketplace for going to great lengths to review all arrivals: The vogues of the library market change frequently because librarians emphasize new directions as well as simply replace old books. Editors must therefore discover new writers and illustrators as well as ensure that the division's backlist continues to feature books which circulate well and retain a reputation for "quality."

Concerning the number of new books chosen each (fall and spring) publishing season, several editors mentioned that a triennial assessment of the market, and the firm's share and economic position, had produced a current guideline of approximately 25-30 new books per season. All the interviewees stressed, however, that their year-round evaluation of manuscripts and the necessity of relying on authors to originate and deliver acceptable works makes it impossible to dictate the exact size of the list. At the same time, it is important to note that this library-oriented children's division is less subject to marketing and sales department approval for the publication of new titles than any other division in the company. One reason for its independence is the absence of any substantial role for the firm's trade force in this division's activities, for librarians order books directly from institutional wholesalers.

Guidelines. Two words used by several editors to characterize the guidelines they use in selecting books were "variety" and "balance." A primary reason for the varied assortment of new books is a feeling that librarians might be loath to buy several books on the same topic or directed at the same age category from one company's list. The editors added that since they know librarians classify children according to different age groupings (encompassing years three to twelve) and different interests, the division should try to balance these categories in the hope that librarians will need all the books on the list. An added impetus towards a "varied" list in terms of age (or grade) levels and subject matter lies in the different interests of the division's editors. Although every editor interviewed admitted to certain likes and dislikes in developing manuscripts, all stressed a preference for working on different kinds of books to vary routines and expand their creativity.

The editors maintain they select individual titles without any formal guidelines. This state of affairs would be consonant with the client relationship, since adhering to specific guidelines could be construed as taking a formulaic approach to what both librarians and these editors like to portray as an artistic endeavor. However, they did state that plot, writing style, characterization, and illustrations (in picture books) are the most important characteristics. The nonformulaic, individual nature of each title was stressed: Broad leeway is allowed for plot (required to be successful "on its own terms"), a personal style is demanded of author and illustrator, and depth and believability are required in characterization. One editor noted a general dislike for anthropomorphic portrayals. All agreed that series books and easy readers produced from word lists are likely to be hopelessly formulaic. Cartoonish illustrations were similarly seen to be generally unacceptable.

Regarding a work's moral point of view, the editors decried titles which are obviously dogmatic or moralistic, though they did note that a book which has no redeeming moral or social value will be rejected. Drugs, abortion, racial discrimination, homosexuality—these and other controversial subjects have been treated in library market-oriented children's books. The confidence of the editors in dealing with such sensitive areas can be traced to an aspect of the client relationship which was raised by several respondents—the support librarians give publishers by acting as buffers between them and complaining community groups.

The Client Relationship and Audience Images. One broad notion regarding selection that the editors implicitly accepted was that the nature, extent, and complexity of a work should vary with the expected age of the reader, according to general conceptions of childhood and childhood interests (acquired, in part, from librarians). However, when asked about the kind of image they have of the "people who read" their books, they all admitted they are not concerned with thinking in such terms. One of the editors, after saying that "we don't have an image," added that children who visit the library get more of "what they really want" than in a department store, since librarians choose books which they know from experience children will like. When three editors did try to characterize their audience, they simply projected an image of readers who would logically correspond to their firm's book list, e.g., "multifaceted," "probably pretty good readers." Even the library market's audience image can thus be seen as a reflection of the publisher's interpretation of the demands of and possibilities in the client relationship.

THE MASS MARKET PUBLISHING FIRM

Answers to the same interview questions by editors for a mass market book publisher oriented to retail sales reflected a very different conception of the client relationship and the definition of a "children's book." This publisher's orientation to the mass market is intimately connected to a trade book tradition for the entire company: The children's division was created with the intention of relying on the firm's already effective sales force to place juvenile titles in the same book, department, and chain store outlets that carry the company's popular adult books.

Editors for the mass market publisher described an environment quite different from that portrayed by the library market's selectors in conceptualizing their client relationship. Both groups did note a dearth of advertising and promotion by both types of children's book publishers (which continues for reasons of cost and industry inertia). However, the library market selectors pointed out that, in place of direct promotion, they rely on librarians to introduce their books to children and parents. The mass market-oriented interviewees, by contrast, stressed that clerks in most of their distribution outlets have little knowledge or time to introduce particular titles to customers.

This situation in the mass market has led to a demand from buyers (representing distribution outlets or jobbers who buy books from publishers) that the juvenile works they purchase essentially "sell themselves." "Lines" (groups of titles in similar formats) and—more rarely—individual titles that have proven sales records are bought repeatedly by outlets. Exterior characteristics (format, cover attractiveness, general subject) are of primary importance; buyers' criteria also include color and competitively low prices (usually from under $2 to around $4.95—about $4 lower than in the library market) as crucial factors for acceptance. The importance of a book's similarity to others with good mass market "track records" was underscored by respondents, for it is much easier to sell a new title to a store or jobber representative if it is introduced as an addition to a popular line. And, as described by one mass market publishing executive, "If you can get them in [stores, particularly enough stores to justify the necessarily low price] you can sell them."

The importance of salespeople for this publisher is another feature which distinguishes it from the library-oriented firm. Here, the sales force is crucial for getting books into the stores and to the jobbers. The salespeople who service major accounts do not usually talk to buyers in terms of lines. Rather, they deal in "programs"—packages of books which are tailored to the individual "turnover" and profit requirements of each outlet. The strong influence of the sales department places the editors for the mass market in the position of having to convince their sales force to wholeheartedly recommend their new titles to buyers as books which will sell themselves. In view of this aspect of the firm's client relationship, it should not be surprising that these editors, in contrast to the library market's, believe their division is *more* dependent on the opinions of the marketing and sales force than any other in the company.

In this particular firm, the marketing orientation was further strengthened by the dual assignment of the company's marketing vice president to the position of juvenile division publisher. While he suggested that this combination of roles was an historical accident, the sales manager and others mentioned the importance of the publisher's marketing expertise in helping the division respond quickly and properly to the mass market environment. This contrasts with the library market (where the publisher was an editor) and points up the different primary requirements of the two client relationships. Other structural contrasts also reflect differences in client relationship. For example, it will be recalled that the library-oriented firm's editors and readers are allowed to work on different types of books with the aim of fostering creativity. By contrast, editors for the mass market-oriented publisher are assigned to one of four separate sections which, for reasons of efficiency and predictability, produce particular lines targeted for particular age levels. In two of these sections, the editorial supervisors also perceived their role as that of marketing expert.

Selecting Books for the Mass Market. These appropriately contrasting organizational responses to very different client relationships have fostered divergent approaches to the selection and production of juvenile books. The library-oriented firm's procedure is a strict selection process, in which special readers and editors choose manuscripts by authors who frequently publish through the firm, by other known talent, or even by "over the transom" discoveries. The publisher here mainly confirms (making sure that a manuscript is an economically feasible "good book") and oversees (making sure the list is "balanced"). In the mass market case, however, most of the titles are originated by the editors and section heads themselves, at the specific request of the publisher (who ties the particular number of books needed to reports on what buyers are willing to outlay). Reliable talent is then recruited to complete the job; sometimes the editors themselves write picture book copy. Such a procedure allows for a high degree of control over the final product and—just as important—helps reduce costs, since the writers or illustrators can be paid lump sums or very small royalties for following directions or well-plotted formulas. In those cases where the books do not originate with the firm's editors, they are usually developed by its several "name" author-illustrators, who are under long-term contract and whose names bespeak "track record" to salespeople and buyers alike.

Guidelines. Besides having the already noted requirements regarding price and color illustrations, the mass market-oriented selectors preferred easily recognizable and admittedly formulaic stories and characters; favored cartoony drawings and anthropomorphic characterization; and championed the series book format. These and other guidelines (quite at odds with those favored in the library market) cultivate the "instant appeal" (and, hence, "self-salability") of lines. Writing style and character depth, both considered extremely important in the library market, were not deemed important by the mass market-oriented editors. They seemed to feel that since these content characteristics are not evident to the stores' agents (who, unlike librarian reviewers, do not read the books) nor probably to the adult or child customers (who are "sold" immediately on the subject and other visible "track record" elements), they can be sacrificed in favor of reduced costs (through the hiring of inexpensive writers).

The Client Relationship and Images of the Ultimate Audience. When editors in both firms were asked about their images of "the people who read" their books, all uniformly denied any knowledge of their ultimate audience. One mass market-oriented executive observed, and people in the library market also noted, that no market research is carried out and "We're really flying by the seat of our pants." Another editor characterized as "parlor wisdom" the mass marketing selectors' assumption that parents usually choose books for younger children (with or without the children present) and that adolescents have more access to books on their own.

Nevertheless, all of the editors articulated guidelines and acted as if they did have clear impressions of their ultimate audience. Actually, in both markets, those implicit impressions are largely reflections of the requirements of the children's respective purchasing agents and of opportunities which they perceived from their client relationships. However, the mass market editors felt that the books they publish are generally those which children want. In fact, the company's trade publicity director even contended that because parents know their children better than librarians do, mass market books are the more likely to give children what they really want. Recall that the exact opposite opinion was voiced by an editor for the library market.

CLIENT RELATIONSHIPS AND THE
DISTRIBUTION OUTLETS:
LIBRARIES AND RETAIL STORES

THE LIBRARY MARKET DISTRIBUTION OUTLET

In the library market, selection perspectives are reinforced through the activities of a "System Coordinating Office" (SCO), comprised of several librarians who set juvenile library policy guidelines for the system's forty-six branch librarians. The coordinators are in continual direct or indirect contact with representatives of library market publishing firms. The head coordinator, well aware of the promotional tactics directed to her and her SCO associates, contended such actions are two-way, that by allowing publishers to influence her and to promote books to the branch librarians through her, she receives the opportunity to make a mark on their editorial activities and, by extension, to participate in the definition of "good books" of high quality.

The little contact between branch librarians and the publishing world, combined with a correspondingly small degree of association between coordinators (because of their administrative positions) and children, has led to some tension between the two groups regarding selection guidelines. Both coordinators and branch personnel cited the library's "General Statement of Objectives" as mandating selection according to the goals of "literary quality" and "child enjoyment." However, the groups differed in their relative emphasis upon each of these goals, with the coordinators emphasizing "literary quality" and the branch librarians tending to emphasize a book's potential "enjoyment" and (more particularly) its "popularity." Tension between the coordinators and branch librarians is mitigated through a book selection process which, though giving the SCO ultimate control, allows the branch librarians some freedom of choice. The procedure, which entails a two-tiered (system-level and branch-level) operation, has been encouraged by the inundation of the Coordinating Office with "review copies" from the publishers. This practice of sending complimentary (or highly discounted) copies of new titles to large library systems with the understanding that each book will be read by at least one librarian has the cumulative effect of perpetuating the requirement to judge a title after reading it (or trustworthy reviews of it) and not simply after superficially noting its author, publisher, and general subject.

As might be expected, preferences articulated in the SCO-based selection tier of the library system were similar to those stated by editors in the library market-oriented publishing firm. Respondents even noted where particular selection trends and perspectives were shaped by their major suppliers, for example, regarding a relatively recent influx of "problem books" with titles concerning issues like divorce or sexual conflicts. Guidelines in the second tier (the branch libraries in the library system) shift from the SCO's focus on artistic aspects of content and on critical acclaim to a concern with the projected popularity of a title's subject matter or (more rarely) its author's track record. This emphasis on "popularity" seldom clashes with the SCO's primary concern with "quality," however, because it can only be applied to books which have been screened by the coordinators for quality before arriving at the branch level. Nevertheless, pressures are sometimes felt by librarians to purchase books considered exceptionally good by coordinators but which the branch staff feels will be difficult to "sell" to a large number of children. In addition, branch librarians have sometimes gotten into open (though usually unsuccessful) arguments with their superiors over the latter's refusal to accept titles which are extremely popular in the mass market. Examples include the "Nancy Drew" series and picture books by Richard Scarry. Perhaps the clearest evidence of the library coordinators' preference for the books of library market-oriented publishers is the finding that 48% of 1,927 titles received from these firms during 1974-1975 were accepted for general branch circulation, while only 96 mass market titles were received and only 29% of these ordered. In addition, the SCO head commented that mass market firms send libraries only those titles which they feel are potential "crossover" material.

THE MASS MARKET DISTRIBUTION OUTLETS

The situation in the mass market book and department stores examined was quite different. Of the 54 new titles purchased by the bookstore chain during 1974-1975, 53 (98%) were from mass market publishers. A less systematic survey of the department store yielded similar findings. This domination by mass market products was reduced somewhat by the purchase of several popular, older titles from the library market. Here too, however, selection criteria quite different from those of the library system were also employed.

Despite such substantial differences between the mass market and library market outlets, the influence of the client relationship is analytically similar in both places: The relationship exerts a powerful reinforcing and guiding influence on selectors' approaches to books. In the interest of brevity, the present discussion will use only the bookstore chain for illustration.

Unlike the library market outlet, the bookstore chain has only two selectors (a chief juvenile buyer and an assistant), who purchase the same books for all of the organization's branches. The chief buyer emphasized the savings obtained through centralized purchasing and space allocation for each store. With space at a premium (only 10% is designated for juveniles), each title must be "justified" in terms of its ultimate profitability. This is done by projecting the frequency with which a title "turns" in relation to its per unit profit and the cost of the space it occupies.

The juvenile buyer noted that these organizational requirements are applicable to nonjuvenile books as well. However, he pointed out that while retailers order adult "trade" and paperback titles in anticipation (or as a result) of publishers' advertising and publicity, juvenile books are generally expected to sell themselves. The buyer accepted the dearth of promotion by children's book publishers, and the ignorance of store clerks about them as traditional "givens," to be taken into account rather than overcome by publishers or retailers. The influence of the major client relationship is evident in this perspective which, basically, leaves to the publisher decisions about publicity and public awareness of children's books for the mass retail market. This industry-wide "path of least resistance" directs the buyer to firms which reinforce this perspective and produce hardbacks and paperbacks that "sell themselves." Interestingly, this also helps to discourage competition from children's book publishers oriented to the library market. The same buyer noted that salespeople from library market-oriented children's book publishers (whose primary aim for visiting is to sell adult titles to the chain) do not expect their firm's juvenile selections to be ordered and so do not try very seriously to promote them to retail outlets. It seems clear that the cumulative consequence of this self-inhibition is to clear the field for mass market publishers. Also reinforcing the mass market firms' dominant position is the buyer's reliance on the "line" concept as an aid in efficient selection of juvenile books, since it is quite expensive and risky for a publisher without a mass market track record to create a line for that arena.

From the client relationship between the producers and distributors of children's books, we have derived differences in the organization structure, perspectives, and policies followed in all areas of the library and mass market segments of this industry. These findings strongly support the organizational perspective that factors other than the ultimate audience exert substantial influence on decisions about mass media content. Indeed, most of the editors interviewed maintained an image of their readers shaped by organizational demands and opportunities which were, in turn, determined by their organizations' major client relationships. These dynamics should be generalizable to other mass media complexes.

THE CLIENT RELATIONSHIP AS A COMMUNICATION SYSTEM

In view of the necessity for stable organizational operations (March and Simon, 1958; Tuchman, 1973), it is significant that the client relationship—and the production and distribution dynamics which characterize it—was found to be the primary factor in shaping the routinized activities of media management and patron organizations in each industry segment. The crucial influence of the client relationship upon these processes follows from continuous patron-management interactions which comprise a stable communication system through which the mutual requirements and opportunities of each member are perceived and acted upon.

We found that editors were more concerned than librarians or bookstore representatives with receiving feedback about their counterparts in the client relationship. The publishing people were also more active and initiatory with respect to using the relationship to reinforce certain perspectives about the marketplace. This difference in the extent of feedback and control efforts by the producer and distributor organizations in both segments can be attributed to the differential importance of each to the various types of organizations involved here. For while the solvency of the publishing firms in both segments is dependent on continued patronage by their clients, the clients' solvency is relatively unaffected by the publishing firms'. The publishers' need to maintain influence over their outlets' selection perspective also can be understood in this context. Having organized their activities and power bases around the current rules of the client relationship, the producers try to maintain their power by maintaining those rules. The client relationship helps them to achieve this aim.

REFERENCES

BREED, W. (1955). "Social control in the newsroom: A functional analysis." Social Forces, 33:326-335.

CANTOR, M. (1971). The Hollywood TV producer: His work and his audience. New York: Basic Books.

DENISOFF, R.S. (1975). Solid gold: The popular music industry. New Brunswick, N.J.: Transaction Books.

EPSTEIN, E.J. (1973). News from nowhere. New York: Vintage.

GERBNER, G. (1969). "Institutional pressures on mass communicators." Sociological Review, Monograph No. 13:205-248.

GIEBER, W. (1964). "News is what newspapermen make it." In L. Dexter and D. White (eds.), People, society, and mass communication. New York: Free Press.

HIRSCH, P.M. (1972). "Processing fads and fashions: An organization-set analysis of cultural industry systems." American Journal of Sociology, 77, 4(January):639-659.

——— (1969). The structure of the popular music industry. Ann Arbor: University of Michigan Institute for Social Research.

LANES, S. (1971). Down the rabbit hole: Adventures and misadventures in the realm of children's literature. New York: Atheneum.

MARCH, J., and SIMON, H. (1958). Organizations. New York: John Wiley.

POWDERMAKER, H. (1951). Hollywood: The dream factory. Boston: Little Brown.

TUCHMAN, G. (1972). "Objectivity as strategic ritual: An examination of newsmen's notions of objectivity." American Journal of Sociology, 77, 4(February):600-639.

——— (1973). "Making news by doing work: Routinizing the unexpected." American Journal of Sociology, 79, 1(July):110-131.

TUROW, J. (1976). "Client relationship and mass media policy: A comparative case study of mass market and library market production and distribution in children's book publishing." Unpublished Ph.D. dissertation, University of Pennsylvania.

WHITE, D.M. (1950). "The gatekeeper: A case study in the selection of news." Journalism Quarterly, 27, 4(fall):383-390.

Chapter 5

WHEN CULTURE BECOMES A BUSINESS

William N. McPhee

Most of our mass culture today is created for money, for profit. Commercialism is not new; money has always followed artistry. But for artistry to follow money, for profit to become the whole point of culture, is new on this scale. Not bad, simply recent: no one knows the consequences.[1]

For example, two aspects of commercial culture seem to have profoundly conservative consequences. They are that the audience (1) gets what it wants, and (2) wants what it gets.

The first is due to feedback from audience to producers. In extreme degree it is the alleged "slavishness" of producers to box office, best-seller lists, top-tens, polls, ratings, and so on. Let us define the degree of this dependency on feedback, as the degree to which

(1) A given type of cultural material is produced in proportion that, and only in proportion that, it is currently being consumed.

This process is notoriously circular, however. In the 1940's and 1950's, for example, did consumers demand bigger and bigger autos, or did Detroit *supply* bigger and bigger autos? Products teach consumers what to want, notably through advertising. In fields like television, moreover, audiences "take what's on." The producer's alternatives command attention by sheer accessibility. A second process, therefore, is the degree to which

(2) A given type of cultural material is consumed in proportion that, and only in proportion that, it is currently being produced.

This is the reverse of feedback, a kind of "forward feed" from production to consumption. At the extreme, it is like force feeding.

* Thanks are due to the National Science Foundation for support under Grant GS–221. This is Publication *38* of the Institute of Behavioral Science, University of Colorado. The first part of this chapter is based on a note previously published in *Studies in Public Communication*, August, 1962.

[1] Some of the most prolific periods in the history of drama and opera were, for example, rather commercialized. Most of the work was bad but, paradoxically, classics like Shakespeare date from such periods.

From J. Berger, M. Zeldich, and B. Anderson (eds.), **Sociological Theories in Progress**, Vol. 1. Boston: Houghton Mifflin, pp. 227-243, 1966. Reprinted with permission of author and publisher.

The two processes together would be circular, producers following consumers and consumers following producers. That would go nowhere. Hence our conservative prognosis when culture does the same.

The point, however, is that no one really knows the consequences. This chapter illustrates by showing that, as a matter of fact, the circular processes above have the *opposite* of conservative consequences. The businessman in mass culture may think he is "playing it safe" by constantly adjusting to feedback from audiences, but this may be the source of his ulcers. And audiences may think they are staying with what is "familiar," by taking whatever is available, but this may be the source of their bewilderment at changes in popular culture. For such processes lead, not to stability, but to instability.

□ **1. A SIMPLE MODEL**

Consider the production of a type of cultural material, say, rock-n-roll music. Call this material type i. Then picture its production, for example, when rock-n-roll was first becoming popular in the early 1950's, as having two components:

$$\begin{pmatrix} \text{Production} \\ \text{of material} \\ \text{of type } i \end{pmatrix} = \begin{pmatrix} \text{A portion inde-} \\ \text{pendent of con-} \\ \text{sumption of } i \end{pmatrix} + \begin{pmatrix} \text{A portion de-} \\ \text{pendent on con-} \\ \text{sumption of } i \end{pmatrix}$$

Noncommercial predecessors of rock-n-roll, for example, have (under names like rhythm-n-blues) long been created by Negro jazz and Southern folk musicians for their own enjoyment, independent of a small market that long existed also under the name "race" music, attracting commercial production in South Chicago, for instance.[2]

To put all this formally, let p_t be the total production of this type of material, for both reasons, at a given time, t. Then p_{t+1} will be production of the same in the next time period, say, next month or next quarter of the year. Let u_t and u_{t+1} be the corresponding levels of "use" or consumption of the same material, by the public, in this time period and next period, respectively. Then let production consist of the two components in the diagram above.

$$p_{t+1} = a + cu_t, \tag{1}$$

where a and c are constants having the following connotations:

$a =$ "artistic" production independent of popular consumption, i.e., regardless of demand.

$cu_t =$ "commercial" production, a proportion c of current consumption motivated by the latter.

[2] Background on popular music in this chapter is due to unpublished studies of that industry in the mid-1950's by Philip Ennis, Rolf Meyersohn, and Sidney Spivak at the Bureau of Applied Social Research, Columbia University.

Of course life is never this simple. This is purely an analytic device for thinking simply about such problems.

Next, let use or consumption of this material be an analogous process, the only difference being that we make it responsive to current rather than previous production (time subscripts are here the same on both sides):

$$u_t = b + dp_t, \tag{2}$$

where b and d are constants with the following connotations:

b = "basic" audience or use for this material, its irreducible following regardless of current fashions in production.

dp_t = "deutero" (secondary) audience, purely derivative from production of the material, in proportion d to that production.

Another connotation of d is the degree of "dependency" of audiences on what is produced for what they consume, for example, the passivity of watching whatever is on television instead of pursuing one's own interests.

A note discusses how such constants can be estimated for particular cases, either from aggregate data on production and consumption or from the behavior of individuals.[3] Here we concentrate on the theoretical consequences.

□ 2. "ALL OR NOTHING" PROBLEMS

One kind of consequence is particularly exasperating in mass culture, because it is so irreversible. It is the intolerance of that culture, a given field of it, for pluralism. Detroit started with perhaps fifty different tastes in cars, but by the 1950's was down to one car, merely labelled variously. Radio in the 1920's started heterogeneously, but by the late 1940's had virtually the *same* "top ten" as it had had a decade previously, despite a world war in between![4] Television broke up this pattern, with great pluralistic vitality, in the early 1950's. But by the end of a decade, about half of the nighttime programs fell into one action-adventure category, whether westerns or easterns in locale, that not even modern factor analysis could differentiate.[5]

This cannot be villainy nor stupidity, for every pressure is on television, indeed, its commercial and political life may depend on *not* letting one kind of fare "take over" like this. Instead, each and every kind of fare should be

---

[3] Linear regression analysis would be the efficient procedure for aggregate data. For individual data, as in a panel survey, a method is given in working papers on project NSF, GS–221, Institute of Behavioral Science, University of Colorado.

[4] I have not bothered for this chapter to find the exact years, but one pre-war and one late-1940's pair of polls showed the *identical* programs in the top ten, merely the order changed slightly.

[5] Technically, cluster analysis was used to try to differentiate finer categories for the media simulation model of the Simulmatics Corporation, New York, based on audience preferences reported by the TVQ panel of the Home Testing Institute (New York). The dominant category in television has probably changed since.

able to find an equilibrium, a niche in which it can maintain itself, somewhere in between commanding all the audience or none of it. The enemy of that kind of pluralism, however, is any process that has no equilibrium short of "all or nothing."

To examine what determines equilibria, let us substitute (2) above for u_t in (1). This gives

$$p_{t+1} = a + c(b + dp_t). \tag{1a}$$

This can be rearranged into a linear difference equation in one variable, production, and otherwise constants (in parentheses):

$$p_{t+1} = (cd)p_t + (a + bc). \tag{3}$$

Now let $\bar{p}$ be the level of production which will make this equation "hold still." That is, we desire some $\bar{p}$ such that, if $p_t = \bar{p}$, then also $p_{t+1} = \bar{p}$. Making those two substitutions,

$$\bar{p} = (cd)\bar{p} + (a + bc),$$

simple rearrangement shows this can be satisfied by

$$\bar{p} = \frac{a + bc}{1 - cd}. \tag{4}$$

This can be shown[6] to be (a) the only level at which production will stay *steady*, other than at zero, and (b) the level toward which production always *returns* after disturbances, except for unstable cases below that go to infinity.

Of immediate concern in this equilibrium, (4), is its denominator, $1 - cd$. First, the minus sign means that this can be very small, go to zero as cd goes to 1. Then "equilibrium" is academic: it would be at infinity! For cd even to approach 1 would be disastrous culturally. For as this makes the denominator very small, it blows up the ratio in (4). That makes production $\bar{p}$, a huge multiple of what quantities in the numerator, a = artistic interest and b = basic audience uses, would ever warrant on their own. The humanist who has not recently tried dividing by (virtually) zero, can picture it for himself as blowing up the tiny a and b of rhythm-n-blues music, in the 1940's, into the nationwide phenomenon of commercial rock-n-roll, in the 1950's.

Commercial is the word for it. The phenomenon rests on c = commercial responsiveness to consumption trends and, vice versa, on d = deutero (secondary) audiences stimulated by the production fashion, the wide attention it commands. For example, the rock-n-roll spiral began with city teenagers picking up the music from Negro radio stations. Their requests stimulated wider distribution of recordings, the success of those invited major artists

---

[6] Goldberg, Samuel, *Introduction to Difference Equations* (New York; Wiley Science Editions, 1961), Chapter 2.

and recording companies to bring out their versions. Then teenagers across the country heard the commercially-adapted versions, and off it went.[7]

Technically, c is near 1 when production is almost perfectly geared to consumption. Indeed, c is like a correlation coefficient between production and consumption in the original expression (1). And d is near 1 when consumption is almost wholly dependent on what is offered in production. This is so if the market for the material does not exist before production and arises in response only to that production — to fashion, accessibility, and, especially, to the very *real* appeal of professional presentation. If both conditions prevail, c and d both near 1, their product is near 1. Then a "magnification factor," rearranged as the left term below in our equilibrium,

$$\frac{1}{1 - cd} (a + bc),$$

blows up basic merit, a and b, beyond all reason. So unbelievably, in fact, that ASCAP called in the Department of Justice against rock-n-roll and its predecessors, convinced that only human villains could so wreck an industry.[5]

□ 3. "ABORTIONS" AND "RUNAWAYS"

Suppose, moreover, that commercialism takes the form of *anticipating* trends, that is, $c > 1$ or overcorrelation of production with (rising) consumption. And suppose that audiences do the same, $d > 1$, jumping on the bandwagon of "what's new." Recall the basic difference equation (3),

$$p_{t+1} = (cd)p_t + (a + bc), \tag{3}$$

and let it be given some starting production at time zero, p_0. Then production in subsequent periods follows by applying this rule (3) over and over again, for example,

$$p_1 = (cd)p_0 + (a + bc)$$
$$p_2 = (cd)p_1 + (a + bc).$$

Note that one can substitute the right side of the first expression for p_1 in the second, obtaining

$$p_2 = (cd)[(cd)p_0 + (a + bc)] + (a + bc)$$
$$= (cd)^2 p_0 + (cd)(a + bc) + (a + bc).$$

[7] Based on Sidney Spivak's study cited in note 2.

[5] Reference is to the extensive litigation initiated by ASCAP complaints to the Department against BMI, the rival composer's society. The charge, never proved and indeed dubious in all data I have seen, was that BMI was in collusion with radio stations (its original founders in 1940) to promote non-ASCAP music.

By the identical procedures,

$$p_3 = (cd)p_2 + (a + bc),$$

and substituting the previous value for p_2

$$p_3 = (cd)^3 p_0 + (cd)^2(a + bc) + (cd)(a + bc) + (a + bc).$$

Comparing this result with those for p_2 and p_1 before, a pattern seems to be emerging. It is that at any future time, call this time t again, results would apparently be

$$p_t = (cd)^t p_0 + (a + bc)[(cd)^{t-1} + (cd)^{t-2} + \cdots + (cd) + 1].$$

This conjecture is easily shown to be correct.[9] The terms in brackets on the right form a geometric series. Its sum is well known to be the expression in brackets on the right below:

$$p_t = (cd)^t p_0 + (a + bc)\left[\frac{1 - (cd)^t}{1 - cd}\right].$$

Note that two of the three terms on the far right were previously shown to define the equilibrium, $\bar{p} = (a + bc)/(1 - cd)$. So we may write

$$p_t = (cd)^t p_0 + [1 - (cd)^t]\bar{p},$$

whose meaning is clearer when rearranged as

$$p_t = \bar{p} - (cd)^t(\bar{p} - p_0). \qquad (5)$$

This says production at any future time, t, would be the equilibrium value, $\bar{p}$, except that we usually start out of equilibrium, for example, below it by the amount $-(\bar{p} - p_0)$, or above it by the amount $+(p_0 - \bar{p})$. This disequilibrium, due to the starting point or to a disturbance, is then being *multiplied* by $(cd)^t$. Multiplied literally, by $(cd)(cd)(cd) \ldots$, t times!

This is not good for ulcers. First note what (5) implies for a new product, trying to break into the field. Its starting p_0 is below the equilibrium eventually warranted, $\bar{p}$. Then the pattern of minus signs is such that, if there is a large $(cd)^t > 1$, that pushes it *further* down, p_t declining still further. In practice in mass culture, this "aborts" the process right there. New material cannot decline like this, it must go up or out.

Meanwhile, consider other material artificially above its equilibrium, the starting p_0 greater than warranted $\bar{p}$. Then (5) above can be rearranged to read:

$$p_t = \bar{p} + (cd)^t(p_0 - \bar{p}). \qquad (5a)$$

---

[9] By mathematical induction.

Now the lucky start or artificial disturbance that lets p_0 be greater than the warranted $\bar{p}$ can be *magnified* by large $(cd)^t$ up to, yes, up to anything the Justice Department will permit. No wonder the talent in mass culture thinks that "breaks" (in our terms, the starting p_0 versus $\bar{p}$) matter in commercial culture.

However, all this depends on *how* commercial the field is, since every field must be commercial in some degree to support itself. Table 1 illustrates by tabulating our measure of commercialism, *cd*, when different values of it are raised to higher powers (as time raises *cd* to a higher power with each successive period).

■ TABLE 1 / Consequences over Time, $(cd)^t$, for Various Starting Values

cd	$(cd)^2$	$(cd)^3$	$(cd)^4$	$(cd)^5$
1.50	2.25	3.38	5.07	7.61
1.25	1.56	1.95	2.44	3.05
.75	.56	.42	.32	.24
.50	.25	.13	.06	.03
.	.	.	.	.
.	.	.	.	.
− .75	+ .56	− .42	+ .32	− .24
−1.25	+1.56	−1.95	+2.44	−3.05
−1.50	+2.25	−3.38	+5.07	−7.61

Inspection shows what is easily proved, namely,

$$1 > cd > -1, \tag{6}$$

is an absolute requirement for stability. If it is not met, no equilibrium is possible and this is a "runaway" process. Moreover, inside or outside these bounds, the value of

$$| cd | = \text{a direct measure of the magnitude of instability}$$

(the vertical bars meaning absolute magnitude, of course). This last result is the crucial point, whether the former bounds are technically passed or not. Commercialism, as defined here, virtually *means* instability.

□ 4. FASHIONS

On the next point, the simple analytic model above is not wrong, but not realistic enough to be convincing. Let the production process be the same, but now capable of *satiating* the audience as follows. First let the abbreviated notation on the left below, defined on the right,

$$\sum_t (p - b) = \sum_{T=0}^{t} p_T - (t)b \qquad (7)$$

be the cumulative sum, from some past time 0 up to the present time t, of the amount that production in each period, abbreviated to p, exceeded the amount that basic audience or basic uses would have warranted. For the warranted amount would have been $p = b$ and thus $(p - b) = 0$ in that period, if production had been only to service the basic market. When production is less than the basic market warrants, on the other hand, $(p - b)$ accumulates negatively as a measure of underproduction, neglect of the material.

Now let the consumption process be as before, except with this "past history" of production modifying the degree that current production stimulates consumption, as on the far right below:

$$u_t = b + d[p_t - \sum_t (p - b)]. \qquad (8)$$

This says that use of the material — its consumption by the public — still is in proportion d to production. But effects of production in the current period, p_t, can be *attenuated* by the cumulative degree that production has been more than warranted by basic audiences in the past. Or if the material has been neglected, that past neglect now *intensifies* the stimulus value of current production.

Next, substitute (8) for u_t in the original production equation (1). That now becomes

$$p_{t+1} = a + c[b + dp_t - d \sum_t (p - b)]. \qquad (9)$$

Collecting terms (with constants in parentheses for clarity) yields

$$p_{t+1} = t(bcd) + (a + cb) - (cd) \sum_{t-1} p. \qquad (10)$$

The solution of this, for production at any future time, will have a nonintuitive form. So, it is better first to look at the problem inductively. For simplicity, let

$$p_0 = 0$$
$$p_1 = k$$
$$a + cb = k. \qquad (11)$$

Then the first eight periods of production (if these were quarters of the year, it would be the first two years) are tabulated in Table 2.

■ TABLE 2 / First Eight Results of Formula (10) with Definitions (11)*

$p_1 = k$

$p_2 = k + (cd)\,b$

$p_3 = k + (cd)(2b - k)$

$p_4 = k + (cd)(3b - 2k) - (cd)^2 b$

$p_5 = k + (cd)(4b - 3k) - (cd)^2(3b - k)$

$p_6 = k + (cd)(5b - 4k) - (cd)^2(6b - 3k) + (cd)^3 b$

$p_7 = k + (cd)(6b - 5k) - (cd)^2(10b - 6k) + (cd)^3(4b - k)$

$p_8 = k + (cd)(7b - 6k) - (cd)^2(15b - 10k) + (cd)^3(10b - 4k) - (cd)^4 b$

---

* Notably $k = a + bc$

Results should be read *down*, to see what happens as time progresses. At first, things seem to go all right. The main component of production is

$$k = a + cb = \begin{cases} \text{Independent artistic production} \\ + \\ \text{Commercial response to basic needs} \end{cases}.$$

In due time, however, components with negative signs enter into the sum whose net is production. The former do not mean that the level of production turns negative, or even down at all. But its previously steady (monotonic) growth now begins to "wobble." For as time progresses, *oscillatory* components enter into production, finally dominate and collapse it when commercialism, *cd*, is strong.

This conclusion was evident with the simpler model before, when $(cd)^t$ was tabulated with d negative. This corresponds to the case of satiation, for in satiation, the audience is not attracted but is repelled by overproduction. That made $(cd)^t$ a "saw-toothed" sequence, first positive, then negative in sign. The present model is much more realistic, *not* oscillating at first and only gradually developing negative components, "sour notes," as the process matures. But the conclusions are the same. Overproduction that leads to audience satiation, here not by d negative but by its application to a past sum that can *turn* negative by cumulation, leads to oscillatory pathologies. If these are strong, the process will soon come crashing down to "below zero" (where, mercifully, we stop, as mass culture does too, although the mathematics continues into divergent oscillation).

These oscillatory collapses correspond to fads and fashions. So, it is interesting to prove that such fashions are in direct proportion to our measure of commercialism and audience dependency on it, the magnitude of *cd*. The present process in (10) can be written for two successive time periods, and these subtracted, as below:

$$p_{t+1} = t(bcd) + k - (cd) \sum_{t-1} p$$
$$p_t = (t - 1)(bcd) + k - (cd) \sum_{t-2} p$$
$$\overline{p_{t+1} - p_t = (bcd) - (cd)p_{t-1}.} \tag{12}$$

This is an oscillating difference equation. Its equilibrium is the place where it settles down, if oscillation is damped out (before mass culture abandons the material, as it too often does in the face of downtrends). For the future equilibrium would be surprisingly benign:

$$\bar{p} = b. \tag{13}$$

Alas, the road to this peaceful outcome is a wild one. If commercialism is at all strong, in our terms cd greater even than .25, then the solution has the (nonintuitive) form:

$$p_t = (cd)^{t/2}[cos(t\theta + x)]y_0 + b, \tag{14}$$

in which we refer the technical reader to an easy text [10] for all details except one substantive point. The cosine function in brackets oscillates benignly, stays in bounds. But its steady oscillation is *multiplied* — both figuratively and literally — by the measure of commercialism, now $(cd)^{t/2}$. If cd is less than 1, the oscillation will be damped out over time; if cd greater than 1, increasingly magnified as time progresses. And at any value, whether the process is technically divergent or not, cd, or commercialism, governs the amount of oscillatory instability — the fad and fashion component — in a process that would otherwise have the benign conclusion, $p_t \rightarrow b$.

□ 5. "OUTVOTING" PHENOMENA

The last, however, is a hopeful possibility. Overproduction leading to satiation, if not too wildly oscillatory, could damp the process back down to a reasonable equilibrium. Thereby satiation could curb the "all or nothing" prospects otherwise. This sometimes does happen. For example, former fashions in popular music were stopped by satiation, but have come back to small positive equilibria in the permanent repertory of that music.

Items in that repertory, however, its "standards" corresponding to the classics that account for most sales in serious music, make up only a minority of the sales in popular music. Why is that? By objective indicators, the popular music of the 1930's and 1940's was better than, for example, that of

---

[10] Goldberg, *op. cit.*, pp. 138–142 and p. 172.

the 1950's.[11] Moreover, since adult consumers have seen the best efforts over decades, the best music should sell best now. The obvious answer is that such adults no longer buy popular music, only teenagers buy it. What is not obvious is how that teenage market has come to be the *only* market for popular music.

In the early 1920's and before, sales of sheet music to musically trained adults set the trends. Adults were still dominant in the Broadway type music of the late 1920's and early 1930's, and were still participating heavily in the dance audiences which set the pace in the late 1930's and early 1940's. Teenagers and their records had begun to play a major role, however, and by the 1950's they were controlling in the market, nearly all the market that was left by the end of that decade. What was called popular music changed accordingly, from adult jazz and Broadway musical styles to a kind of "pre-music" for teenagers.

How could this happen, our national (only native) music degenerate to the level of the least mature, least trained ears in the population? [12]

Picture a system in which one is allowed to vote, here to register his cultural choice by buying something, not just once per person but as many times as he pleases. Specifically, suppose the number of times one votes is in proportion to how well he *likes* the existing regime, the existing fare in a culture. And conversely, in proportion that another person does *not* like the existing regime (the fare offered does not suit his cultural taste level), in that degree suppose he votes fewer times. He is progressively *disenfranchised*, then, in proportion that he would otherwise register protesting votes. That would be a political joke, a George Orwell nightmare. It is no joke, alas, but the real nightmare of the way we vote in commercial culture.

Picture the population as divided into only two types, for simplicity, in proportions b_i and b_j, respectively. They might be .20 teenagers and .80 adults, for example, with

$$1 = b_i + b_j \qquad (15)$$

as the total relevant market, say, all people who enjoy popular music. Now in political voting, each person gets only one vote. In cultural voting under commercial conditions, however, the respective votes are

$$v_i = b_i u_i,$$
$$v_j = b_j u_j, \qquad (16)$$

[11] By measures such as the musical training of (a) the composers and (b) the performers of top hits. The decline of ASCAP in reference 8, for example, was virtually synonymous with the decline of musically trained composers. The chief performers in the 1950's were singers of little beyond high school age (and training) themselves.

[12] Note, however, our later discussion of the consequently larger market for *other* kinds of music in the 1960's. The overall picture of American consumption of all kinds of music has improved despite (indeed because of) the relegation of popular hit music to teenagers.

where v_i is the number of votes for material of type i, for example, for teen-age music, and u_i has the same meaning as before, some measure of how fre-quently material of type i is "used." It could be the number of records bought. So votes are numbers of people *multiplied* by their frequency of use of their material.

The above expression (16) neglects use of material of type i by other than persons of type i. For example, it neglects purchases of teenage music by adults. This portrays the case of incompatible audiences as the general problem. A prime example today is television's attempt to serve audiences as incompatible as are women and children of grade-school education versus mature men of college education. The question then becomes, in determining the future evolution of that culture, who will "outvote" whom?

Voting is the word for it in any culture run by, or at least for, its audiences. This voting aspect is made explicit by changing the notation on the right in otherwise the same production equation as before:

$$p_{i,t+1} = a_i + c v_{i,t}, \tag{17}$$

where it is now necessary to add subscripts other than those for time, to note that this is for type i material. For example, $v_{i,t}$ means the votes for material of type i at time t. These votes are determined by (16). In its discussion we did not burden the reader with time subscripts, but $v_i = v_{i,t}$ and $u_i = u_{i,t}$, are both variable over time.

Next, let frequency of use, $u_{i,t}$, be determined by

$$u_{i,t} = 1 + d \sum_t (p_i - p_j), \tag{18}$$

in which the right hand term is an abbreviation for

$$\sum_t (p_i - p_j) = \sum_{T=0}^{t} (p_{i,T} - p_{j,T}), \tag{19}$$

and means "the cumulative amount that production of material of type i has exceeded that of material j from some point in the past, $T = 0$, up to now, $T = t$." What this idea in (18) implies is that the present use of the material, $u_{i,t}$, is some average unit of use which we set equal to 1, plus some proportion d of the cumulative degree that this material has been *more* accessible than the rival material in the past, $p_i - p_j$ being the difference in a given past time period. In this the interpretation of d can change:

> If $p_i > p_j$ in the past, then d has an interpretation like that before, of use derived from accessibility, now as a *habit* of depending on this medium or market, say, on television or popular music, to serve mostly i tastes.

If $p_i < p_j$ in the past, however, then the sum on the right of (18) will be negative. Then d will mean a degree of disuse, a dishabituation to this medium or market, due to objectionable j material predominating there.

All this is very similar to the satiation case. But now it is satiation with p_j, not because it exceeds its warranted audience, b_j, but because it overwhelms the material one prefers himself, p_i. And a mechanism is made explicit for expressing displeasure at this, *underuse* of the medium or market whose majority fare has stereotyped it as j in taste.

To see the consequences, first substitute (18) for u_i in (16), and then the result of that for $v_{i,t}$ in (17). We do so for two consecutive periods for material i:

$$p_{i,t+1} = a_i + b_i c + b_i cd \sum_t (p_i - p_i)$$

$$p_{i,t} = a_i + b_i c + b_i cd \sum_{t-1} (p_i - p_i). \tag{20}$$

These become meaningful if we subtract the two, to see the difference in production of material of type i that arises each time this process applies:

$$p_{i,t+1} - p_{i,t} = b_i cd(p_{i,t} - p_{j,t}). \tag{21}$$

The result on the right here follows because, after subtracting the sums on the right in (20) up to time $t - 1$, there is nothing left but current production, at time t. Let us rearrange the resulting expression (21) in the form shown on the first row below. Then, on the second row below, we write an analogous expression for $p_{j,t+1}$, the production of the *rival* material of type j. It was derived in an identical manner:

$$p_{i,t+1} = (1 + b_i cd)p_{i,t} - (b_i cd)p_{j,t}$$

$$p_{j,t+1} = -(b_j cd)p_{i,t} + (1 + b_j cd)p_{j,t}. \tag{22}$$

Persons working in a mass culture industry often complain about "the system." Expression (22) agrees it is a system: as soon as competition enters, the fate of each type of material depends on the other, and vice versa.

It is merely a change of notation to write (22) in matrix form:

$$\begin{pmatrix} p_{i,t+1} \\ p_{j,t+1} \end{pmatrix} = \begin{pmatrix} 1 + b_i cd & -b_i cd \\ -b_j cd & 1 + b_j cd \end{pmatrix} \begin{pmatrix} p_{i,t} \\ p_{j,t} \end{pmatrix} \tag{23}$$

Indeed, the reader unfamiliar with matrix multiplication can easily see how it works by reconstructing (22) from (23). The latter can be written more succinctly as

$$P_{t+1} = MP_t, \tag{23a}$$

where *capital* letters denote the corresponding vectors (columns) and matrix (square table) in (23). Notably, M is the matrix in the center of (23).

Now suppose we are given some starting production levels at time 0

$$P_0 = \begin{pmatrix} p_{i,0} \\ p_{j,0} \end{pmatrix}. \tag{24}$$

Then one can apply the rule given by (23a), as shorthand for (23) which is equivalent to (22). That permits writing the next steps succinctly as

$$P_1 = MP_0$$
$$P_2 = MP_1,$$

and then substituting the first expression for P_1 in the second,

$$P_2 = M(MP_0)$$
$$= M^2 P_0.$$

By similar procedures one finds that

$$P_3 = M^3 P_0,$$

and it is not hard to see why the standard solution is

$$P_t = M^t P_0. \tag{25}$$

A note gives technical references for expanding M^t and the results obtained in our present case.[13] Expression (25) above can then be expanded into full matrix form like (23) before. That translates by definition back into ordinary algebra as in (22). This gives the solution in ordinary algebra as:

$$p_{i,t} = p_{i,0} + b_i[(1 + cd)^t - 1](p_{i,0} - p_{j,0})$$
$$p_{j,t} = p_{j,0} + b_j[(1 + cd)^t - 1](p_{j,0} - p_{i,0}) \tag{26}$$

If this outcome seems nonintuitive, one can imagine what the dynamic behavior of a real mass culture system is like. Even a simple case such as popular music is hopelessly too complex to understand intuitively (and thus one can see why "villains" are blamed).[14]

[13] See Goldberg, *op. cit.*, pp. 225–241, especially pp. 230–231. Our case in which $b_i + b_j = 1$ simplifies to:

$$M^t = \begin{pmatrix} 1 - (1 - k^t)b_i & (1 - k^t)b_i \\ (1 - k^t)b_j & 1 - (1 - k^t)b_j \end{pmatrix},$$

where $k = 1 + cd$.

[14] See note 8.

In our simple theoretical case, however, the key results can be excerpted as

$$p_{i,t} = \cdots\cdots\cdots + (1 + cd)^t(p_{i,0} - p_{j,0})$$
$$p_{j,t} = \cdots\cdots\cdots + (1 + cd)^t(p_{j,0} - p_{i,0}).$$

(26a)

First, note the far right-hand terms. In the upper row for i material, suppose that it starts (at $p_{i,0}$) ahead of j material (greater than $p_{j,0}$). Then the right-hand term will be positive and contribute still *further* growth to p_i. The corresponding right-hand term in the lower case will be negative and still further depress growth of p_j, as a function purely of "bad breaks" at the start, $p_{i,0} > p_{j,0}$. This system, we recall, was one in which each audience votes (buys) a number of times in proportion to offerings of its own material, as opposed to the other taste. If so, the outcome is completely a function of the system's *initial* history.

At the start of television, for example, suppose that women and children and less educated persons "outvoted" men and mature people and the more educated, as the former did. Then the system would have evolved toward the interests of the former, as television did until recent intervention.[15] Or, suppose a device is introduced in popular music whereby young people without musical training can outvote mature people with musical training, as happened when cheap recordings supplanted sheet music. Then the system evolves toward the tastes of the former.

Initial conditions matter in *all* culture, however, as (26) itself shows. The critical new thing added in commercial culture is that

$$(1 + cd)^t$$

can scarcely escape being greater than 1, for c and d are both positive under commercial conditions. If so, we are faced with a divergent process, for example, a sequence like $(1 + cd) = 1.50$, then $(1 + cd)^2 = 2.25$, next $(1 + cd)^3 = 3.38$, and so on. That *multiplies* any initial imbalance, $p_i - p_j$, into grotesquely exaggerated consequences.

What stops it? Nothing, mathematically, and in much actual culture, nothing does until long after the outvoted people have withdrawn, as adults have from popular music.

Yet here lies a healthy consequence of unhealthy processes: one practical way that pluralism is achieved is for the outvoted people, driven out, to have to start their own cultural systems! The *New York Times* grew up in the era of the penny press, FM radio had its opportunity from the worst era in radio's

---

[15] Most of the material of the early 1950's, notably live drama and comedy, was supplanted in the late 1950's, notably by material appealing to children (adventure) and women (family series). Unlike popular music, however, television is sensitive to political and public pressure for balance, and has in the early 1960's restored material appealing to the mature (notably news in depth) and men (notably sports). See "Survival Theory in Culture," in McPhee, W., *Formal Theories of Mass Behavior*, for an analysis of trends from the early to the late 1950's.

(and popular music's) history, and in the 1960's mass markets have begun to emerge for a kind of popularized good music that was voted out, excluded, by both teenagers and classicists. Pay television may be the next example. When *the* market cannot remain pluralistic, plural markets are forced to come into separate existences. The voting system above tends to that result.

□ 6. "EQUAL" CULTURES

The only other possibilities, with the present model, are interesting but, in the end, sad. They occur when either c or d turns negative. Then their product is negative, and that makes

$$(1 + cd) < 1,$$

and thus the sequence over time now becomes

$$(1 + cd)^t \rightarrow 0.$$

For example, when $[1 + (-.25)] = .75$, the sequence over time is .75, .56, .42, . . ., down to an asymptote at zero. Then the system *will* reach a stable equilibrium, retaining a kind of pluralism discussed later. Of the two possible conditions for this stable outcome, the first

$$c < 0,$$

or "negative commercialism," would occur in high fashion, for example, where creative designers are expected *not* to cater to what is already popular (as if repelled by it). In mass culture, innovating disk jockeys are known to behave this way. As they put it, they "get off" what is already popular onto the new. A more common situation in commercial culture, however, is the second possibility for a stable outcome,

$$d < 0,$$

which, when applied in our original equation (18) for use or consumption, gives the following version

$$u_{i,t} = 1 + (-d) \sum_t (p_i - p_j),$$

in which an explicit minus $-d$ has been entered to clarify its import. Namely, the fact that p_i has been the majority fare in a given era from some past time 0 to the present time t, in this case *detracts* from its frequency of use in the next period. And the previously neglected p_j benefits, in an analogous equation, from its previous neglect.

In the general case this would be an audience preference for what has not been overdone recently, as in symphony music. But with our earlier assumption (16) about incompatible audiences, it is like the progression on the newspaper sports pages, first, baseball fans getting satiated with that, then football fans with that, then basketball fans with that; but by then the baseball fans are ready to go again.

With any of the above mechanisms at work, cd is negative, so $(1 + cd)^t$ is going to zero during the era in question, and an equilibrium will emerge from (26) at

$$\bar{p}_i = p_{i,0} - b_i (p_{i,0} - p_{j,0})$$
$$\bar{p}_j = p_{j,0} - b_j (p_{j,0} - p_{i,0}). \tag{27}$$

Recalling that $b_i + b_j = 1$, we can substitute in the lower equation $b_j = 1 - b_i$. Rearrangement will then show that the right sides of both equations are the same. That is, if after this substitution, we subtract the lower equation from the upper, results are

$$\bar{p}_i - \bar{p}_j = 0$$
$$\bar{p}_i = \bar{p}_j, \tag{27a}$$

and thus the final equilibrium, if ever reached, would be *equal* production of both kinds of material. And that result would be independent of the sizes of the audiences, b_i and b_j. So each kind of material would be equally produced no matter how unequal the audiences!

To see why, recall that the production equation in this model depended mainly on "votes" for the material, $v_i = b_i u_i$. Now if equilibrium production is equal, then $b_i u_i \rightarrow b_j u_j$. (They are exactly equal, if differences in artistic production are negligible.) That means the numerically smaller audience develops a much higher rate of use or consumption, because its tastes are being better served, so that its total votes just about equal those of the numerically larger audience. Or put another way, the numerically larger audience is being so ill served by production that its rate of consumption becomes so small or "thin" as to have no more weight in total sales than that of the minority.

PART II

QUANTITATIVE DATA COLLECTION AND MODELING

Chapter 6

THEMES OF MEASUREMENT IN COMMUNICATION RESEARCH

Peter V. Miller

THIS CHAPTER AND THE THREE TO FOLLOW IT concern several aspects of measurement in communication research. Simply put, the task of measurement is to assign numerals—or, more generally, symbols—to objects, events, people, and so forth according to a rule. But the neatness of this definition belies the complexity of the measurement process. A multitude of operations is involved in assigning numerals, and there is more than a little intricacy in devising the rules by which assignments are made.

We will take a "theme and variations" approach to managing the complexity. Measurement error and the structure of scaling models constitute the themes to be introduced and embellished in this section of the volume. Issues involved in collecting information and considerations in using it, in other words, serve to tie these chapters together.

This strategy omits some of the more familiar measurement topics in the communication field, such as the classic attitude measurement techniques (Thurstone, Guttman, Likert, and others). Our discussion of reliability and validity—a sine qua non of writings on measurement—will center on some issues which are sometimes neglected when these topics are mentioned. In other words, this is a rather specialized collection of ideas on measurement. Readers desiring a more general treatment of the subject may consult profitably the work of Guilford (1954), Nunnally (1967), and Torgerson (1958), among others.

FIRST THEME: ERRORS IN THEORY AND PRACTICE

Attaching numbers to phenomena of interest is never accomplished with absolute accuracy. One can handle this problem through a "deterministic" approach, discarding cases which do not conform to a scale pattern, or through a "probabilistic" method which deliberately introduces an error component into the measurement theory. Of the two, we are probably more familiar with the models featuring a stochastic, chance, or error component. Each observation is assumed to be composed of a "true" portion and an error resulting from a myriad of circumstances which operated when the measurement was carried out. One can express the measured score as a simple additive function of the "true" value for the object, event or person, and the error:

$$M = T + e \qquad\qquad [1]$$

The smaller the numerical value for the error term, the more *reliable* the measurement is said to be. This straightforward conceptualization of measurement is complemented by some equally simple assumptions about the nature of the errors. They are supposed to be "random misses"—pushing the value of the measure up or down with equal probability, and cancelling out in the long run (Hays, 1973). Although they may exist, *systematic* measurement errors—ones which are correlated with the "true" portion of the measure—do not receive much attention.

Random errors are bad enough, as Bohrnstedt and Carter (1971) cogently argue. They demonstrate that regression estimates are robust when least squares assumptions such as homoscedasticity are violated, but also that measurement error wreaks havoc with the estimates. Correction for attenuation in analysis variables is recommended to handle the reliability problem, but few investigators bother to take this action. Bohrnstedt and Carter reach this dismal conclusion:

> many of the published results based on regression analysis in the sociological literature are possibly distortions of whatever reality may exist. Our plea is for sociologists engaged in substantive research to confront the unreliability of their measurement instruments.

If simple unreliability causes this much trouble, one can imagine the difficulties associated with errors which do not conform to the traditional assumptions. Take the case of errors which are correlated with the "true" part of a measured variable. Siegel and Hodge (1968) discussed this problem as evidenced in census data. They observed that the variance of the estimates on years of education for the population in the decennial census was *smaller* than that obtained from the *same* respondents in the Current Population Survey (CPS), a sample survey conducted several times each year. The import of this finding is revealed when one learns that the CPS measurement procedure is more painstaking than the one in the census, and the resulting CPS estimates are considered to be of higher quality—closer to the "true" value of the parameter. Now, the fact that the *variance* of the CPS estimate is greater than that for the census presents an interesting quandary. For if we treat the CPS figure as the true value (a procedure regularly followed by the Bureau of the Census), its variance should be strictly less than the census value, or else the assumption of random measurement error is not tenable.[1]

A simple algebraic manipulation of Equation 1 (see Siegel and Hodge or Gulliksen 1950, Ch.1) indicates that the variance of the measured score is equal to the variance of the true score, plus the error variance, *plus* the *covariance* of the true score and the error. The covariance is assumed to be zero when we treat measurement errors as random. But since the error variance is always a positive number, the only way for the measured score variance (here treating the census value as the measured score) to be equal to the sum of the true score and error variances when the true score variance is *greater* is if there is a *negative correlation* between the true score and the error. This implies for this example that there is a negative correlation between the CPS score and the error. Remember that the estimates for both the CPS and census were obtained from the *same* respondents, so sampling error does not enter into our calculations.

What is the mechanism for this finding? Siegel and Hodge explore a number of path models to examine the error-true score correlation. They argue that the source of the problem lies in the nature of the item used to measure years of education in the CPS. It offers a choice of yearly categories, with a definite floor and ceiling. Errors, therefore, consist of overestimates for those with little schooling and underestimates for those with many years of education. Notice that the thrust of either type of error is "against the grain" of the true values and the overall result is a negative correlation of error and true score. It is possible to imagine many other circumstances in which a similar result might obtain. A more general lesson is that the simplifying assumption of random measurement error may not accord with reality.

ERRORS IN COLLECTING OBSERVATIONS

Errors may enter into the measured score in any of several stages in the measurement process. A good deal of attention has been given to those errors which may occur in the process of scaling already collected observations. Different formulae have been proposed for assessing the amount of error in Guttman scales, for example, and building scores via regression provides a convenient estimate of least squares fit. Item analysis, split-half and test-retest reliability assessments are routine procedures in scale building.

We have been somewhat less systematic about dealing with errors which happen while the original observations, from which the data are made, are collected. There are manuals on experimental procedure, interviewing, participant observation, and content analysis, but few programmatic evaluations of how reliable or standardized the data-gathering situations themselves are. Rosenthal's (1966) work on experiments is an exception to the rule. It might be interesting to examine some more recent ideas on collecting observations, both to redress the imbalance and to continue our discussion of non-random measurement error. First, there will be a look at collecting data through direct observation. Then, we will use a review of a program of research on interviewing methods as a springboard to a broader treatment of some implications for measurement theory of improved measurement techniques.

The rekindling of interest in the study of communication organizations in recent years has made the techniques of direct observation of behavior increasingly important for data-gathering. Runkle and McGrath (1972) point out that observational or field studies are necessary in cases where one is interested in making statements only about a certain ongoing, observable social system, and where it is important to preserve as much as possible the "natural" progression of behavior in the system (as opposed to manipulating some aspect experimentally). A number of organizational studies in this volume attest to the richness of the information obtained by the observational method. Rather than relying solely on retrospective accounts of decisions, actions and reasons for them, these researchers attempt to understand the process of the organizational action by watching it as it happens.

The necessity of this approach is obvious if one considers the questions which often confront investigators conducting organizational studies. For example, a recent effort in which I participated but which is not reported in this book was one of several studies of the media in the 1976 presidential election, administered by the Social Science Research Council. In conjunction with a panel survey of voters in two cities, a team of investigators studied the local news organizations in those areas during important campaign periods. The flow of work in these news operations was charted, and the impact of campaign events was assessed over time. It would have made little or no sense to administer a questionnaire at a given point in the campaign in the hope of discovering behavioral patterns. The burden of memory would be too great for specific event recall, and general patterns of action are often difficult or impossible for participants to describe.

Reiss (1971) notes that observation, when conducted according to explicit procedures which permit replication and when designed so that the effects of observing are measurable, does not have the stigma of "subjectivity" often attached to the method. Of course, there must be a clearly formulated problem for investigation in order for these conditions to obtain. Serendipity is an added benefit of systematic observation; one should not simply go "feeling around" in an organization in the hope of a surprising discovery. Reiss offers some valuable insights into the mechanics of study design and administration using systematic observation, as well as some examples of studies conducted with this method which less imaginative investigators might consider impossible.

There is a marked similarity between many of the techniques of systematic observation and sample survey methods, such as sampling for observation and formatting the instrument. The many problems of self-report—memory error, social desirability bias, and so forth—clearly are *not* applicable to the observation situation. These matters, however, are the subject of some recent research in survey methodology. At a recent conference on health survey research methods, discussion papers dealt with, among other topics, "respondent burden" and reducing measurement error through sampling schemes which allocate measurement resources in a maximally profitable fashion. Bradburn (1977) noted that techniques are required to alleviate the effort and stress respondents encounter in survey interviews. Kalsbeek and Lessler (1977) pointed out that increasing sample size only has an impact on sampling error and *simple* (random) measurement error. A dual sampling scheme was outlined in which a cheap, but faulty measurement process is assigned to one group and a more costly and effective measurement technique is allocated to the other group. Depending on the relative anticipated sizes of the simple measurement error and the nonrandom error, and the cost of cheap data relative to expensive data, the best survey design, they argue, may be one which only uses cheap, faulty data but relatively large sample sizes, a design which collects only expensive, accurate data with a small sample size, or the double sampling scheme which corrects the faulty estimates with the more expensive accurate ones.

These ideas are combined in a program of research conducted by Cannell and colleagues in the health area over the past two decades. Cannell and I review much of this work and extend the methods to research on media use in a later chapter. It is sufficient to note here that the purpose of the interviewing research was to discover standardized techniques for interviewers to follow in communicating to respondents the measurement objectives of the survey. The methods do not deal with question wording, but rather the instructions and feedback provided by interviewers to respondents concerning the questions and their answers. Additionally, a method for increasing respondent motivation has been developed. The product is a way to alleviate, or at least make more sensible, the respondent's burden, and an improved measurement technique for use in a double sampling scheme, if need be.

The availability of these methods raises the issue confronted by Siegel and Hodge which we reviewed earlier. If interviewing or other measurement techniques are somehow improved, the estimates which result from them should show smaller variances than poorer methods applied to the same people. We need good size Ns to verify this result, and sampling errors should not be allowed to confuse the issue, but it is not possible to hold that a technique is improved (producing estimates closer to the true value) and simultaneously admit that the variances of its estimates are greater than those of some relatively crude method. At least, it is impossible to cleave to those two propositions under the assumption of random measurement error (but, see Note 1).

Table 1 shows the variances for some selected scores from interviewing research reported by Cannell, Oksenberg, and Converse (1977), and from a media use survey I conducted this past spring. We are comparing variances from respondents interviewed with experimental interviewing techniques and those

TABLE 1
MEANS AND VARIANCES FOR SELECTED MEASURES PRODUCED BY
TWO INTERVIEWING STYLES IN HEALTH AND MEDIA USE STUDIES[1]

	Experimental Interviewing Technique		Control Group[2]	
	Mean	*Variance*	*Mean*	*Variance*
Health Data:				
1. Number of Food Items Consumed Yesterday	27.06	126.59	24.4	104.48
2. Number of Sicknesses Mentioned for Last Two Weeks	.73	.85	.77	.97
3. Total Mentions to Open Health Questions[3]	79.3	531.87	64.05	415.83
Media Use Data:				
1. Number of TV Programs Watched Yesterday	3.97	3.66	3.04	2.17
2. Number of Minutes Spent Watching TV Yesterday	197.5	152.6	156.9	104.4
3. Number of Messages Recalled about Natural Gas Shortage from TV	2.69	2.64	2.30	1.40
4. Average Time Spent Listening to the Radio (minutes)	151.39	179.19	138.16	205.27

1. See Miller and Cannell in this volume for the sources of these data.
2. Respondents in this condition were interviewed with techniques normally prescribed for survey research, without the special interviewer training provided for the experimental condition. See Miller and Cannell for details.
3. Includes food eaten yesterday, chronic health conditions reported, symptoms of illness.

exposed to more typical interviewer behavior. As one can see, the variance of the scores is almost always greater in the experimental (improved) condition than in the control group. It seems intuitively reasonable that the more standardized interviewing techniques should produce higher quality information, and we have some empirical verification for this belief in other characteristics of the responses and respondent reactions to the interview conditions. The reader will have to judge this for himself when perusing the Miller and Cannell chapter. But if the experimental techniques really are better, then we appear to have another case of the correlated error phenomenon investigated by Siegel and Hodge. One must assume, of course, that the Ns for these comparisons (approximately 100 in each cell) are not too small to invalidate the conclusion, and that the people in the experimental and control conditions are similar enough to make attributing the differences to sampling error the wrong approach. The fact that the result is found so many times with such different questions in totally different studies gives us more confidence in the correlated error inference.

The upshot of all of this gazing at variances is that a question has been raised in different settings by investigators with very different interests concerning the nature of the measurement process. Can one blithely assume that measurement errors are random, paying no more than lip service to the possibility that systematic errors as well as the random variety contaminate our measured scores? Corrections for attenuation, rare as they are now, will not suffice to correct our estimates when correlated error is involved in the score. The price we pay by ignoring the issue is the one noted by Bohrnstedt and Carter: our published results may not reflect what is really going on in the world.

We are not totally lost if it turns out that correlated error is an issue we must confront on a regular basis. The well-known conceptual advancement provided by Campbell and Fiske (1959) in the multitrait-multimethod matrix, coupled with the high-powered mathematics of Joreskog's (1970) confirmatory factor analysis, along with path analysis with unmeasured variables, provide the tools for finding good estimates of relationships among variables even in the presence of nonrandom error. Apart from being correlated with the "true" value of a measured variable, error for the variable may be correlated with the measured values of other variables, or with the errors associated with other variables. When analyzing all of these, the correlated error can produce fictitious results. See Alwin (1974) for a discussion of the multitrait-multimethod approach to the nonrandom error problem, and Andrews and Crandall (1976) for an example of the technique using quality of life data.

SECOND THEME: DATA-MAKING

The other chapters in this section, by Kline, and Greendale and Fredin, take up the problem of measurement at a point after the information collecting period. They discuss familiar concerns of scaling observations, with a heavy reliance on the encyclopedic work of Clyde Coombs in his *Theory of Data* (1964). Although there are many, one of the chief benefits of contact with Coombs's ideas is the way in which his typology of all behavioral data enables one to think about the subject on a different level from the typical concerns of level of measurement and appropriate statistics. He offers the facility to conceptualize observations in terms of many different scaling models, and clearly makes the point that there is no necessary interpretation of a given recorded observation as some particular kind of data. Although we are accustomed to speak of "data gathering" or "data collection," a major lesson of Coombs's book is that data are *made*—not born at the time of observation. This doesn't make the subject of errors in information gathering unimportant; rather, it emphasizes the investigator's freedom to conceptualize the scaling stage of measurement in a number of different ways.

The theory of data seeks the basis of data in a geometric structure consisting of three dimensions. First, Coombs posits that each datum requires an "individual" (construed broadly to include people and other entities which play the role of "acting, deciding, or responding") and a stimulus. Both of those are represented in the theory as *points* in a psychological space. There are two sets of points—individuals and stimuli—from which data may be formed, and one of the key dimensions characterizing a scaling model is whether one or both sets of points are to be mapped onto the scale. Do we wish to assign numerals to individuals, to stimuli, or to both?

The second attribute on which the theory is built concerns whether stimuli are judged in relation to other stimuli or in absolute terms. For example, one might be asked to indicate the more preferred of *two* alternatives, or to say whether a *single* stimulus is acceptable. In the former case, the judgment may be seen as a comparison of *distances* between the individual's "preference point" (the most preferred position) and the points representing the stimuli presented for choice. Thus, one is comparing two pairs of points—two dyads—on their relative distances. (One of the points, that corresponding to the individual's ideal position, is stationary in the comparison and the stimulus points are contrasted to it.)

In the situation where the individual is to judge the acceptability of a single stimulus, we are dealing with only a single pair of points—one for the individual and one for the stimulus. The second dichotomy of interest, then, is whether a pair of points or a pair of dyads is involved in the datum. Do we know the individual's choice among stimuli, or only his response to one?

The third dimension in the typology has to do with another characteristic of the judgment the individual makes concerning stimuli. On the one hand, he may be asked to establish an *order* relation among points or dyads. This happens, for example, when individuals pass or fail arithmetic problems (an order relation for an individual and a stimulus point), or when a judgment of the more preferred of two stimuli is requested (ordering two individual-stimulus dyads). On the other hand, the individual may be called upon to establish a *proximity* relation. In this case, he renders information on whether a point or dyad "matches" or falls within a certain range of a criterion point or dyad. One might judge whether or not a political candidate, a candy bar, or a newspaper is acceptable. The decision reflects a proximity relation on a pair of points, an individual's preferred position on candidates, candy or newspapers and a point for the given stimulus. If the stimulus comes close enough to the preference point, it is deemed acceptable; if not, it is rejected. Comparing dyads, one could indicate whether or not one of two stimuli is preferred over the other (but not the actual preference, which is an order relation). The third dimension in the theory, to sum up, concerns the nature of the response to the stimulus: Does the individual order or match in responding?

The three dimensions in the theory are combined to form a fourfold classification, with each of the cells bisected. Quadrant I data consist of order or proximity relations among pairs of *dyads,* the points being from different sets (individuals *and* stimuli are scaled). Quadrant II features data made up of relations among pairs of *points* from different sets. In Quadrant III, the pairs of points are from the *same* set, and Quadrant IV data consist of relations among dyads whose points are from the same set. In each of the four cells, relations either among points or dyads may be order or proximity judgments.

Quadrant I is called "preferential choice" or rank order data and its archetypal scaling model is Coombs's own "unfolding" model. Quadrant II is "single stimulus" data; an example would be Guttman's scalogram analysis. Quadrant III is called "stimulus comparison" data—psychometric measurements comparing weights or tones is an example. Finally, Quadrant IV, "similarities" data, is exemplified by the various multidimensional scaling models. The reader should consult Coombs's treatment of the data theory for a fuller explanation of each of the Quadrant characteristics.

Kline's model of cognitive structure in a chapter to follow features data from Quadrant I and Quadrant IV. In explaining how individuals learn to identify objects, he relies on similarities data. The individual is said to perceive objects through a series of paired-comparisons judgments in which one pair is judged to be more similar than another. The dimensions by which these judgments are made become internalized, and individual weights are attached to them. Thus, some individuals will place more stress on a particular characteristic when identifying a given object than others will. Once objects have been identified, the individual's preference among them is described by Quadrant I data. We develop preference points for classes of objects, and each object can be evaluated (rank ordered) in relation to the ideal point. When different individuals use the same dimension for rank ordering the objects—i.e., when their rank orders unfold according to the same J (joint individual-stimulus) scale, they may be said to be cognitively "in tune" with regard to these evaluations. Runkle (1956) argued that this cognitive similarity leads to better communication concerning the evaluated objects. Data concerning student-teacher similarity in unfolding supported his hypothesis; Kline explores the idea with a very different data set.

Briefly, unfolding is a method for assigning metric scores to individuals and stimuli on a joint scale, given a set of rank orders of the stimuli. Recovering the metric information is too detailed a process to describe here, but the first step is to find the dominant unidimensional continuum which fits the set of individual rank orders. One first looks for the end points of the scale; all of the individual, or I, scales must end in one of them. Then, two "mirror-image" scales need to be found, each one beginning and ending with the two identified end points. The occurrence of more than one pair of mirror-image scales is sufficient to reject the hypothesis of a unidimensional latent attribute common to the preferences of the particular set of subjects.

The next step is to order the I scales between the two mirror-image scales which serve as the boundaries of the continuum. The correct order is obtained when, comparing two adjacent I scales, a pair of adjacent stimuli is reversed. (See Table 2.) This set of I scales for four stimuli illustrates the rules which must

TABLE 2
AN EXAMPLE OF I SCALES IN ORDER FOR UNFOLDING
ANALYSIS WITH FOUR STIMULI

Scale Number	Preference Order
1	ABCD
2	BACD
3	BCAD
4	BCDA
5	CBDA
6	CDBA
7	DCBA

SOURCE: Coombs (1964), p. 85.

obtain in order for a J scale to be recovered. Each of the individual preference orderings ends with D or A. There are two mirror-image scales (ABCD and DCBA) which bound the set of preference orderings. When moving from the top to the bottom scale, each I scale evidences a reversal in a pair of adjacent points.

The term "unfolding" comes from the notion that each of the I scales (individual rank orders) consists of judgments of distances between the individual's ideal preference point and each of the stimuli. The left end-point of an I scale is the stimulus closest to the ideal, with the other stimuli being progressively less preferred. Thus, an I scale is a "folded" version of a hypothetical J scale, which indicates the ordering of stimuli for the entire set of subjects. One can imagine the J scale as a string with a series of knots in it, one for each stimulus. If we pick up the J scale and fold it at any point, we have created an I scale or individual preference ordering. In the actual analytic situation, however, we have only collected rank orders and the job is to recover a J scale from all of these (*unfold* the string) which indicates the order of the stimuli for all of the subjects. Once this is done, individual points may be placed on the J scale to indicate the preference positions of each person.

The unfolding model is both a scaling criterion and a scaling method. One can use it to obtain metric information on the distances between stimuli, but as it is used in Kline's chapter, it is more of a scaling criterion—a way of judging whether or not a scale is possible to form from the observations. Judging whether people are cognitively similar entails judging whether their preference orders fit on the same continuum. The unfolding model permits us to make this judgment, apart from any observations about the scale metric.

Multidimensional unfolding is also a possibility, although it has not been applied in the sense of Runkle's model of cognitive similarity. See Coombs (1964, Chaps. 5-7), for a thorough treatment of the unfolding model. Greendale and Fredin's chapter, an interesting variant on the agenda-setting theme, illustrates how the investigator can learn new properties of his observations as he moves through the theory of data structure. Rather than simply analyze correlations between issues portrayed in the media and perceived by the public, they examine the *internal relationships* among issues as seen by newspapers and a sample of people who read them. The theory of data points to a number of approaches to examining the issue structure. As outlined by Greendale and Fredin a major choice facing investigators in this case is whether to regard issues as points from the same set or to preserve hierarchical distinctions among them which may be evident in the observations. For example, one may have information on the "major problems" which individuals see facing the country, along with ancillary issues which they have mentioned. Should one treat all of the issues, whether "major" or not, as the same for purposes of analysis? If so, the models of Quadrant IV (similarities data) are appropriate for examining the structure of the observations. Cluster analysis and multidimensional scaling are familiar analytic techniques for dealing with these symmetric relations.

One could treat the relationships among issues as *conditional,* preserving the distinction between major and minor problems, for example. This amounts to regarding major problems as one set of points and minor ones as another set. Now we move to Quadrant I; major issues serve as "individuals" selecting among minor issues ("stimuli"); we could use a variant of the unfolding model to scale the observations. Greendale and Fredin argue for preserving the asymmetric relations found in their observations and compare the issue structure as revealed in media content and individual perceptions. This is an interesting departure from the usual agenda-setting analysis. Another approach not considered by them would be to treat the observations as conditional proximity data, analyzing the matrix through a multidimensional scaling technique which preserved the major-minor relationship among the problems. Coombs illustrates this technique in an analysis of similarities data on psychological journals. The matrix consisted of the number of citations each column journal made to each row publication. Naturally, journals are most similar to themselves, so one would expect each journal to cite itself often. The number of references data allows one to derive the dimensions of similarity and scale the journals on them. One could take the same approach to the analysis of issue structure in agenda setting research. The application of graph theory presented in Greendale and Fredin is another enlightening way to look at and compare the structures.

I have not attempted an exegesis of Coombs's work, but have instead tried to fill in some of the background for later chapters in this section. The range of topics in the Theory of Data is much too broad for adequate treatment here, and first-hand knowledge is certainly more rewarding than any summary. It is a work with which communication scholars should be more familiar.

A NOTE ON FADS

Any treatment of methods, whether new, forgotten, or misused, is prone to the pitfall of hucksterism. At the extreme, this tendency is manifested in arguments for a method as the *only* way to look at the phenomena of interest to the field. To the extent that the argument is accepted, we are likely to find a good deal of research using a given method, whether or not it makes much substantive sense. In recent years, for example, the number of communication research papers featuring path analysis or some form of "causal modeling" seems to have increased exponentially. To be sure, there are some very real and important theoretical and methodological benefits in these techniques; we have seen some of them earlier in this chapter when discussing what to do about correlated error. One could not even adequately conceptualize the correlated error problem without reference to some form of path analysis. Still, there are a striking number of ill-conceived applications of the technique in the literature, and one begins to wonder how much light the method has to shed on problems in the field when it (or any other technique) is selected for its presumed power or elegance seemingly in spite of substantive considerations.

Consider also Osgood's remarks on the semantic differential in his recent book on affective meaning in different cultures (Osgood, May, and Miron, 1975). After publication of *The Measurement of Meaning*, the semantic differential—designed for a very specific and theoretically based measurement purpose—came to be used as simply another attitude measurement technique. Later, bipolar adjectives with seven blanks between them became familiar sights on other sorts of measurement instruments. Factor analysis, the companion technique for the semantic differential, also increased in popularity. As late as last year an article in one communication journal discussed the pros and cons of various factor analytic approaches for semantic differential items.

Models like the ones investigated by Kline in this section are linked intimately with other scaling techniques—multidimensional scaling and unfolding. One has seen a recent upsurge in interest in the former by communication scholars, and the latter is likely to undergo the same sort of transformation. Kaplan (1964) points out that there is a good reason for the rise and fall of popularity of techniques: the methods depend on the state of mathematics at the time. As new possibilities open up, people begin to think about phenomena in different ways. But there is also an unreasoning element of methods for their own sake in these developments. Another of Kaplan's remarks—about little boys who are presented with hammers and are delighted to find that everything needs to be pounded—accurately captures the blind adoption of "new, improved" methods where others would do a better job.

One hopes that we have not fallen prey to the "method mystique" in this section, or elsewhere in this volume. We clearly believe that there are useful things in the models and techniques outlined here, but we do not suggest that any one of them can solve the problems of research in the field. Instead of trying to start a fad, we intend to offer some questions for further research and some different ways of looking at the world.

CODA: QUALITY AND QUANTITY

This volume contains examples of both "qualitative" and "quantitative" research; though it is probably surprising to some readers, none of the qualitative or quantitative chapters has threatened to leave the book in protest. The endless battle between humanists and empiricists, phenomenologists and positivists, will not be fought here. It is a mistake to think of quality and quantity as antithetical or even alternate; quantities are *of* qualities. Further, there is no purely qualitative problem—we may always approach it in quantitative terms. That this entails some degree of abstraction or does not capture every nuance of a phenomenon does not mean that we can say *nothing* quantitatively. The peaceful coexistence of qualitative and quantitative studies in this book reflects these simple facts.

Measurement, of course, has both qualitative and quantitative aspects. Dantzig (1930), in tracing the development of mathematics from early times, noted that the concept of number contains the idea of "matching" (later known as *cardinality*) and the idea of "order" (*ordinality*). We must see things the same or different and more or less in order to count. Generally speaking, the primitive man's ideal of matching a basket of pebbles to a flock of sheep (to make sure he hadn't lost any) is a qualitative decision. When one asks *how* different the basketful of rocks and the flock are, one begins to *quantify* the losses. We rarely make the distinction between cardinality and ordinality when counting, but it is there and points up the intimate relationship between quality and quantity in measuring.

NOTE

1. The reader should remember that this discussion is based on treating the CPS estimate (and, later, examples from interview experiments) as the *true* value of the variable in question. Further, we are dealing with *one item* measures, rather than those constructed from several questions. Nunnally (1967) points out that, in the case of multi-item measures, more reliable scores generally have *larger* variances than less reliable ones because the covariance among items (which indicates reliability) in the better measures adds to the overall variance of the resulting score. The less reliable measure, with less covariance among test items, would have a smaller overall variance. In the text, I raise the variance issue to sensitize readers to the general problem of correlated error, which may arise in the context Siegel and Hodge point out, or in the case of interrelationships among variables.

REFERENCES

ALWIN, D. (1974). "Approaches to the interpretation of relationships in the multitrait-multimethod matrix." In H. Costner (ed.), Sociological methodology, 1973-1974. San Francisco: Jossey-Bass.

ANDREWS, F. and CRANDALL, R. (1976). "The validity of measures of self-reported well-being." Social Indicators Research, 3(1):1-19.

BOHRNSTEDT, G.W., and CARTER, T.M. (1971). "Robustness in regression analysis." In H. Costner (ed.), Sociological methodology, 1971. San Francisco: Jossey-Bass.

BRADBURN, N. (1977). "Respondent burden." Discussion paper presented at the Biennial Conference on Health Survey Research methods, Williamsburg, Virginia, May 4.

CAMPBELL, D.T., and FISKE, D.W. (1959). "Convergent and discriminant validation by the multitrait-multimethod matrix." Psychological Bulletin, 56:81-105.

CANNELL, C., OKSENBERG, L., and CONVERSE, J. (1977). "Striving for response accuracy: Some experiments in new interviewing techniques." Journal of Marketing Research, 14:306-315.

COOMBS, C. (1964). Theory of data. New York: John Wiley.

DANTZIG, T. (1930). Number: The language of science. New York: Macmillan.

GUILFORD, J.P. (1954). Psychometric methods. New York: McGraw-Hill.

GULLIKSEN, H. (1950). Theory of mental tests. New York: John Wiley.

HAYS, W. (1973). Statistics for the social sciences. New York: Holt, Rinehart and Winston.

JORESKOG, K. (1970). "A general method for analysis of covariance structures." Psychometrika, 57:239-251.

KALSBEEK, W., and LESSLER, J. (1977). "Total survey design: Effect of nonresponse bias and procedures for controlling measurement errors." Discussion paper presented at the Biennial Conference on Health Survey Research Methods, Williamsburg, Virginia, May 2.

KAPLAN, A. (1964). The conduct of inquiry. Scranton, Pa.: Chandler.

NUNNALLY, J. (1967). Psychometric theory. New York: McGraw-Hill.

OSGOOD, C., MAY, W., and MIRON, M. (1975). Cross-cultural universals of affective meaning. Urbana: University of Illinois Press.

REISS, A. (1971). "The systematic observation of natural social phenomena." In H. Costner (ed.), Sociological methodology, 1971. San Francisco: Jossey-Bass.

ROSENTHAL, R. (1966). Experimenter effects in behavioral research. New York: Appleton-Century-Crofts.

RUNKLE, P. (1956). "Cognitive similarity in facilitating communication." Sociometry, 19:178-191.

RUNKLE, P. and McGRATH, J. (1972). Research on human behavior. New York: Holt, Rinehart and Winston.

SIEGEL, P., and HODGE, R. (1968). "A causal approach to the study of measurement error." In H. Blalock and A. Blalock (eds.), Methodology in social research. New York: McGraw-Hill.

TORGERSON, W. (1958). Theory and methods of scaling. New York: John Wiley.

Chapter 7

COMMUNICATING MEASUREMENT OBJECTIVES IN THE SURVEY INTERVIEW

Peter V. Miller
and
Charles F. Cannell

THE SAMPLE SURVEY PROVIDES an interesting focus for inquiry in communication. The survey may inform us about aspects of dyadic communication, while the resulting data have often dealt with questions concerning mass communication. This chapter seeks to explore and link these two interests; in it, we describe recent work on communication in the survey interview which has important implications for the measurement of a number of phenomena, including mass media use and effects.

Placing survey methodology in the context of mass communication research is not a new idea. Developments in survey methods and in the study of mass communication have often been made simultaneously. One needs only to note the pioneering work of Lazarsfeld and colleagues on panel surveys dealing with media effects (Lazarfeld, Berelson and Gaudet, 1948; Berelson, Lazarsfeld and McPhee, 1954), "sociometric" sampling to study the social context of media effects (Katz and Lazarsfeld, 1955), and audience analysis techniques (Lazarsfeld, 1959), to see that the method and the substantive interest have enjoyed a

AUTHORS' NOTE: Survey data on mass media use presented in this chapter were collected when the first author was Assistant Professor of Communication, Purdue University. We would like to thank the department for support in this work, and to thank, in particular, several students who participated in the Practicum in Survey Research Methods during which this research was carried out: Stephen Goldman, Ray Robison, Marla Scafe, Ina Siler, Jean Smith, Teresa Lou Thompson, Henry Tkachuk, Chuck Wood, and C. Newburger.

"symbiotic" relationship. Of course, business decision-making by media entre-
preneurs has necessitated the collection of data by survey. The well-known
"readership" survey is a good example, as is the more recent rating survey
undertaken for the electronic media. A readership study was the subject of
Gallup's doctoral thesis (1928) at the University of Iowa.

Naturally, not all advances in survey methods have come about through
association with mass communication studies. For example, a large amount of
work in this area has been accomplished in connection with studies of health.
This considerable body of literature is largely unfamiliar to communication
scholars, even though the problems addressed in the research are clearly relevant
to their methodological concerns. A particularly important aspect of this work
focuses on the conduct of the survey interview. Communication between
interviewer and respondent, both verbal and nonverbal, is at the heart of
questions concerning data quality. Communication problems in the interview
itself may also be a source of interest in their own right.

We will begin with a review of some research on interviewing in the health
area. Some findings from a pilot study of mass media use which employed some
of the techniques developed in health research will conclude the presentation.

COMMUNICATION IN THE INTERVIEW

Communication between survey respondents and interviewers consists in large
measure of questions and answers, of course. But, in addition to asking
questions, interviewers provide information for respondents; on survey auspices
and purpose, confidentiality, the nature of the interview, and appropriate
respondent behavior. In addition, interviewers traditionally are supposed to
achieve and maintain "rapport" with respondents—to encourage self-disclosure
and to be warm and permissive toward even the most outlandish opinions.
Besides answering questions, respondents are likely to seek information on how
best to perform their task in the unfamiliar survey situation. They may also
engage the interviewer in conversation on topics tangential to the objective of
the survey.

The ground rules for some of this communication may be prescribed by the
study staff. For example, interviewers may be provided with statements to read
to respondents concerning the study sponsorship and goals, how the respondent
was selected, and what safeguards will be taken to ensure the confidentiality of
responses. In survey organizations which maintain a permanent field staff, the
directions on handling these items of information probably do not vary
considerably from study to study. Most, if not all, surveys have an interview
protocol which specifies the wording and order of questions and, perhaps,
recording instructions and transitions between topics or question types.

Interviewing techniques involved in instructing and motivating the respondent, however, are not likely to be covered by procedures established for the

study. General dictates, such as being understanding and not formulating answers for the respondent (or otherwise allowing personal bias to interfere) are often part of basic interviewer training. But how to judge response adequacy, when to ask a probing question and which one to ask, and how to get the respondent to work hard to give accurate and complete information are questions often left to the interviewer to resolve. Poorly worded questions, presumably, are salvaged by interviewers with experience and good judgment through explanations and probing questions. Cannell and Kahn (1968) argued that interviewing skill, in fact, consists in the ability to go beyond the prescriptions of study directors to handle spontaneously the issues we have just discussed. The implication—often overlooked—for those conducting surveys is that differential skill leads to various levels of data quality. Since expertise is not uniformly distributed in an interviewer corps, between-interviewer variance can become a sizable portion of total survey error. Procedures to reduce this component of error might involve more intensive training to inculcate good instinctive technique. For the study director who does not wish simply to close his eyes and hope that the interviewers are performing adequately, this would be the traditional remedy.

EASING THE INTERVIEWER'S BURDEN

Another approach to this problem is to remove from the interviewer much of the responsibility for spontaneously coping with a given questionnaire—to standardize a good deal of the behavior which would otherwise differentially contribute to total survey error. Efforts in this direction might include carefully specifying the instructions which respondents are to receive concerning what is expected of them and how to perform the task. A common technique for motivating respondents would be desirable, as would rules for judging response adequacy and for providing feedback on respondent behavior. Naturally, one can never take into account all of the possible contingencies which may arise in the course of an interview. But, with sufficient pretesting, many seemingly idiosyncratic communication issues may be placed within a common framework for interviewer action, as we will see below.

Such a method recognizes that the interviewer's technique is not really separable from situational factors involved in the survey—the subject matter, the sample composition, and the manner in which questions are formulated. Interviewers should not be given the responsibility for ensuring good measurement; study directors should not expect tedious or confusing questions to obtain valid and reliable responses through the application of some mysterious interviewer technique which they neither understand nor appreciate. The burden of measurement should be borne, as much as is possible, by those who formulate the study objectives. In practice, this means that communication of measurement objectives—casually entrusted to interviewers in many studies—must be embodied in the survey director's own product, the questionnaire.

THE CRITERION: REPORTING ACCURACY

To be able to judge the efficacy of any "improvement" in interviewer performance, one must examine differences in response characteristics. This entails looking beyond the subject matter of a survey to the basic response tendencies at work in the question-answer process. In reporting experiences and events, for example, we must be concerned about under- or overreporting likelihoods. For attitudinal items, the respondent's position may be based on little or no information, or the response may reflect current "socially accepted" ideas. Generally speaking, we are interested in increasing response validity by combating these potential errors through better interview communication.

In studies where validity information on the events of interest was available, several reporting tasks with predictable response errors have been identified. As one might expect, the longer the period of *time* between the event to be reported and the interview, the more likely the event is to be underreported. The effects of memory lapse are marked even within a two-week period, as Cannell and Fowler (1963) found with regard to reports of doctor visits. Thirty percent of documented doctor visits which occurred two weeks prior to the interview were found to go unreported in the National Health Survey. Neter and Waksberg (1965) noted substantial underreporting of actual household repairs and alterations when the recall period was lengthened from one to six months.

Salience of the event to be reported, measured in a variety of ways, has a considerable impact on response validity. When hospital stays are long, they are more likely to be mentioned even if they occurred long ago (Cannell, Fisher, and Baker, 1965). Respondents who have visited a physician frequently for a chronic illness report the illness more accurately than those with fewer visits (Cannell and Fowler, 1963). The effects of time on reporting of the household repairs in Neter and Waksberg's (1965) study were greatly reduced when the repairs cost more than $20. It appears that the importance of the event to the respondent, his involvement with it, is a noteworthy condition for accurate reporting of the experience in an interview.

Finally, perceptions of *social desirability* are likely to influence the reporting of an event. If the experience is embarrassing or threatening to the respondent, it is likely to go unmentioned in the interview. Similarly, events which put the interviewee in a good light may be overreported. Voting fits in this category (Parry and Crossley, 1950), as do reports of the size of savings accounts (Ferber et al., 1969). Genito-urinary conditions and mental illnesses are subject to substantial underreporting (perhaps as few as 25% valid reports), while causes of asthma or stomach ulcers are underreported much less frequently (Cobb and Cannell, 1966).

If time, salience, and social desirability are not the only barriers to accurate reporting, they seem to represent a particularly important subset of them. Experiences and attitudes which are the stuff of much mass communication research are apt to be subject to response errors involving one of these mechanisms. But what can the survey practitioner do to increase accurate reporting in the face of these obstacles? In this regard, it is well to recognize that under- or overreporting biases are compounded by traditional survey interview procedures. The typical interview does not inform the respondent well about either the general goals of the survey, nor about his responsibilities in connection with particular questions, as Cannell, Oksenberg, and Converse, (1977) point out. The feedback provided respondents by interviewers is just as likely to reinforce poor response behavior—e.g., cursory answers or refusals to answer—as it is to reward the respondent's hard work (Marquis and Cannell, 1969). Tape recordings of interviews reveal that the interviewer's reinforcement utterances and probes could be much more appropriately utilized to increase response validity. Another problem is that respondents tolerate the interview, but do not have enough psychological investment in it to report embarrassing events.

In sum, cognitive and motivational problems beset the respondent in any survey interview because of the demands of the question-answering task. Interview techniques should help to alleviate these difficulties rather than further obfuscate the issues. This involves giving the respondent better information on how to perform adequately in the interview, motivating him to expend the effort required to reduce the effects of the reporting biases we have just discussed, and providing positive feedback when accurate and complete information is obtained.

INSTRUCTIONS, FEEDBACK, AND COMMITMENT

The first modification in the "typical" interview protocol which has been shown to be useful in improving response validity is the provision of instructions on the respondent role. Being interviewed is not a familiar experience for most survey respondents, and orientation to the kind of behavior required is apt to be very useful. The instructions should deal with general features of the interview, as well as the demands of specific questions. For example, respondents may wonder just how accurate they should be in their answers. Is a report of *average* behavior sufficient when talking about yesterday's activities? General instructions might emphasize that the information sought should be as accurate and complete as possible. They might also suggest approaches to the interview which will aid in fulfilling the demands of the respondent role. The behavioral recommendations might look like this:

> Some people want to know what they can do to give accurate and complete information. We find that people do better when they *think carefully* about each question, *search* their memory, and *take their time* in answering. People also do better if they give *exact* answers, and give as much information as they can. This includes important things as well as things which may seem small or unimportant. Also, please tell me if a question is not clear, and I will read it again.

Notice that the information sets up standards for response accuracy and offers ideas on how to achieve the desired result. Other standards might be appropriate for other survey objectives—as when we wish only the respondent's first impression on a given issue—but the point is to tell the interviewee *something* about what is expected of him and how he might approach the task. The seriousness and importance of the interview may be impressed upon the respondent, and more considered and complete answers may result.

In addition to general information, suggestions may be made on performance with regard to certain types of questions. For example, when the objective is a report of the frequency of a given experience (say, doctor visits or movie attendance), we might emphasize in an instruction just prior to the question that *exact* information is needed. In other words, ranges or approximations are not sufficient. This instruction is designed to lead the respondent to make the effort to have explicit recall of different events, rather than to rely on a vague impression.

On open questions, the instruction might emphasize the *specificity* of the desired information, or its *completeness.* Hence, when asking for symptoms of illnesses or the names of television programs viewed on a given day, we have an interest in getting the respondent to recall as much as possible, and to give more than general impressions. Communication of the response objective is likely to increase the chances of getting a codable answer.

Behavioral recommendations in this case might include telling the respondent to take time in answering, and to think carefully. These suggestions assist the respondent in doing a better job. They also serve as a basis for reinforcement of appropriate behavior.

It is also possible to tell the interviewee that a general impression or best estimate is the response goal for the question. Such an instruction is particularly useful in the case of personality test items for which we want first impressions. When asked for a general affective statement toward a class of people or an institution, careful examination of specific details concerning the group or entity is likely to make the general judgment more difficult. Information on the general nature of the response required is apt to be helpful in such a case. Of course, this information is a common feature of many self-administered questionnaires dealing with attitudes.

In addition to telling the respondent about the overall and specific question response objectives, communication in the interview should include *feedback* to the interviewee on how well the objectives are being met. We mentioned earlier that Marquis and Cannell (1969) found that much of the reinforcement given respondents by interviewers is *not contingent* upon what we might consider appropriate response behavior. In part, this reflects a lack of clear objectives for respondents in the typical survey interview; also, interviewers are not trained on how to differentiate between poor and adequate response behavior. The result is that an expression of interviewer approval (e.g., saying "OK, "Uh-huh," or making positive references to responses) is just as likely to follow a refusal to answer, or a hasty, incoherent, or incomplete response as a more considered answer. Secondary or probe questions may be used frequently by some interviewers and never by others. When the response objectives are clearly stated, however, it becomes possible also to standardize the kinds of feedback interviewers are to provide, depending upon the character of the response. Here are a couple of examples of the instruction—feedback linkage, taken from questionnaires dealing with health and media use.

SICKNESS EXPERIENCES

Q1. *Let me just mention that to be most accurate you may need to take your time to think carefully before you answer.* (PAUSE) Have you been sick in any way within the last two weeks?

IF R	1a. In what ways were you sick?
SAYS YES	1b. *Uh-huh, I see. This is the kind of information we want.* Were you sick in any other ways within the last two weeks?
IF R	1c. You answered that quickly. Were you sick in any way
SAYS NO	at all in the last two weeks?
WITHIN 5	1d. (ANY MENTION) *Thanks, this is the kind of information*
SECONDS	*we want.*
IF R SAYS	1e. Were you sick in any way at all within the last two
NO AFTER	weeks?
5 SECONDS	1f. (ANY MENTION) *Thanks, this is the kind of information*
	we want.

TELEVISION WATCHING

Q2. *On this next question, we'd like to get numbers as exact as possible.* How many hours did you personally spend watching television yesterday?

EXACT	2a. *I see . . . thanks.*
NUMBER	
APPROX-	2b. Can you be any more exact about the number of hours?
IMATION	2c. (EXACT NUMBER) *I see . . . thanks.*
NO RE-	2d. Let me repeat the question. How many hours did you
SPONSE,	personally spend watching television yesterday?
DON'T KNOW	
	2e. (EXACT NUMBER) *I see . . . thanks.*

The instruction within the main questions and the subsequent reinforcement statements are italicized in the examples. In the health question, the instruction seeks a carefully considered response by suggesting that the respondent spend some time thinking before responding. Following these directions elicits a positive response from the interviewer when accompanied by an affirmative answer (sickness tends to be underreported). A quick "No," however, results in a reminder from the interviewer to take a little more time, and the question is repeated. For those with a more considered negative response, another sort of feedback—repeating the question—is called for. For any affirmative response, the interviewer thanks the respondent and reiterates that such a response is what is desired.

To sum up the health example, the interviewer is providing feedback to the respondent based upon the latter's outward manifestation of thought about the answer, and upon the actual response. Since the tendency on a question of this kind is to underreport, due to the memory effort involved and perhaps the salience of the topic, the instruction, reinforcement, and probing provisions are designed to combat this inclination. The respondent may learn about what is expected and also have this information recapitulated by way of a reinforcing statement or probing question (the latter implies that the task has not been completed). The probe consists of a repetition of the original question, which serves to remove misunderstandings the respondent may have about the information desired, and lets him consider the matter again.

In the television watching example, the objective is precision. The instruction calls for an *exact* number, which leads the interviewee to review the day carefully to reach a summary answer on the time allocated to the activity. When a range or approximation (e.g., "3 or 4," "about 5") is obtained, we repeat the precision objective. If exactness is achieved, before or after the probe, the interviewer provides positive reinforcement. In this example, or in the health question, when the response objective is not attained on the second try, the interviewer is instructed to move to the next question without any feedback utterances or nonverbal cues.

Knowledge of, or assumptions about, the probable reporting tendencies for each question are essential if appropriate instruction—feedback linkages—are to be established. This is straightforward in some cases, like questions dealing with matters which occurred some time prior to the interview, but more difficult in others. Many attitudinal items do not allow a reasonable reporting prediction, and the best that can be done is to urge and reinforce a well-considered response. In general, however, investigators must devote a good deal of effort to understanding the response demands in their questions and to tailoring instructions and feedback to those demands. The results of the effort are both better and standardized communication of measurement objectives to survey respondents. It is not necessary (and probably not desirable) for each question with a similar objective to be prefaced by the same instruction. Words may be varied, or one instruction, with brief reminders, may handle an entire set of questions. Variety in feedback is also desirable, as respondents may grow tired of being thanked for providing "exact information." Within limits, interviewers may be given a choice of reinforcement statements to use. The essential mechanism, however, is the teaching of respondent role through instructions and feedback.

The final interviewing technique we wish to discuss in this paper is *commitment* of the respondent to good role performance in the interview. This procedure seeks to motivate the interviewee to expend the necessary effort for accurate reporting by having him make an overt agreement to fulfill response objectives. Lewin (1958), Bennett (1955), and others have shown that people who state their intention to act in a certain way, in response to a request for the intention, are more likely to follow through on this plan than those who are asked for cooperation but not for the public agreement. Hence, after a few introductory questions, respondents are asked to sign a form, as in Exhibit 1, committing themselves to render accurate and complete information. The

EXHIBIT 1
COMMITMENT PROCEDURE EXAMPLE

That's the last of this set of questions. The rest of the questions are on how media like newspapers, TV and radio fit into your daily life. We are asking people we interview to give us extra cooperation and that they try hard to answer accurately so we can get complete and accurate information about this topic. You are one of the people we hope is willing to make the extra effort.

Here is an agreement which explains what we are asking you to do. (HAND AGREEMENT) As you can see, it says, "I understand that the information from this interview must be very accurate in order to be useful. This means that I must do my best to give accurate and complete answers. I agree to do this."

We are asking people to sign this agreement and keep it for themselves so that we can be sure that they understand what we are asking them to do. It is up to you to decide—if you are willing to agree to do this, we'd like you to sign your name here (POINT OUT LINE). Down below there is a statement about confidentiality and I will sign my name here (POINT OUT LINE).

(IF R HAS NOT ALREADY SIGNED) Are you willing to make the extra effort to continue the interview?

AGREEMENT

I understand that the information from this interview must be very accurate in order to be useful. This means that I must do my best to give accurate and complete answers. I agree to do this.

_____
Signature of Respondent

All information which would permit identification of the people being interviewed as a part of this project will be held in strict confidence. No information that would allow identification will be disclosed or released to others for any purpose.

_____
Signature of Interviewer

interviewer, in return, also signs the form—promising confidentiality—and returns it to the respondent *to keep.* The respondent's anonymity is preserved in this way, but if interviewees are reluctant to sign for other reasons, they are allowed to initial the agreement. Interviews with potential respondents who refuse to sign or initial the agreement are terminated, but the number of such cases has been very small in the several studies using the commitment procedure.

The combination of instruction, contingent feedback, and commitment attacks the various problems of respondent understanding and motivation outlined earlier. Through these modifications in the survey instrument, the investigator removes the burden of measurement communication from the interviewer. At the same time, the study director must assume responsibility for—and should understand—the measurement that goes on in the field operations. Demands of questions on memory or willingness to respond must be taken into account and their effects anticipated in instructions and feedback. Interviewers, meanwhile, must receive sufficient training in the techniques so as to handle them naturally. Decision-making on response adequacy must be taught, so that contingent feedback is properly utilized.

Confronting these techniques *de novo,* some readers may feel that the standardization involved in these procedures comes at too high a price—i.e., interviewer dissatisfaction or respondent irritation. The argument here is that interviewers will feel stifled and mechanical when using the modified instrument because the techniques lack a provision for achieving rapport. While we cannot reject these notions in every case, it is clear from the research to be presented shortly that the general tendency is for interviewers to adapt well to the new techniques and for respondents to work harder with *more* interest and positive affect toward the interview experience.

Basic Interviewer Training

In addition to learning the features of the new techniques, interviewers should acquire a few related skills. First, they should learn to read the interview to the respondent *slowly*—at the rate of perhaps two words per second, on the average. While the pace seems unnatural at first, the benefits in increased respondent understanding more than outweigh the temporary disadvantages. Reading practice overcomes the initial difficulty. Secondly, interviewers should be sure to place an upward inflection at the end of every question, so as not to bury the interrogative nature of the phrase in a too quick or casual delivery. A downward inflection is apt to sound to the respondent like the interviewer really doesn't expect an affirmative answer.

THE IMPACT OF INTERVIEWING TECHNIQUES
ON REPORTING ACCURACY

HEALTH DATA

Table 1 presents information on the effects of the techniques we have discussed on various types of survey reporting. The summary of the procedures given above was based on a program of research in which various techniques have been compared in experimental field conditions. The data in Table 1 are taken from one of the series of studies (Oksenberg, Vinokur, and Cannell, 1976), in which several randomly assigned groups of respondents were interviewed with different combinations of instructions, feedback, and commitment. The respondents were drawn from a homogeneous population (adult white women in the Detroit metropolitan area) so as to standardize health *experience* as much as possible. Differences between the groups could then be more confidently attributed to *reporting* variance, and not to actual differences in the health of those in different conditions.

As one can readily see, the data are very supportive of the notion that the addition of the various interviewing techniques lead to higher reporting of health events which are expected to be underreported. The increase in responses to 16 open questions included reporting of more health symptoms and conditions, as well as acts undertaken by the respondent to maintain health status. Data from national health validity studies, as well as our expectations concerning reporting behavior suggest that these items should be underreported. The average reporting increases associated with the combination of experimental manipulations can be interpreted, therefore, as *accurate* reporting. The same goes for the test of reporting specificity, indicated by the details of activity curtailment. As we add the new techniques to the interview, respondents are more precise when presented with the difficult memory task of relating the dates on which illness inhibited normal activities.

On a response task likely to be embarrassing (pelvic region symptoms), respondents provide more information as experimental techniques, and in particular, commitment, are added to the interview. Respondents were also observed to make greater effort in the interview—checking calendars, medicines, etc.—when the experimental manipulations were present. The overall impression we get from these results is that respondents are working harder when they are informed of the response objectives and motivated by commitment to the interview. They also appear to be more honest in reporting experiences which are likely to go unmentioned because of embarrassment. Let's turn now to some evidence from a very different substantive area—mass media usage.

AN EXPERIMENT ON MEDIA USE REPORTING

The data include reports of the type and frequency of contact with various media, as well as details of information obtained. Television and radio usage is

TABLE 1
RESPONDENT PERFORMANCE ON HEALTH ITEMS BY VARIOUS INTERVIEWING PROCEDURES

Performance Measures	A Control**	B Instructions	C Instructions + Feedback	D Instructions + Feedback + Commitment	Percent Increase in Reporting (D-A)
Number of mentions, 16 open questions[a]	62.82*	68.08	70.42	75.30	20%
Dates of activity curtailment[b]	.49*	.55	.62	.74	51%
Checking Outside[a] Information Sources	.75*	1.32	1.93	2.28	204%
Number of Items Reported for Pelvic Region[a]	.66*	.67	.69	.89	35%

SOURCE: Oksenberg, Vinokur, and Cannell (1976).

* Scores are means for the different experimental treatments.

** The control group received only the question stimuli. Interviewers were instructed to refrain from extemporaneous explanatory remarks or feedback.

a. Scores based on 194, 176, 174, and 183 respondents, respectively.

b. Scores calculated only for those reporting an instance of activity curtailment in the "last three months," yielding 90, 84, 84, and 86 respondents, respectively.

often defined in terms of *time spent,* either on the average or on the day preceding the interview. Newspaper reading is generally partitioned into exposure to various sections of the paper (e.g., front page, sports page, women's section), since publishers wish to know the popularity of these aspects of the product. Those interested in comparing people primarily exposed to print media with those who more often use the television and radio (with regard to their voting stability or cultural sophistication, for example) often want to know how many books and magazines the respondents have read. Examples of all of these types of measures are in the instrument constructed for a pilot study in Lafayette, Indiana, directed by the first author in the spring of 1977.[1] Respondents were randomly assigned to two groups; in the control condition, student interviewers were trained in basic interviewer techniques and instructed to be "good interviewers"—to apply whatever techniques of explanation, feedback, and motivation they thought necessary to achieve good reporting on the basic questions. The experimental group, interviewed by the same interviewers, received identically worded questions, but interviewers were trained to "stick to the instrument," reading instructions and feedback as required, and implementing the commitment procedure.

In the media use study, then, we combined all of the experimental techniques reviewed heretofore in the experimental condition, and instructed interviewers to "do their best" in the control condition.[2] While many of the interviewers were new to the business, all were participants in a class on interviewing techniques, or had taken classes in interpersonal communication. The instructions for the control condition probably simulate well the conditions encountered by many survey interviewers who receive a modicum of basic training and an exhortation to do well. The comparison between conditions is thus a test of standardized communication in the interview with what might be termed "normal" interviewer behavior. We cannot tell in this design which of the new techniques—instructions, feedback, or commitment—or which combination of them is making the most difference in reporting. But we have already seen that each makes a contribution in the health study, and it seems reasonable to treat the three innovations in combination rather than individually. Improved communication of measurement objectives is our goal, not a piecemeal evaluation of single aspects of this process. Instructions are not complete without feedback, and commitment gives a motivational advantage in the respondent role-learning task. The respondents for the pilot study were white adult women in a probability sample from middle-class neighborhoods in Lafayette, Indiana. A total of 209 respondents were interviewed with 102 in the experimental condition.

REPORTING BIASES IN MEDIA USAGE DATA

What hypotheses should we entertain concerning response behavior in questions on this topic? First, it seems clear that much of mass media use will be difficult to remember, since it is often a "secondary activity" performed while other actions (housework, conversation, traveling, for example) are occurring. In other words, we are likely to have a *salience* problem in reporting of media use. Radio and television contact may be "wallpaper" phenomena, and so time-spent estimates on these activities are likely to be understated. This is contrary to the arguments of others (Bechtel et al., 1972; Losciuto, 1972) who say that TV time allocation is *over*reported. The difference lies in the interpretation of activity while "in contact" with the medium. If the respondent is not *really* watching (i.e., actively processing information) while in the same room with the TV set, some would say that they are not *really* spending any time with the medium. Time spend watching is not likely to be characterized by full attention, but one may still consider the time allocation report as valid whether anything was learned or not. Ultimately, the decision on whether the time allocations are under- or over-reported depends on the manner in which the measure is to be used—as a predictor of other behavior or knowledge or as a criterion. When we wish to predict information gain, a measure stressing the "attentive" watching is desired. When time allocation itself is of interest, it matters less how "hard" the respondent is working while in contact with the medium. The difficulty is that most investigators simply measure time spent without instructions to the respondent (or a clear idea themselves) on whether attentive or sporadic watching is desired. In this study (see the earlier example), we specified in the instructions that an *exact* amount of time was desired (that the respondent should carefully consider *all* contact with the medium). This action combats the tendency to underreport the time when contact with TV or radio was a secondary activity.

In other questions with a possible salience problem, we requested *all* the information possible on details from television and radio programs, and newspaper articles. These open questions are clearly subject to underreport, and we expected the experimental condition to show higher mean scores for these items. Several questions with a possible *social desirability* bias were also explored. In two of these (a report of the number of books read in the past few months, and a report of reading the editorial page of the newspaper "yesterday") we anticipated *overreporting* by those in the control condition. An underreporting bias was expected for a question on whether the respondent had ever attended an "X-rated" (read "pornographic") movie.

Table 2 presents the basic difference findings of the media use survey. Consider first the items for which the reporting task involves problems of memory lapse and salience. In reports of watching TV on the day preceding the interview, as well as time spent viewing television and time listening to the radio, there are marked differences between the two conditions. In each case, the experimental condition produces higher reporting. In estimates for newspaper reading and radio listening, a higher percentage of respondents in the experimental condition answer affirmatively, but the differences between conditions are small.

TABLE 2
EFFECT OF INSTRUCTIONS, FEEDBACK AND COMMITMENT
ON VARIOUS MEDIA USE REPORTING TASKS

	Experimental Condition	(N)	Control Condition	(N)
Exposure to Media and Time Spent				
Percent reporting TV watching "yesterday"**	86%	(102)	66%	(107)
Time spent (mean)**	197 minutes	(88)	157 minutes	(71)
Percent reporting radio listening "yesterday"	67%	(102)	65%	(107)
Time spent (mean)**	157 minutes	(68)	89 minutes	(69)
Percent reporting Newspaper reading "yesterday"	83%	(102)	77%	(107)
"Average" TV time (mean)*	215 minutes	(98)	177 minutes	(106)
"Average" radio time (mean)	151 minutes	(97)	138 minutes	(106)
Items Subject to Social Desirability Bias:				
Percent reporting editorial page reading "yesterday"*	38%	(84)	55%	(70)
Percent reporting ever attending "X-rated" movie	61%	(101)	51%	(106)
Number of books read in last three months (mean)*	3.9	(99)	5.3	(104)
Details Recalled from Exposure to Media				
Details from newspaper article read yesterday (mean)*	1.89	(85)	1.44	(82)
Details from radio program heard yesterday (mean)	1.22	(68)	.97	(71)
Details about Gas Shortage:				
Percent reporting any details from TV in last month*	62%	(102)	49%	(107)
Number of details (mean)	2.7	(63)	2.3	(52)
Percent reporting any details from newspaper in last month	48%	(102)	47%	(107)
Number of details (mean)	2.4	(49)	2.0	(50)
Details about Local School Closings:				
Percent reporting any details from TV in last month	58%	(102)	56%	(107)
Number of details (mean)	1.8	(59)	1.7	(60)
Percent reporting any details from newspaper in last month	61%	(102)	55%	(107)
Number of details	2.1	(62)	1.9	(59)
Number of TV programs watched "yesterday" (mean)*	4.0	(89)	3.0	(71)
Number of book titles recalled	2.9	(61)	2.8	(65)

*$p < .05$
**$p < .01$

Three items involving possible social desirability bias demonstrate another impact of the improved interviewing techniques. Two questions on which we anticipated an overreporting bias—reading the newspaper editorial page and the number of books read in the last three months—show markedly *lower* reporting in the experimental condition. On the other hand, X-rated movie attendance (a question subject to probable underreport) was reported by a substantially *greater* number of respondents exposed to instructions, feedback and commitment. The effect of the methods, judging from these results, is not simply to increase reporting; it appears that the experimental condition produces more *accurate* answers, whatever the predicted direction of the bias.

In open questions requesting details of programs on TV and radio, learning about different topics (the natural gas shortage during the winter of 1977 and possible permanent school closings in Lafayette, Indiana) in newspapers and on TV, details from newspaper articles, and book titles, we find higher reporting in the experimental condition. The differences are not always large, but they consistently indicate that the improved interviewing technique produces the greater effort required to perform well in these memory tasks. Note that while the mean numbers of book titles recalled does not differ between conditions, the *ratio* of *titles* to the number of *books* reported read is substantially higher in the experimental than in the control group (75% to 50%). This supports the notion that social desirability bias accounts for the numbers of books difference between conditions.

Overall, the data in Table 2 buttress the health findings presented earlier, indicating more accurate reporting behavior when interview communication is improved through instructions, feedback and commitment. Consistent and sometimes rather large differences were apparent between respondents exposed to the new techniques and those asked the *same* questions, but without the improved measurement context. Both underreporting and overreporting biases are affected by the techniques. The implication for those interested in media usage variables is that many survey estimates of these behaviors are probably inaccurate, and the magnitude of bias is likely to be large. We were dealing with only 200 homogeneous cases in this pilot study; larger, more heterogeneous, Ns and more far-flung field operations were probably subject to substantially greater problems in data collection. Naturally, the problems with univariate measures carry over to *relationships* with other variables; errors may produce pseudo-findings when variables are correlated. We will see an instance of this situation shortly.

A CLOSER LOOK AT THE MEDIA USAGE DIFFERENCES

There are a number of alternative explanations for the difference findings just presented on media usage. One simple but important issue to resolve is whether the two respondent groups, even though randomly assigned, are actually similar on variables which may affect the estimates. For example, the reports on time-spent with television on the day preceding the interview would likely depend on how much time respondents had to spend at home. Women who work, attend school, or are otherwise occupied outside the home would be expected to report less time watching TV than their counterparts who leave the house less often. If those occupied outside the home were disproportionately represented in one experimental condition or the other, the estimates for TV time might be due to this factor, rather than the interviewing techniques.

Examining the demographic characteristics of the experimental and control groups, we find only slight differences in years of education and age (the respondents were all white women, of course). Respondents in both conditions were classified according to their self-reported occupation, with those working full-time, students, and those occupying more than one role (e.g., housewife *and* student) in one category and housewives, retirees and disabled persons in the other group. This variable seeks to describe the "home orientation" of the women respondents—the likelihood that they would be spending time in the home as opposed to other places. Approximately 7% more of the respondents in the control condition were occupied outside the home. Could it be that the differences in TV time estimates between conditions is due to this overrepresentation of housewives, disabled and retired women, or those of low education, in the experimental group? Since these women spend more time at home, the probability of their viewing television is somewhat greater than it is for others.

Table 3 summarizes the results of a multiple classification analysis (Andrews, Morgan, and Sonquist, 1967), in which the TV time estimate for the day preceding the interview was predicted by the type of interview, occupation and education (dichotomized at 12 years and below 13 years and above). The grand mean of number of minutes watching television is 179.1; those with high school education and below reported viewing about 11 more minutes than that, while those with at least some college reported spending nearly 20 minutes less. Those in the control interviewing condition reported 22 minutes less than the grand mean and the women interviewed with the improved techniques said they watched nearly 19 minutes more. The deviations from the grand mean for those working, students or other, and housewives, retirees and disabled were −26.9 and +32.8, respectively. Unadjusted for the effects of other predictors, each one has a considerable impact on the time-spent estimates, with occupation showing the greatest effect.

The adjusted deviations and betas in the second column of Table 3 indicate the effect of individual predictors, controlling for others. As is readily apparent, the impact of the interview technique does not diminish when controlling for the occupation and education of the respondents in both groups. Occupation still has the largest impact, but one cannot attribute differences in time estimates between experimental conditions to this important factor. In an analysis of variance, both interview type and occupation showed significant main effects ($p <$ .05), although education did not. These findings are not surprising—we would be

TABLE 3
THE EFFECT OF INTERVIEWING TECHNIQUES, OCCUPATION AND
EDUCATION ON TIME SPENT WATCHING TELEVISION
(Multiple Classification Analysis)

Grand Mean = 179.1	*N*	*Unadjusted Deviation*	*ETA*	*Adjusted Deviation*	*BETA*
Interview Type:					
Control Condition	73	−22.2		−21.3	
Experimental	87	18.6	.15	17.9	.15
Education					
≤ 12 years	101	11.4		12.9	
≥ 13 years	59	−19.6	.11	−21.9	.13
Occupation					
Working, Student, Other	88	−26.9		−25.8	
Housewife, Retired,					
Disabled	72	32.8	.22	31.5	.21

Multiple R^2 = .08
Multiple R   = .29

surprised if occupation and education were not related to TV time. The interesting aspect of the analysis is that when the experience of the respondents is even further standardized in analytical controls, the effect of the improved interviewing techniques remain strong.

If demographic differences between the groups do not explain the interview technique effect, what sort of explanation should we seek? It might be that the TV time difference is due to better recall of their viewing by the respondents in the experimental condition. If not, one might argue that the higher reporting in the experimental condition is simply a product of a "desire to please" the interviewer. Table 4 addresses this point. In another multiple classification analysis, we looked at the effect of the experimental manipulation on yesterday TV time reported, controlling for the *number of television programs* the respondent could recall watching the preceding day. The idea is that the improved interviewing techniques might lead to better recall of the programs seen, and thus to the higher (and more accurate) estimates of time spent. Time in front of the TV, after all, is organized by programs, and so using the number of programs recalled as a covariate should reduce the impact of the interviewing techniques.

The results of the MCA are supportive of the notion that the difference between interview forms is the result of better recall inspired by the new techniques. When we control for the numbers of programs recalled, the effect of the interviewing manipulation is practically "washed out," while the effect of

TABLE 4
THE EFFECT OF INTERVIEWING TECHNIQUES AND OCCUPATION ON
TIME SPENT WATCHING TELEVISION, CONTROLLING FOR NUMBER OF
TV PROGRAMS REPORTED (COVARIATE)
(Multiple Classification Analysis)

Grand Mean = 179.1	N	Unadjusted Deviation	ETA	Adjusted for Other Independents and Covariates	BETA
Interview Type					
Control Condition	73	−22.2		− 8.3	
Experimental	88	18.4	.15	6.9	.06
Occupation					
Working, Student, Other	89	−26.6		−20.0	
Housewife, Retired, Disabled	72	32.8	.22	24.8	.17

Multiple R^2 = .41
Multiple R = .64

occupation is only slightly reduced. The beta for interviewing condition is very small (although our prediction improves substantially: R^2 = .41). It appears, thus, that people exposed to the new interviewing techniques are not simply making up information to please the interviewer; instead, the TV time differences reflect more *effort* on the part of the respondents in the experimental condition.

Space does not permit a thoroughgoing analysis of each of the differences we have encountered between experimental conditions. One additional analysis, however, may help us to understand further how the effect of the interviewer manipulation comes about. Consider the "X-rated" movie finding, in which this experience—likely to be embarrassing for some people to admit—is reported more often by those in the experimental condition. The analysis presented in Table 5 focuses on the people for which reporting X-rated movie attendance is likely to be threatened. We have partitioned the respondents into two groups: one consisting of those with 12 years or less of education and the other with 13+ years. The hypothesis is that those with high education are less likely to be embarrassed reporting "pornographic" movie attendance than those with less education. The "Hi-Ed" group is likely to be more cosmopolitan and less self-conscious about sexual taboos. The "Lo-Ed" people, on the other hand, are more likely to find this type of event embarrassing to admit—particularly to a younger college student interviewer.

The upshot of this hypothesis is that the experimental interviewing techniques should have more impact among the "Lo-Ed" group (where

TABLE 5

THE EFFECT OF INTERVIEWING TECHNIQUES ON
REPORT OF X-RATED MOVIEGOING, BY EDUCATION

		Lo-Ed (0-12)		
		Interview Type		
		Control	Experimental	
Ever Attended X-rated Movie?	Yes	36 (50%)	40 (68%)	76
	No	36 (50%)	19 (32%)	55
		72	59	131

Phi .18
$\chi^2 = 3.5$

		Hi-Ed (13+)		
		Interview Type		
		Control	Experimental	
Ever Attended X-rated Movie?	Yes	18 (53%)	21 (51%)	39
	No	16 (47%)	20 (49%)	36
		34	41	75

Phi .02
$\chi^2 = .01$

underreporting is more apt to be a problem) than in the "Hi-Ed" group (since Hi-Ed respondents are likely to report this behavior anyway). The cross tabulations in Table 5 bear us out on this point, as the relationship between reporting and interview type is much stronger in the "Lo-Ed" group than in the other. Specifying the finding in this way, we can understand a little better the circumstances within which the improved interviewing techniques do their work.

THE PRICE OF ERROR IN ONE RELATIONSHIP

Before leaving the media use data for other information on the effects of instructions, feedback, and commitment, we should look at one final aspect of measurement upgrading through these techniques: the effect on relationships between variables. It is clear that errors of measurement in one variable have repercussions when that item is related to another. A correlation among the errors may account for some of two variables' relationship, or error may result in a finding of no relationship where one actually exists. The latter is the case when we examine the relationship between occupation, as constructed earlier, and the report of time spent watching television yesterday *within* the control and experimental conditions. We have seen earlier that occupation is a strong predictor of TV time, as we would expect intuitively. (See also Szalai, 1972). Within the control condition, however, occupation is *not significantly related* to the time estimate (in an analysis of variance, F = 1,29, 1 d.f., sig .26). MCA reveals a beta of .13, and R^2 of .02.

By contrast, occupation is strongly related to the time estimate for respondents interviewed with the improved techniques. The ANOVA results are: F = 6.4, 1 d.f., sig .01. In MCA, the beta is .26, and R^2 .07. These results add one more piece of evidence to the collection which points to the value of working to standardize and upgrade the communication of measurement objectives in the interview.

COORIENTATION BETWEEN INTERVIEWER AND RESPONDENT

Chaffee and McLeod (1973) have summarized the coorientational perspective on interpersonal communication. Of particular interest here are two outcomes of communication proposed by the model which may help to further evaluate the experimental manipulation in the media usage study. *Agreement* and *accuracy*— both *inter*personal measures—assess the extent to which partners in communication arrive at the same idea independently and the extent to which one individual's perception of the other's position on an issue matches the other's actual idea. For example, an interviewer and respondent, rating the respondent's effort in the interview, may independently *agree* on the rating. Whether they agree or not, the respondent may come to know what the interviewer thinks about the respondent's effort. He may more accurately perceive the interviewer's thinking as a result of interaction in the interview.

We would expect greater accuracy on the part of respondents in the experimental condition with regard to the interviewers' thinking on respondent performance. Remember that the improved interviewing techniques tell the respondent clearly what is expected of him and reinforce good performance. Hence, respondents interviewed in this way are more likely to understand what interviewers are thinking about their effort in the interview. We may also find that respondents and interviewers more often *agree* on perceptions of the respondent's effort in the experimental condition.

To test these propositions, we asked respondents and interviewers to fill out a form at the end of the interview describing their ideas about the interaction. Included were questions on the effort expended by the respondent, her accuracy in answering, honesty, and degree of favorability toward the interview. Each party rated their own ideas and also what they thought the *other* person thought about that question. Correlating these perceptions, we find that there is more accuracy in the experimental condition concerning the respondent's effort and accuracy in the interview. The Tau B difference for agreement ratings is .21 to .15. For accuracy, the difference is .26 to .17. The coorientation model seems particularly appropriate for analyzing the results of communication in interviews, although it has never been applied this way before to our knowledge. The behavior ratings were also used in a *discriminant function* analysis, attempting to identify the perceptions which best distinguished between the two interviewing conditions. Added to the list of ratings mentioned above were perceptions by the respondent of how difficult the interview task was, and how accurate the respondent thought she was supposed to be when answering questions. These two items and the interviewer's perception of the respondent's *effort* best distinguished between the control and experimental groups (had the highest standardized discriminant function coefficients). Respondents evaluated the questions in the experimental conditions as more difficult than those in the control group (even though they were the *same* questions). They also said that more accuracy in answering was required in the experimental condition. As mentioned earlier, interviewers felt that respondents expended more effort in the interview with instructions, feedback and commitment.

CONCLUSIONS

We have seen the effects of improved interviewing techniques, in two subject areas covering a range of question types. Manipulation checks through coorientation and discriminant function analyses confirm that respondents better understand the survey task when they are given instructions and contingent reinforcement and motivated through commitment. The case of a simple relationship between occupation and time spent watching television demonstrate the advantage of more accurate, standardized data collection procedures. Underreporting biases due to problems of memory and salience, as well as over- and underreporting due to social desirability are reduced by the improved communication in the interview. Biases in common measures of media usage have been highlighted.

Little has been said about the maintenance of "rapport" in the interview: affective responses to the interview by the interviewee and warmth and permissiveness by the interviewer. The tradition in interviewer training, it seems to us, has placed too much emphasis on "rapport" at the expense of poor measurement. Interviewers certainly should be pleasant and accepting of complete, relevant answers. Too often, however, permissiveness extends to behaviors detrimental to good measurement; interviewers accept and even reinforce incomplete and irrelevant responses in the interest of maintaining "good" affective relations. This misplaced emphasis on rapport loses information and probably does not appreciably affect the respondent's feelings about the interview experience. In our research, respondent evaluations of the more "businesslike" interview are just as positive and often more positive than those concerning the "chatty" interview. The evaluations differ on how difficult the task is, and how accurate the respondents feel they should be. This knowledge of response tasks, emphasizing the importance and seriousness of the survey task, is precisely what we wish to inculcate by communicating measurement objectives to the respondent.

What about the *skill* of interviewing? Some interviewers may believe that the standardizing of communication techniques makes the interviewer an automaton with no contribution to data quality. It is true that a good deal of responsibility for measurement is removed from the interviewer's shoulders by implementing the new techniques. But interviewing skill is still required for judging response adequacy and utilizing the appropriate feedback. Interviewing skill is the basis for the new techniques, and investigators still depend heavily on interviewers for proper measurement. The difference is that interviewers do not have to bear the burden of the survey director's mistakes. With practice, the interview schedule becomes easy to use, and interviewers say they are happy to be relieved of the responsibility for "ad-libbing" to achieve response objectives.

The implications of this work for mass communication research are important. Data quality is an issue in many studies of media usage, particularly those done under private auspices to get data for advertising purposes. Response biases in common measures, as we have seen, require attention apart from the actual wording of items. Those conducting research in marketing or advertising, as well as those studying mass communication from academic perspectives have to be aware of how communication in the interview itself has an impact on findings. The cost of adopting the more standardized approach is primarily a better understanding on the part of investigators of the response objectives and demands of their questions. It seems a small price to pay.

NOTES

1. Some of the questionnaire items were measures used in studies conducted as part of the Surgeon General's investigation into television and violence (Comstock and Rubenstein, 1972). Several open-end questions were structured like "message discrimination" measures (Clarke and Kline, 1974). The questionnaire is available from Miller upon request.

2. The type of interview to be taken was assigned to the address of the respondent. The order in which the experimental and control interviews were taken was determined by respondent availability.

REFERENCES

ANDREWS, F., MORGAN, J., and SONQUIST, J. (1967). Multiple classification analysis. Survey Research Center, University of Michigan.

BECHTEL, R., ACHELPOHL, C. and AKERS, R. (1972). "Correlates between observed behavior and questionnaire responses on television viewing." In G. Comstock and E. Rubenstein, Television and social behavior. Washington: U.S. Government Printing Office.

BENNETT, E. (1955). "Discussion, decision, commitment and consensus in 'group decision.' " Human Relations, 8(3):251-273.

BERELSON, B., LAZARSFELD, P. and McPHEE, W. (1954). Voting. New York: Free Press.

CANNELL, C., FISHER, G., and BAKER, T. (1965). "Reporting of hospitalization in the health interview survey." Vital and Health Statistics, 2(6).

CANNELL, C., and FOWLER, R. (1963). "A study of the reporting of visits to doctors in the national health survey." Survey Research Center, University of Michigan.

CANNELL, C., and KAHN, R. (1968). "Interviewing." In G. Lindzey and E. Aronson (eds.), The handbook of social psychology. Reading, Mass.: Addison-Wesley.

CANNELL, C., OSKENBERG, L.E., and CONVERSE, J. (1977). "Striving for response adequacy: Experiments in new interviewing techniques." Journal of Marketing Research, 14:306-315.

CHAFFEE, S., and McLEOD, J. (1973). Interpersonal perception and communication. American Behavioral Scientist. 16(4).

CLARKE, P., and KLINE, F.G. (1974). "Media effects reconsidered: Some new strategies for communication research." Communication Research, 1(2).

COBB, S., and CANNELL, C., (1966). "Some thoughts about interview data." International Epidemiological Bulletin, 13:43-54.

COMSTOCK, G., and RUBENSTEIN, E. (1972). Television and social behavior (Vols. 3 and 4). Washington D.C.: U.S. Government Printing Office.

FERBER, R., FORSYTHE, J., MAYNES, E., and GUTHRIE, H. (1969). "Validation of a national survey of consumer financial characteristics: Savings account." Review of Economics and Statistics, 51:436-444.

GALLUP, G. (1928). "An objective method for determining reader interest in the content of a newspaper." Unpublished Ph.D. dissertation, State University of Iowa.

KATZ, E. and LAZARSFELD, P. (1955). Personal influence. New York: Free Press.

LAZARSFELD, P. (1959). "Latent structure analysis." In S. Koch (ed.), Psychology: A study of a science. New York: McGraw-Hill.

LAZARSFELD, P., BERELSON, B., and GAUDET, H. (1948). The people's choice. New York: Free Press.

LEWIN, K. (1958). "Group decision and social change." In E. Maccoby, T. Newcomb, and E. Hartley (eds.), Readings in social psychology (3rd ed.). New York: John Wiley.

LOSCIUTO, L. (1972). "A national inventory of television viewing behavior." In G. Comstock and E. Rubenstein (eds.), Television and social behavior (Vol. 4). Washington, D.C.: U.S. Government Printing Office.

MARQUIS, K., and CANNELL, C. (1969). "A study of interviewer-respondent interaction in the urban employment survey." Survey Research Center, University of Michigan.

NETER, J., and WAKSBERG, J. (1965). "Response errors in collection of expenditures data by household interviews: An experimental study." Bureau of the Census, Technical paper No. 11.

OKSENBERG, L., VINOKUR, A., and CANNELL, C. (1976). "The effects of instructions, commitment and feedback on reporting in personal interviews." Survey Research Center, University of Michigan.

PARRY, H., and CROSSLEY, H. (1950). "Validity of responses to survey questions." Public Opinion Quarterly, 14:61-80.

SZALAI, A. (1972). The use of time. The Hague: Moutou.

Chapter 8

COGNITIVE SIMILARITY AND COMMUNICATION
BETWEEN PARENTS AND ADOLESCENTS

F. Gerald Kline

THIS CHAPTER EXAMINES THE CONCEPT of *cognitive structure* within the framework of two models. The first model is applied to the problem of how people develop and maintain cognitive representations of, and interrelationships among, objects in the perceived environment. The second concerns the *match* between individual cognitive structures and the implications of this for dyadic communication. In the latter case, we will see that the model is actually a scaling technique whose characteristics are found to be isomorphic with the components of a theory of cognitive structure.

"Recent research has in part abandoned the descriptive approach (to cognitive components and associated interrelationships among them) and turned to the problem of cognitive dynamics, in which the emphasis is primarily on (cognitive) change." (Zajonc, 1968: 338.) In this paper we will agrue for a static, descriptive approach that can also account for cognitive change, a point we will return to later. (Also see Scott, 1969: 261).

In his survey of "Cognitive Theories in Social Psychology," Zajonc (1968) defines *cognitive structure* as "any form of interdependence among cognitive elements, whatever their definitions, which has motivational, affective, attitudinal, behavioral, cognitive consequences." For example, Abelson and Rosenberg (1958) considered the elementary units of cognitive organization to be "cognitive representations of things, concrete and abstract," to which verbal labels can be attached. Asch (1946) says that a structure consists of attributes organized in a Gestalt-like way. He took his experimental results as proof that the list of characteristics (attributes) he used was not simply an equally weighted additive array. Some traits, he argues, are central and have a greater impact while others are peripheral and have little impact. Wishner (1960) has shown that some of the configurational effects found by Asch (1946) are a function of empirical correlations among traits and Hays's (1958) model of trait independence describes the dimensionality of the cognitive space in terms of the implicative relations among cognitive units.

Zajonc (1968: 328), referring to his earlier research, says,

> The term "cognitive structure" refers to something . . . ephemeral (although potentially recurrent). . . . The components of cognitive structure are *attributes.* For purposes of analysis, it is assumed that a person perceives objects and events in terms of psychological dimensions. A *psychological dimension* is one's capacity to map consistently a set of responses on a collection of stimuli that is itself ordered. A specific act of "perceiving" or "cognizing" a given stimulus object or event is regarded as involving the projection of the stimulus onto a set of psychological dimensions. These projected values, attributes, are the elements of the cognitive structure under analysis. . . . The set of all (his) attributes is called cognitive universe, and a single cognitive structure by itself is simply an *organized* subset of the individual's cognitive universe which has reference to a specifiable entity.

Another common approach is the "measurement of meaning" technique (Osgood, Suci, and Tannenbaum, 1957) for describing cognitive structure. It has been used by Triandis (1960a, 1960b) and Shibuya (1962) for relating communication effectiveness to semantic differential profiles as measures of cognitive structuring.

Another effort to specify a cognitive structuring has been made by Scott (1969). The structural properties of his model are defined by dimensionality, attribute articulation, attribute centrality, evaluative centrality, centralization, image comparability, affective-evaluative consistence, affective balance, and image ambivalence. Many of these terms relate to the primary interests of those doing experimental research in attitude change.

Scott also introduces the concept of *cognitive domain* to cover instances of phenomenal objects which the person perceives as functionally related (Scott, 1969:262). Borrowing this term, we define the cognitive domain as the set of external stimuli toward which the individual orients himself when considering a particular topic in a given situation.

Turning from the individual cognitive structure models, this brief literature review finally focuses on a little-discussed approach used by Runkel (1956) to link structures *across* people. He argued that people with similar ("co-linear") cognitive structures exchange symbols in a similar semantic context. The structural match facilitates efficient communication by insuring that the symbols invoked by the individual parties have the same meaning for each. The means for judging cognitive similarity lies in whether or not the individuals use the same psychological dimension in evaluating stimuli relevant to the topic of interest. The judgment is made using the "unfolding" model developed by Coombs (1964).

The characteristics of cognitive structure seen in the research above, in sum, consist of *attributes, elements* (functions of attributes) and their interrelationships. Subsequently, we will develop a formal model incorporating these items. The multidimensional model deals with intrapersonal cognitive framework; thereafter, we will look at an abbreviated—unidimensional—form of the general model in examining data linking structures *across* people (an application of Runkel's approach). Ideally, we could ascertain cognitive fit on a multidimensional level, but data are not readily available, and the matching algorithm is not developed.

THE MODEL

A weighted *Euclidean* model of the organization of elements in r-dimensional space, we stipulate, is isomorphic with characteristics of cognitive elements in a person's cognitive structure relative to r-attributes.

Several terms need definition. The first of these is a cognitive *element*. Noting the relevant literature referred to above, but placing emphasis jointly on the stimulus sampling terminology specified by Atkinson, Bower, and Crothers (1965), and the *Theory of Data* terminology of Coombs (1964), an element is a cognitive representation associated with an external stimulus which is sampled from the cognitive domain. This element, according to Coombs (1964:326) is thought of " . . . as a particular combination of attributes, an r-tuple, which constitutes the input." (See Torgerson, 1958:26.) The simplest cognitive element consists of a psychologically meaningful differentiated point on a single attribute dimension. More complex cognitive elements would be the intersection of two or more projections from values differentiated along two or more attribute dimensions. During the process of orientation the individual will relate each of the stimuli sampled from the cognitive domain to a particular internalized cognitive element. A cognitive element may be considered an "ideal point" for the stimulus in the cognitive domain—a specification of the properties (values) of an equivalence class. Any particular stimulus which is sampled may not match this ideal cognitive element $|c_{tij}|$ (where t represents time, i the individual, and j the element) perfectly, however. A particular stimulus, then, is another r-tuple, q_{tij} which will fall at a distance, $|p_{tij}| = |c_{tij} - q_{tij}|$, from the ideal of the nominal class. If this distance p_{tij} is less than some admissible prescribed amount on each dimension $|e^{(d)}_{tij}|$ the stimulus is assimilated and identified as a member of the class and tends to become endowed with the properties of that class. This is how we *identify* an object as that object.

The second of our primitive terms is an *attribute.* An attribute refers to a particular characteristic or property of an object. It is a property that is capable of further subdivision or differentiation (i.e., it can be continuous). We shall use the term "dimension" in referring to a particular attribute. (See Torgerson, 1958:248). Thus, the concept *attribute* can refer to aspects like the shape of a stimulus object, its color, size, or spatial position. Several psychologically meaningful points may be differentiated along any particular attribute for the individual.

Over time the individual will accumulate a large number of cognitive elements—combinations of attributes which may be used to orient him to a wide variety of cognitive domains. The *interrelations* of these cognitive elements make up the cognitive structure which accounts for consistency in the individual's orientation to topics or situations over time. This orientation is accomplished by relating a set of stimuli sampled from a cognitive domain to a set of cognitive elements. For any particular stimulus, these relationships can be referred to as a definition of the stimulus. When all of the sampled stimuli within a cognitive domain have been defined, a set of cognitive elements in r-dimensional attribute space will represent the topic or situation for the individual.

This cognitive structure includes a third primitive term, the *individual's psychological preference point* with regard to a cognitive domain. This concept is defined as a point that orders the cluster of cognitive elements that define the cognitive domain.

Once phenomenal objects have been identified through association with cognitive elements, a class of elements may be compared through their relationships to the preference point—a preferred combination of attributes for that class of elements. For example, a set of elements might consist of job opportunities available to an individual. Each element is the intersection of a number of attributes by which the person identifies it. All of the elements, however, may be seen as related to the preferred combination of attributes (the preferred job) and, depending on their closeness to the preference point, the job-elements will be more or less favored. In this sense, the preference point *organizes* the elements in the class. The preference point may be "moved" by the activation of additional cognitive elements during the process of orientation. At some point in the process, however, the preference point begins to dominate the positioning of new cognitive elements. The point becomes a "psychological anchor" toward which newly activated cognitive elements may be assimilated or contrasted. The preference point becomes particularly important for the individual in placing himself with regard to others for any specific cognitive domain.

Three distance functions may be used to define the relationships which exist between the terms which have been defined above. Every cognitive element is related to values along one or more attribute dimensions. So the first of our distance functions is the *psychological distance (from "zero") of each cognitive element along each attribute dimension.* This is the extent to which each element possesses the attribute.

Every cognitive element is separated from every other element by some distance in the cognitive space. Following the terminology used by Carter (1965), we define the psychological distance *between* elements as the *pertinence relation,* based on the attributes to which each of the elements are related.

The third distance function is the psychological distance between the preference point for each cognitive domain and each of the cognitive elements which make up the cluster which defines the domain. Again using Carter's terminology, this distance is the *salience relation.* Here we assume that the preference point is equivalent to Carter's "I," the individual in the orientation situation.

Assume that all attributes potentially relevant to cognizing an element are available to each individual. Assume, further, that the infinite number of combinations of attributes which constitute cognitive elements are made available to everyone. The expansion of the cognitive universe in which all share allows us to place each individual situation under the umbrella of the model.

It is our supposition that the organization of n-elements (objects) in some r-dimensional (attributes) space for a particular cognitive domain (class of elements) has a preference point for the cognitive elements which defines that domain. The point is the ideal combination of attributes in that particular situation. There is no stipulation that the same elements will necessarily be activated each time a person orientates himself to a particular cognitive domain.

We now move to the formal characteristics of the model.[1] Comparing the relations among elements in the Euclidean model and the metric relationships among elements in the cognitive structure model, we stipulate that there is an isomorphism between the elements or points in the Euclidean model and the cognitive elements (see Note 1); between the dimensions implied by the dimensional representation and the cognitive attributes; and between the metrics of the two models.

It is difficult to standardize the individual preference points across people, to continue the general statement of the model. To move toward a solution to the problem we have relied on work by Carroll and Chang (1969, 1970) who postulate an individual differences model for choice behavior. Their approach can be related to our theory of cognitive structure. Carroll and Chang do not discuss concepts which might be related to our notions of cognitive domain or stimulus sampling. They simply assume an input of stimuli during the process of perception. They assume that each stimulus is evaluated along several attribute dimensions. Our model differs from their formulation in that we do not assume that a particular stimulus is directly evaluated along the attribute dimensions.

Instead, as we have noted above, a specific stimulus is defined by its association with a cognitive element which represents an ideal point in a nominal class. Only through its association with a cognitive element can a stimulus be said to be related to a position (value) of a particular attribute dimension. Our theoretical differences with Carroll and Chang are not serious, but they will lead to some differences in the interpretation of data analyzed using their model.

We will use our terminology in the discussion to follow. The reader may wish to refer to Carroll and Chang's original work for a discussion of this model from the viewpoint of these authors. We assume that an individual's cognitive space may be represented as consisting of a set of r dimensions (attributes) and a set of cognitive elements projected from values of these dimensions. We shall use x_{jd} to represent the value of the jth cognitive element on the dth dimension (so that j ranges from 1 to n and d ranges from 1 to r). Similarity judgments for each subject are assumed to be related in a simple way to weighted Euclidean distance in this space. (Of course, these judgments cannot take place until each stimulus sampled has been associated with a particular cognitive element. Then the task of performing similarity judgments is assumed to involve evaluating the distances between cognitive elements in the individual's cognitive space.) In particular, it is assumed that:

$$s_{jk}^{(i)} = L(d_{jk}^{(i)}) \qquad [1]$$

where $s_{jk}^{(i)}$ is the similarity of the jth and kth elements for the ith individual, and L is a linear function (which negative slope). The term $d_{jk}^{(i)}$ refers to the "modified" euclidean distance assumed to exist between the jth and kth elements for the ith individual. The "modified" Euclidean distance for the ith subject is given by:

$$d_{jk}^{(i)} = \sqrt{\sum_{1}^{r} w_{id}(x_{jd} - x_{kd})^2} . \qquad [2]$$

This formula differs from the usual Euclidean distance formula only in the presence of the weights, w_{id}, which represents the saliences or "importances" of each dimension to each individual. Another way of looking at this formula is to say that the $d_{jk}^{(i)}$'s are ordinary Euclidean distances computed in a space whose coordinates are:

$$x_{jd}'^{(i)} = w_{id}^{1/2} x_{jd} \qquad [3]$$

that is, in a space that is like the x space except that the configuration has been expanded or contracted (differentially) in directions corresponding to the coordinate axes. This is the kind of transformation that would, for example, convert circles into ellipses with major and minor axes parallel to the coordinate axes, or spheres into (parallel) ellipsoids in three dimensions. On a practical level, this means that some attributes are more important than others for perceiving objects, and the important attributes vary from person to person. I may judge an occupation primarily on its flexibility and freedom, while others might place greater weight on the financial rewards.

If we are not interested in reducing the dimensions used by our subjects to some parsimonious set (usually three or less because of the three-dimensional character of our perceptual capabilities), then we can define the location of cognitive elements activated by each person in a common space. That is, we can "superimpose" the cognitive maps for each subject, where the maximum dimensionality of the common map consists of all attributes used by all people. There would be many zeroes in each person's "r-tuple" where particular dimensions were not used. The attribute dimensions do not need to be orthogonal to each other. Where the cosine of the angle between many of these attributes becomes small, it is conceivable that by using an algorithm such as that specified by Carroll and Chang we would get a reduced space measure of meaning (see Osgood, Suci, and Tannenbaum, 1957). But this parsimony asks for its payment a diminished specificity when we attempt a procedure to develop a common space for our subjects.

We have specified the formal characteristics of multidimensional weighted Euclidean model and have argued for the isomorphism between it and our set of primitive terms. Let us now turn to a simpler model, having only one attribute, which will be useful in judging the similarity of cognitive structures between people in predicting communication outcomes. If we take the above model and view it as a one-dimensional, rather than r-dimensional, solution we would be dealing with the most important, most greatly weighted, attribute used to make discriminations among objects. We would still be faced with developing a matching algorithm for this solution for one person and some other solution for a second person. Another approach we could take, one that loses some of the richness of a multidimensional perspective of phenomenal stimuli, is to force a person to choose a "discriminating attribute" for making judgments among objects. If we could do this and also jointly determine whether two persons are using, or not using, the same dimension, we would have lost some information but gained in achieving the algorithm for matching dimensionality. Runkel (1956) has provided us with this possibility with an adaptation of Coombs' (1964) unfolding model. Here a person makes judgments about objects such that the absolute distance between the jth stimulus point and the ith individual's ideal point is:

$$|p_{ij}| = |c_{ij} - q_{ij}| \qquad [4]$$

and his preference for stimulus j over stimulus k denotes that:

$$|p_{ij} - p_{ik}| \leqslant 0 \qquad [5]$$

Solving for a set of simultaneous inequalities of the above statement (5), where $i = 1, \ldots, m$ and $j, k = 1, \ldots, n$, is the equivalent of the unfolding technique.

Returning to the primitive terms from the multidimensional model we would still have attributes, in this instance a "discriminating" one; we would have cognitive elements, the objects that were evaluated by our respondents; and we would have individuals' psychological preference points. The distance functions would be between the preference points and the different points on the attribute for each object.

Now, we will discuss the utility of this model in predicting facilitation of communication. Runkel (1956:179) hypothesized that "similarity of structure between two cognitive fields increases the efficacy of communication between them." Runkel tested this hypothesis using a unidimensional unfolding model as a basis for measuring whether individuals had similar cognitive structures. He referred to individuals who shared the same attribute dimension for ordering stimuli as having orientations which are "co-linear." When individuals used different attributes, as defined by their lack of fit to the same J-scale, they were "non-co-linear." He was able to demonstrate that students who were "co-linear" with their instructors in evaluating course objectives were likely to learn more from those instructors.

This approach to predicting communication effectiveness differs in one important respect from previous efforts. Other research has concerned itself with whether persons who share similar attitudinal positions on topics will share more effective communication with individuals with opposing positions. Selective perception or selective exposure are predicted to occur when conflicts in positions on topics exist between persons attempting to communicate with one another. Our concern is not with the consequences of any particular position on a topic which an individual may develop in orienting himself to a cognitive domain. As we have pointed out above, such positions can be regarded as preference points in a multidimensional cognitive structure. We maintain that it is the underlying *cognitive structure* in this instance, indicated by the important dimension for evaluation which does more to facilitate communication than the particular location of preference points. Thus, in attempting to make predictions of communication effectiveness, it is more important to have a measure of similarity of cognitive structure rather than measures of similarity of positions on topics.

APPLICATION OF THE MODEL

In this initial application of our model we followed Runkel in basing our measurement of similarity of cognitive structure upon Coombs's unidimensional unfolding model. We used procedures initially developed by Coombs and elaborated by Runkel to estimate the cognitive similarity of pairs of individuals based on their rank ordering of six stimuli.

The data being offered to elucidate our notions is part of a large field experiment conducted to examine information acquisition by adolescents

(Kline, Miller, and Morrison, 1974). The research design treats the adolescent household as the sampling point while the data point consists of dyadic relationships between the adolescent and his or her father and mother. Three measures will be looked at here. The first, cognitive similarity, is based on the unfolding of preference rankings for six jobs[2] by the adolescent and the mother and the adolescent and the father. The second, a measure of reciprocal talking, is the adolescent's report of talking to the mother and/or the father, and the parent's report of talking with the adolescent. We have reciprocal talking when both report talking to the other about jobs and no reciprocal talking if either reports no talking. Finally there is a measure of shared perception, or common view. This is based on asking the adolescent what job he or she is going into when finished with school. This was paired with what the mother or father thought the adolescent wanted to do. The jobs nominated by the adolescent and the parent were compared. If they were in the same Duncan SES decile category they were scored as having a common view.[3]

If our notions are correct, we should find that cognitive similarity will be related to this common or shared view. As Runkel would hold, the similarity of the cognitive structure facilitates communication outcomes like common view. In addition, the actual amount of communication (reciprocal talking) between parent and child should predict common view. The product of cognitive similarity and reciprocal talking should result in the highest probability of common view.

To restate, we wish to explain common view (CV) of job claim by parent and adolescent by a combination measure (RTCS) of reciprocal talking (RT) and cognitive similarity (CS) as well as each of these variables separately. The equation would look like this:

$$\mu_{cv} = \beta_0 + \beta_1 (RTCS) + \beta_2 (CS) + \beta_3 (RT) + e. \qquad [6]$$

Each of the variables in equation 6 is dichotomous and as such present certain analytic problems, particularly in the case of CV. RTCS is coded 1 for pairs who are both cognitively similar and reciprocally talking pairs, respectively, and 2 if otherwise. CV pairs are coded 1 if both parties choose jobs in the same category and 2 if not. With CV a dichotomy there is no theoretical justification for positing a joint normal distribution with the predictor variables, regardless of their measurement form; and the dependent variable $P(CV = 1)$ is restricted in range to $0 \leqslant P(CV = 1) \leqslant 1$. Additionally the additivity assumptions are inappropriate with two or more predictors. To get around these problems we will employ a log linear regression model which calls for a logit transformation on $P(CV = 1)$ (DuMouchel, 1974). The equation will look like this:

$$\log_e P(CV = 1)/P(CV = 2) = \beta_0 + \beta_1 (RTCS) + \beta_2 (CS) + \beta_3 (RT) + e \qquad [7]$$

and use a maximum likelihood estimation procedure for $\beta_0, \beta_1, \beta_2,$ and β_3 that will maximize the probability that $P(CV = 1)$. [4]

DATA ANALYSIS

Table 1 displays the distribution of our four basic variables. At the outset we can see that we have reasonable distributions for each measure, except perhaps for talking. We find mothers slightly less often cognitively similar with their children than fathers when it comes to jobs; but mothers do more reciprocal talking and have a greater likelihood of agreeing on what job plans the adolescent will pursue.

Dividing the adolescents by sex, we find no great differences in relation to fathers or mothers except that mothers talk with girls slightly more often and girls have less common view with fathers. There is also a tendency toward more joint talking and similarity for mothers and girls.

There are major differences when it comes to age. We partitioned our adolescents into younger (14-15) and older (16-17) and found that for father/adolescent pairs there was an upward shift in all of our measures with age. For mother related pairs there was a drop in cognitive similarity and in the joint measure of talking and similarity. There was an increase in the proportion of pairs who were reciprocally talking and who held a common view.

Turning now to Table 2 we can examine how well each of our predictors does in maximizing the probability of a common view between father and adolescent and mother and adolescent.

TABLE 1

SEX AND AGE AS THEY RELATE TO COGNITIVE SIMILARITY, RECIPROCAL TALKING AND COMMON VIEW ABOUT OCCUPATIONAL CHOICE WITH MOTHER AND FATHER (%)

			Father		
	All	*Boys*	*Girls*	*Younger*	*Older*
Cognitive Similarity	47	48	45	42	50
Reciprocal Talking	75	74	75	70	79
Common View	29	32	26	24	31
Reciprocal Talking and Cognitive Similarity	38	39	37	29	45
			Mother		
Cognitive Similarity	40	40	40	47	34
Reciprocal Talking	85	81	90	80	90
Common View	36	36	36	31	40
Reciprocal Taling and Cognitive Similarity	34	31	37	37	31

TABLE 2

| | Mother/Adolescent Common View | | Father/Adolescent Common View | |
| | (1) | (2) | (3) | (4) |
	Reg. Coeff.*	Est. Prob. of Having a CV (Overall = .35)	Reg. Coeff.	Est. Prob. of Having a CV (Overall = .30)
Reciprocal Talking and Cognitive Similarity?				
Yes	+.47 N = 80	.46	+.35 N = 83	.38
Overall	(+.32)		(+.27)	
Cognitive Similarity?				
Yes	−.46 N = 95	.25	+.04 N = 102	.30
Overall	(−.37)		(+.04)	
Reciprocal Talking?				
Yes	+.10 N = 203	.37	−.00 N = 163	.30
Overall	(+.16)		(−.00)	

NOTE: The coefficient in parentheses is standardized for equal numbers of respondents in the "Yes" and "No" cell. The coefficient above is the coefficient calculated for the actual number respondents in the "Yes" cell.

The equations are not statistically significant. Additionally we find that none of the individual predictors are. The individual coefficients for each category are found in columns 1 and 3. Our RTCS measures are in the predicted direction and are of about the same magnitude for mother and father pairs. However, for the mother-adolescent dyads cognitive similarity alone seems to diminish CV while reciprocal talking makes no difference.

An examination of columns 2 and 4 is also instructive. The probabilities at the top of the columns, .35 and .30 respectively, represent the probability of a common view between parent and adolescent when the three predictors take on their average value in the sample. The probabilities below represent the probability of having a common view when being in that particular category. Thus, for those mothers and adolescents who are cognitively similar and talking (RTCS = Yes) there is a slightly higher probability of having a common view (a 30% gain). For the Father/Adolescent column (4) one can see a little gain (27%) for the category, RTCS = Yes, but nothing for CS or RT.

This very modest support for the notion of similarity of cognitive structure combined with talking back-and-forth between parent and child can be further elaborated by examining our notions across parent and age of adolescent. Table 3 provides this analysis.

An examination of columns 1, 3, 5 and 7 of the table shows that with increasing age the adolescent/parent CV can be predicted most effectively by RTCS. In columns 4 and 8 we can see that if an adolescent and parent are talking and cognitively similar, taken together, there is a probability of .93 or .94 that they will hold a common view. In the same columns being cognitively similar, taken alone, yields a near zero probability of being CV. And, we can see there is no gain in CV with talking alone.

For the younger adolescent our measures are not strong predictors of CV.

TABLE 3

| | Mother/Adolescent Common View | | | | Father/Adolescent Common View | | | |
| | Younger (1) | | Older (2) | | Younger (3) | | Older (4) | |
	Reg. Coeff.	Est. Prob. of Having a CV (Overall = .30)	Reg. Coeff.	Est. Prob. of Having a CV (Overall = .38)	Reg. Coeff.	Est. Prob. of Having a CV (Overall = .24)	Reg. Coeff.	Est. Prob. of Having a CV (Overall = .30)
Reciprocal Talking and Cognitive Similarity?								
Yes	+.41(42)	.40	+3.30	.94(39)	−.69(29)	.13	+3.50	.93(54)
Cognitive Similarity?								
Yes	−3.30(54)	.24	−3.20	.03(42)	+62(42)	.37	−2 70	.03(60)
Reciprocal Talking?								
Yes	+.05(91)	.31	+.09	.40(113)	+.09(69)	.26	−.05	.29(95)
Equation Significance	N.S.		N.S.		N.S.		N.S.	

SUMMARY AND CONCLUSIONS

From the above analyses we have seen that our notions of cognitive similarity supplemented by communication frequency have been productive in attempting to understand the holding of a shared view about jobs by an adolescent and his or her parent. It was particularly clear that age, and its attendant implication for more communication about upcoming vocational choices, was crucial for this topic. One might expect a topic such as family planning to be more dependent on within and across sex differences with the parents.

We have moved through a maze of formulae; delineated two formal models claimed to be isomorphic with a substantive theory of cognitive structure; chose, due to available data and algorithm, a unidimensional model of cognitive structure and fitted sociometric data to it; and, finally, tested our notions of the predictive power of the cognitive structure theory. We would argue that we have made a case for this approach by finding as much as we did with the cruder model of the two discussed. A multidimensional representation of cognitive structure should be better.

We have also tried to make a case for examining measurement, or scaling models, as formal representations of substantive theory. In this case we are using an unfolding model. One can imagine other instances or applications where the emphasis is on theoretical uses rather than data reduction or simple number assignment.

NOTES

1. It will be necessary to have the following definitions for our model.
(1) A *Metric* is a relation, M, satisfying the following seven conditions:
  (a) Its domain is the family of ordered pairs of elements of some well-specified underlying set.

(b) Its range is the set of nonnegative real numbers: i.e., the positive numbers taken together with the number zero.

(c) It is a function: i.e., to each ordered pair from the domain it attaches a *unique* number from the range.

(d) If we let a, b, and c denote generic elements of the underlying set, and if we let M(a, b) denote the number attached to the ordered pair (a) by metric M, then for any elements M(a, a) = 0.

(e) M(a, b) − M(b, a)   (asymmetry)

(f) M(a, b) = M(a, c) + M(c, b)   (triangle inequality)

(g) If M(a,b) = 0, then a = b.

(2) A *Metric Space* consists of a set of points, say a, b, etc., together with the set of distances between the various pairs of points, M(a, b), M(a, c), etc.

(3) A *Dimensional Representation* of a metric space consists of a set of points, a, b, etc., a set of coordinates for each point, say X_{ij} where i = 1, 2, . . . , n; and j = 1, 2, . . . , n, and a function by which the distance between two points can be determined from the coordinates of the two points.

The ordinary Euclidean distance satisfies the properties of a metric. Conditions (a) through (e) and (g) can be easily satisfied whereas condition (f) requires a longer, but not difficult, proof.

2. Each of the respondents was asked to rank the following jobs: plumber, secretary, teacher, police officer, assembly line worker, and lawyer. The question stated, "We are interested in what *you think* are the rankings of the jobs. Now, which is the best job? . . . Next best? . . . (INTERVIEWER RECORD NUMBERS NEXT TO JOB LIST).

3. Job names were assigned codes according to Census designations. They were then given Duncan socioeconomic status scores, and these were collapsed into ten groups. When a parent mentioned a job within the same decile category as the adolescent's nominated job, a score of 1 was assigned to the pair (common view). If the parent and teenager choices did not match, a score of 2 was assigned. Hence, the parent need *not* choose the precise job the adolescent mentioned in order to evidence a common view, under this scoring system. Although a more lenient criterion, this procedure seems fairly to assess the shared knowledge in the dyad, since many adolescent plans are only temporary and the parent would do well to know what kind of job the adolescent would choose in general.

REFERENCES

ABELSON, R.P., and ROSENBERG, M.J. (1958). "Symbolic psychologic: A model of attitudinal cognition." Behavioral Science, 3:1-13.

ASCH, S.E. (1946). "Forming impressions of personality." Journal of Abnormal and Social Psychology, 41:258-290.

ATKINSON, R.C., BOWER, G.H. and CROTHERS, E.J. (1965). An introduction to mathematical learning theory. New York: John Wiley.

CARROLL, J.D. (1972). "Individual differences and multidimensional scaling." In A.K. Romney, R.N. Shepard, and S.B. Nerlove (eds.), Multidimensional scaling (Vol. 1). New York: Seminar Press.

CARROLL, J.D., and CHANG, J.J. (1969). "Relating preference data to multidimensional scaling solutions via a generalization of Coombs' unfolding model." Unpublished paper. Murray Hill, N.J.: Bell Telephone Laboratories.

——— (1970). "Analysis of individual differences in multidimensional scaling via an n-way generalization of 'Eckhart-Young' decomposition." Psychometrika, 35(3).

CARTER, R.F. (1965). "Communication and affective relations." Journalism Quarterly, 42(2):203-212.

CHAFFEE, S.H., and McLEOD, J.M. [eds.] (1973). Interpersonal perception and communication. A special issue of American Behavioral Scientist, 16(4).

COOMBS, C.H. (1953). "Theory and methods of social measurement." In L. Festinger and D. Katz (eds.), Research methods in the behavioral sciences. New York: Holt, Rinehart and Winston.

——— (1964). A theory of data. New York: John Wiley.

DuMOUCHEL, W.H. (1974). "The regression of a dichotomous variable." Internal memorandum, Institute for Social Research, University of Michigan, Ann Arbor.

HAYS, W. (1958). "An approach to the study of trait implication and trait similarity." In R. Tagiuri and L. Petrullo (eds.), Person perception and interpersonal behavior. Stanford, Calif.: Stanford University Press.

KLINE, F.G., MILLER, P.V. and MORRISON, A.J. (1974). "Adolescents and family planning information: An exploration of audience needs and media effects." In J.G. Blumler and E. Katz (eds.), The uses of mass communications. Beverly Hills, Calif.: Sage.

NEWCOMB, T.M. (1953). "An approach to the study of communicative acts." Psychological Review, 60:393-404.

OSGOOD, C.E., SUCI, G.J. and TANNENBAUM, P.H. (1957). The measurement of meaning. Urbana: University of Illinois Press.

RUNKEL, P.J. (1956). "Cognitive similarity in facilitating communication." Sociometry, 19:178-191.

SCOTT, W.A. (1969). "A structure of natural cognitions." Journal of Personality and Social Psychology, 12(4):261-278.

SHIBUYA, Y. (1962). "A study in the relationship between cognitive similarity and communication effectiveness." Japan Journal of Psychology, 4:173-177.

TORGERSON, W.S. (1958). Theory and methods of scaling. New York: John Wiley.

TRIANDIS, H.C. (1960a). "Cognitive similarity and communication in a dyad." Human Relations, 13:175-183.

——— (1960b), "Some determinants of interpersonal communication." Human Relations, 13:279-287.

WISHNER, J. (1960). "Stimulus pooling and social perception." Journal of Abnormal and Social Psychology, 60:365-373.

ZAJONC, R.B. (1968). "Cognitive theories in social psychology." In G. Lindzey and E. Aronson (eds.), Handbook of social psychology, Vol. 1 (2nd ed.). Reading, Mass.: Addison-Wesley.

Chapter 9

EXPLORING THE STRUCTURE OF NATIONAL ISSUES: NEWSPAPER CONTENT AND READER PERCEPTIONS

Susan C. Greendale and Eric S. Fredin

THE RECENT ATTENTION given to "agenda-setting" effects of the media in political communication research (see Chaffee, 1975) has rekindled an interest in content analysis designs, and in constructing the linkages between media messages and audience perceptions. This chapter is an attempt to stake out a new conceptual approach to these issues, emphasizing the *structure* of messages and perceptions.

The standard agenda-setting analysis features a comparison of the media and respondent-generated content distributions dealing with a given substantive area. For example, one might code newspapers over a period of time, picking out references to national issues. Respondents would then be questioned about their perceptions of what the important issues are, and the resulting distribution would be matched against that derived from the newspaper coding exercise. Correlations among the newspaper and reader data are typical of the evidence offered for the agenda-setting effect (however, see McLeod, Becker, and Byrnes, 1974, for a cogent critique).

AUTHORS' NOTE: Data used in this chapter were made available by the Inter-University Consortium for Political Research. The data were collected by the Center for Political Studies, Institute for Social Research, University of Michigan, under a grant from the National Science Foundation, the John and Mary R. Markle Foundation, and the Carnegie Corporation. The authors wish to thank F. Gerald Kline for his comments and suggestions. Of course, he, the collectors of the data, and the Consortium bear no responsibility for the analysis and interpretations presented here. The authors contributed equal effort to this report.

Rather than simple frequency distributions, we recommend an approach which describes the *relationships* among issue categories for both media presentations and audience judgments. Motivation for the structural tactic comes from several sources. The idea was explicitly recommended for content analysis by Merton and Lazarsfeld (1957), although they did not fill in the details. Structuralism, per se, has an extensive intellectual history in mathematics and science; hence, a number of analytic techniques have been developed.

On more substantive grounds, we intuit that much of the news is not really new. Inflation is not new, recession is not new—the novelty is in the changing relationship between them. We could document the number of times newspaper stories considered the U.S. relationship with the Soviet Union, and how often civil liberty concerns appeared in the press. Without making provision to examine the *relationship* between the categories, however, we would never capture the new structure in these issues created by President Carter's "human rights" salvos directed at the USSR. A content analysis of relationships will pick up much more of what is actually new in the news, and the concomitant changing audience perceptions, than will a simple matching of content frequency distributions.

We will first consider some of the facets of the observations which might be used in the relational approach, and then talk about how they are eventually treated as data. Coombs (1964) points out that observations really become data after adopting a "theory" about them. No particular collection of observations necessarily calls for a given data theory. The implications of these statements for content analytic observations will be seen shortly.

TREATING RELATIONSHIPS AMONG CONTENT CATEGORIES

Content analysis is a type of abstraction, and all abstraction involves judgment; decisions must be made about what events in the world (such as spoken answers or written communications) are going to be considered as equivalent—coded in the same category—for purposes of analysis. (See Lewin, 1951, for a discussion of this point.) The complexity of decision increases when we consider relationships among categories in addition to the categories themselves. More things must be defined, and more definitions operationalized. In linguistic terms, we begin to deal with subjects, verbs and objects when the structure of content is examined, rather than with isolated subjects. Edelstein (1974), for example, set up content categories for the ways his respondents talked about political problems which they thought were important. They took a number of approaches to this task: comparing problems on the basis of one or several attributes; relating aspects of problems to their personal lives; or mentioning no relationships between problems and other aspects of the environment. With the exception of the last group, the categorization of responses evidences the linguistic characteristic we just outlined. Some problems are subjects and others objects—they are connected by verbs. Edelstein might have simply coded the subjects and missed these nuances.

We can go beyond the linguistic analogy to some more general ideas on the structure of content analysis observations by considering the ideas of graph theory (Harary et al., 1965). Given two objects A and B—e.g., two content observations—a relation (r) between them can be written ArB and BrA. A relation is *symmetric* if whenever A relates to B, B relates to A in the same manner. A relation is *asymmetric* whenever ArB *precludes* BrA, and vice versa. One can see this in the case of a hierarchical organization in which influence is seen flowing in only one direction between two positions in the structure. So-called "causal" relationships (assumed in path analysis) are asymmetric; if A causes B, B generally cannot cause A.

Applying these ideas to categories which might be derived in a particular content analysis, we can construct an imaginary matrix which has the categories for rows and columns. In the cells, there may be a number of different quantities, depending on whether symmetric or asymmetric relations obtain between the categories. A symmetric matrix will show the same number (be it a frequency count, correlation, or other measure of connection) in cell (i,j) as in cell (j,i), where i and j stand for rows and columns, respectively. A typical correlation matrix with unities in the diagonal (reflecting the relationship between a variable and itself) is a symmetric matrix—one can eliminate the numbers above or below the diagonal and still know how the variables relate to one another. The *asymmetric* matrix, however, only considers the case where category j depends on i (or vice versa). Influence is seen as flowing from either the row or column categories, and the numbers in a cell reflect the extent to which a given category is seen as superordinate to another.

The complexity of written material and oral discourse is not adequately described by either the symmetric or asymmetric matrices, however. We can envision some cases in which a given content category might dominate a second, and other cases where the second may dominate the first. In discussing a national issue, for example, a newspaper editorial may address what is deemed to be the major facet of the problem, and also outline a number of ancillary matters which are connected. A different paper may editorialize on the same subject, but stress a different aspect of the problem and relegate the "important point" in the first editorial to a secondary position. As events progress, little-considered aspects of large problems may come to be seen by *both* papers as the really major part of the difficulty.

Rather than burying these distinctions in a symmetric matrix, which gives all categories equal weight, or assuming that influence can only flow one way, we should take advantage of the *directionality* in the issue structure of a news story or statement of a survey respondent. Preserving the information, one can see the issues which most often seem to dominate the discussion of national problems, those which often appear subordinate, and those which show little or no connection to others. One can map, on the aggregate level, the direction and pattern of relationships among the various issue categories. These maps serve as the basis of comparison between the way newspapers structure national problems and the way readers perceive the connections based upon their perusal of the papers.

As seen from the perspective of Coombs's (1964) theory of data, the symmetric matrix concerns points from the same set (the content categories). At the data collection stage, two points or categories are "matched" by appearing in the same news story or the same survey response. This proximity relation between two points from the same set falls into Quadrant IIIb of the data theory. When the responses are aggregated across individual articles or respondents, one can scale the observations in the symmetric matrix via the models of QIVa, e.g., cluster analysis. The analysis in this case entails comparing the relative similarity of different *pairs* of points. One might find, for instance, that economic references, such as inflation and recession, tend to appear more often together than do other types of content. The result of scaling in the models of QIVa is a mapping of objects (in this case, content categories) in a multidimensional space.

In contrast to the symmetric matrix, the *directional* matrix data fits into Quadrant Ia of Coombs's theory. The difference is that the points are now seen to be from different sets—some categories represent major issues and others are ancillary to them. Although the corresponding rows and columns of the matrix may have the same names, we treat one as the dominant subject matter of an article or piece of discourse and the other as the secondary theme. The observation in the cell indicates how often the category is dominant or subordinate in relation to another, depending upon whether we view the matrix from the perspective of rows or columns. We are interested in three characteristics of the QIa data when applied to content analysis. Comparing dyads in which the points come from different sets, we may find that the dyads have no points in common, or they may have one or three points in common. To exemplify, the first comparison might consist of an inflation—unemployment dyad with a recession—economic policy pair. The second, typical of unfolding analysis, might be an inflation—unemployment, inflation—recession comparison. To get three points in common in two dyads, we have to allow a point (a content category) to be related to itself. Hence, we might observe a pattern in the matrix of content categories such that some category mentions in news stories or reader discourses are *isolates,* and we can compare these situations with the cases where they are connected to other categories. How often is race an isolate and how often linked to other issues, for example. The second kind of comparison, with one common point in the dyads, concentrates on one row or column of the matrix to see the links between a given issue and all of the others. The first type of comparison might lead to a multidimensional scaling of the categories, with the distinction between major and minor issues maintained.

It is important to note the flexibility of the "complementary" approach to the data matrix. Either the "important" issue or its complementary, connected issue may serve as the basis for analysis. Some problems may be cited often as major ones, while more pervasive issues—linked to a number of others—may never attain the distinction of "most important" in the newspaper articles or the perceptions of readers. Further, examining matrices generated by different types of people, one may find that the distribution of major and minor issues changes markedly. A stereotypic example would be the Democrat who sees unemployment as an important issue with inflation associated; his Republican counterpart would view things in the complementary fashion—inflation first and unemployment connected secondarily. While category labels, assigned prior to coding, provide the *denotions* for observations collected in media content and audience perceptions, this structural approach offers one way to discover the *connotations* of the categories: What is associated with what?

To go a step further, we argue that ascertaining the relationships is important to really defining the categories themselves. For an individual, the issue of abortion may be associated with poverty or with moral values. If two people adopt the different connections, their discussion of the issue is likely to proceed on quite different terms. It is important for the analyst to recognize this intuitive difficulty in communication; we strive for exclusive and exhaustive categories, but fail often to recognize the context of their definition provided by the other content codes. If the relations among categories change, their definitions can be seen to change as well.

A SAMPLE ANALYSIS

The secondary analysis which follows uses the same sets of observations to illustrate differences between data using symmetrical relations and data maintaining complementary relations. In the latter instance, some simple analysis strategies will be suggested.

The two sets of observations employed, a national sample survey of 1,575 voters and a content analysis of newspapers, were gathered as part of the 1974 Institute for Social Research (ISR) national election study. Based on the respondents' reports of the daily newspapers which they regularly read, the issues of 96 different newspapers were collected for 10 sample days during the month prior to the election. The front pages of these issues were content analyzed using the story or analogous unit (i.e., column or stand-alone photograph) as the unit of analysis. Approximately 8,800 items on the front pages were classified using a coding scheme in which the first step was determining the "most important problem." Each story or item was assigned to one of 284 problem categories (e.g., unemployment, crime) based on the item's overall content. The most important problem was coded, as well as additional information about story content (involved actors, proposals, etc.) and story placement, and display. Determination of the secondary problem to be coded was made through a coding rule which designated the overall content of the story as most important, thus receiving the label of "most important problem" and then specified that one should begin at the lead of the story, searching through the story until another problem topic was found—the associated or background problem. This coding decision was based on the assumption of a pyramid style of writing which places the most important information toward the top of the story.

The concept of "most important problem" has been used for approximately 20 years by the Institute for Social Research at the University of Michigan, and by various private pollsters such as the Gallup Organization. The value of this methodological concept has been expanded for open-ended questioning by Edelstein (1973, 1974). By using a system of questions "unobtrusive in content but structured in form" (Edelstein, 1973), the respondent is allowed to define a set of topics he deems salient. Edelstein (1974) points out that allowing respondents to select and talk about an important problem sets up a different type of equivalence across respondents. The equivalence is "most important problem," not the problem itself, or the structure of closed questions about a problem. The equivalence was desirable in part because of the cross-cultural nature of his study: asking respondents about particular, normative problems nominated by the researcher may be misleading because while the name may be the same in a different country, at least in translation, they actually may not be the same since the terms may not have the same attributes. In the conceptualization we have outlined, individual terms may refer to problems not actually in the same set. The problems may not have the same type of relations with others for different individuals. This point of equivalence—"most important"—rather than equivalence of topic definitions allows comparisons of communication styles. The method also generates what Edelstein terms "situational responses," not general responses to pre-selected attitude objects. This approach, with the resulting emphasis on relations among issues seems applicable both to content of newspapers, and content of open-ended responses.

The 284 problem codes used in the ISR study were generated from responses gleaned over two decades of sample surveys. This coding scheme for issue topics, while generated from survey responses, was also applied to the analysis of the media content with little difficulty. The few additions to the code which were made to accommodate the media content have not been considered in the analysis here, to allow comparison between the newspapers and the respondents.

Data on the public side were gathered from the personal interviews of a national sample of voters taken during the six weeks immediately following the election. Each respondent was asked to nominate what he or she believed to be the "most important problem facing the nation at this time." These "important problems" were assigned to one of the 284 problem categories in the same coding scheme as used for newspapers. Respondents were then asked what they had read, if anything, in the newspapers about their nominated problem. This information was content analyzed for an important problem which may or may not have varied from their nominated "most important" problem. The issue topic information gleaned from the respondents' "message discrimination" of media about their own most important problem provided information on *auxiliary* or *background* issues. (See Palmgreen, Kline, and Clarke, 1974, and Clarke and Kline, 1974, for more detail on message discrimination.)

For both newspapers and the public, then, we have expressed relations between a "most important" problem and an auxiliary problem. In attempting to match the structure of content in the media and the public, we are searching for an equivalence of operationalization which will yield conceptually similar units of analysis. The relationship that exists between the first and second problems in the newspapers is one based on being in the same article. That the newspaper places both issues into a single context—the story—posits a connection between the two whether explicitly or implicitly made. It is those connections that we have delineated. The relationship among issues for the public is one which provides a good test of the agenda-setting notion. By asking the voters to specify what they had read about their own most important problem, we have asked them to report to us the issue relationships they perceive in the media. If the media do tell people what issue relationships to think about, then this route of questioning should elicit information to support the hypothesis.

The timing of the data collection also strengthens the test of agenda-setting. The entire period of data gathering covered 10 weeks in October, November, and December of 1974. The first four weeks of that time were spent in monitoring the newspapers which our sample read. The remaining six weeks were devoted to the personal interviewing. Such a two-stage collection of data is necessary for agenda-setting research in that it is essential for the media information to be temporally prior to the audience perceptions if the media are, in some way, "causing" the audience to have certain perceptions. The validity of connections found in the data between the newspapers and the respondents, however, is limited by the lack of control of the time gap in the collection of the observations. The collection could be mistimed such that connections between newspapers and respondents are not found because the gap is too long or too short. Connections found could be the result of a spurious relationship. There is also the possiblity that the stability of relationships among issues varies across, and depends on, what events are actually occurring which respondents learn about. This situation is complicated by the fact that each respondent defines his problems and problem relations. A possible result is that the problems and relations given by a respondent may not have appeared at all in the newspapers during the time the newspaper material was gathered. The same kind of reasoning may apply to any part of the observations gathered, either problems or relations between them. However, if it seems plausible to assume some stability of problems and relations over a period as long as several months, comparison will have validity, although other confounding factors mentioned above have to be taken into account.

To reduce the complexity of studying the structure in the data for illustrative purposes, the 284 problem categories were reduced to 28. The collapsing of the content codes was based upon conceptual grouping of categories, but some information obviously was lost.[1] Thus a 28 by 28 matrix of observations was generated which can be treated a number of ways, including as a data matrix with symmetrical relations, or as a data matrix with directional, complementary relations. One 28 by 28 matrix was created using the newspaper material, another using the respondents' comments. In both cases the organization of the matrix is the same. In each cell there is a frequency count of the number of times important problem x is found with auxiliary problem y. In general, the count in cell (i,j) does not equal the count in cell (j,i), and, again, conceptually they can represent different relations. The diagonal contains frequency counts of instances in which the problems mentioned are sufficiently close that in the collapsing from 284 categories, a problem becomes related only to itself, i.e., is an isolate. In the newspaper matrix, approximately 50% of all cases fell on the diagonal; in the respondent matrix, about 59% of the cases fell there.

Using the notions outlined above, we can begin examining relationships between issues. The symmetric relation, which relies solely on the co-occurrence of two issues in the same article or respondents' commentary for its data values, was studied using one of the several possible mathematical procedures suitable for this type of information—a cluster analysis. Other types of data manipulation which seem suitable are metric or nonmetric factor analysis, metric or nonmetric multidimensional scaling, or smallest space analysis. A minimum variance cluster algorithm was applied to the data with distances expressed in Minkowski (1) metric—commonly know as the city-block—because the metric tends to minimize differences particularly for deviant cases, when compared with Euclidean metric. Implications of the metric choice for this analysis are important. With a Minkowski (1) metric, the emphasis is on including all cases into a cluster of cases which are as similar as possible, while a solution based on the squared Euclidean distances, emphasizing deviant cases, would be more likely to find isolates—cases which form their own cluster. The concept of an isolated issue is an intriguing one, but presents real difficulties, and we will discuss it in more detail below.

Looking to the cluster solution for newspapers, we find that there are five clusters of issues defined as occurring together on the front pages. The five clusters are:

Cluster One: Inflation, Unemployment, Recession, Economic Change, Economic Policy.

Cluster Two: Labor, Natural Resources, Consumer Protection, Mass Transit, Agriculture, Shortages.

Cluster Three: National Defense, Mideast Conflict, Foreign Affairs, Russian Relations.

Cluster Four: Government Power, Government Performance and Competence, Values, Campaign Financing, Confidence in Government, Watergate, Democratic Landslide.

Cluster Five: Social Welfare, Abortion, Civil Liberties, Race, Crime, Public Order.

The co-occurrence data matrix for the respondents also produced a five-cluster solution:

Cluster One: Inflation, Economic Policy, Democratic Landslide, Agriculture, Shortages, Recession, Economic Change.

Cluster Two: Unemployment, Labor, Social Welfare, Mass Transit, National Defense.

Cluster Three: Natural Resources, Mideast Conflict, Foreign Affairs.

Cluster Four: Government Power, Confidence in Government, Watergate, Government Performance and Competence, Values, Crime, Public Order.

Cluster Five: Abortion, Civil Liberties, Consumer Protection, Race, Russian Relations, Campaign Financing.

Although both cluster solutions isolate five groups of issues which co-occur, there are some important differences between the two. Note that for newspapers, issues are clustered by broad generic categories (i.e., all economic issues fall into the same cluster and so on). From this analysis, it would appear that the relationships between issues in the media are based upon quite intuitive associations.

However, the relationships among issues for the public are interestingly not so generic, though equally understandable, especially when placed in the context of late 1974. Cluster One for the people, while capturing most of the economic categories, also includes Democratic Landslide, Agriculture, and Shortages, three matters whose relationship to economic problems might be readily inferred. But the inference is problematic. All that can be said about the three noneconomic issues in the ostensibly economic cluster is that they occur more often with the economic issues than with any other kind of issue. Cluster Five, too, is problematic. It is difficult to posit readily the reason these six fairly diverse issues cluster together, but with such an analysis little more than the clustering information is available. They may in fact cluster together simply as a function of all not being related to any other topics. Analysis using the next type of data matrix—the directional relation—produces a different kind of information.

Considering the directional matrices, an issue may be conceptualized in terms of three relations: isolate, prominence, and contextual. For issue A, the isolate relation is ArA, and the diagonal cell of the matrix holds the frequency of occurrence. Isolate issues tend not to be related to other issues, but occur as the only issue in the story. The prominence relation for issue A is ArB where A is the most important problem and B is the associated problem. The contextual

TABLE 1
NEWSPAPER ISSUES BY TYPE OF ASSOCIATION
WITH OTHER ISSUES

Problem	Prominence	Contextual	Isolate
Abortion	25.0%	16.7%	58.3%
Agriculture	25.7	24.0	50.3
Campaign Financing	29.2	17.9	53.0
Civil Liberties	15.4	23.1	61.5
Confidence in Government	21.4	28.2	50.4
Consumer Protection	23.0	15.0	62.0
Crime	21.7	25.9	52.4
Democratic Landslide	53.5	6.9	39.6
Economic Changes	41.3	35.9	22.8
Economic Policy	26.5	29.0	44.5
Foreign Affairs	21.3	32.4	46.2
Government Performance and Competence	28.5	18.9	52.6
Government Power	29.2	40.1	30.7
Inflation	25.2	45.2	29.6
Labor	17.4	8.9	73.7
Mass Transit	25.5	23.5	51.0
Mideast	24.3	18.9	56.8
National Defense	35.7	26.4	37.9
Natural Resources	23.6	25.6	50.8
Public Order	26.4	10.6	63.0
Race	42.7	14.4	42.7
Recession	37.8	33.7	28.5
Russian Relations	37.7	27.8	34.4
Shortages	17.9	37.4	44.7
Social Welfare	23.0	22.7	54.3
Unemployment	37.7	40.1	22.2
Values	29.9	23.4	46.7
Watergate	10.2	8.8	81.0

relation for issue A is BrA, where A is the secondary problem and B is the most important problem. Given the three forms of relations connecting issue occurrence in the articles or respondents' commentary, the research question of how issues vary in the distribution of types of relations they maintain with other issues arises. Issues were classified by the percentage of all their relationships which fall into each of the three types. This form of standardization compares the isolate relation using the diagonals, the prominence using the row marginals, and the contextual using the column marginals.

Of the 28 issue categories, 23 have more than one-third of their mentions as isolates, 15 issues have more than one-half. This, however, may partly be a function of collapsing codes. High isolates include Labor and Watergate (73.7% and 81.0% respectively). Campaign Financing is also a high isolate (53.0%) despite the fact that changes in financing arose out of Watergate. This kind of finding may be useful in explaining the extent to which the public thinks of Watergate as an isolated issue, one which has not affected their general attitudes toward government and politics. There is some evidence from data collected at earlier stages in Watergate that this was true (McLeod et al., 1977). Other high isolate issues are Consumer Protection (62%) and Public Order (63%), a category including protests, demonstrations, and terrorists. Civil Liberties (61.5%) and Abortion (58.3%) are mostly treated as isolated as is Social Welfare (54.3%). While information about isolates alone could be found using a symmetric matrix, information about the following types of relations could not.

Of particular interest may be those problems which most frequently have the contextual relation—the background problems. One pervasive background problem emerges in the newspaper data: Inflation, with 45.2% of its mentions as a background problem, 25.2% as the important problem, and 29.6% as an isolate. Unemployment is also most often found as a background problem (40.1%), but nearly as often it is the important problem (37.7%) and less often as isolated problem (22.2%). Government Power, referring to the power of the government to regulate industries and the size of the federal bureaucracy, is also most frequently a background issue. In contrast, Confidence in Government and Government Performance and Competence are two issue categories which are primarily isolates (50.4% and 52.6%, respectively). Other issues which are frequently in the background are Foreign Affairs (which excludes Russia, Israel, and the Arab countries) and Shortages. These are first isolates, but the contextual relation occurs more frequently than the prominence relation.

There is evidence, then, that an issue which may not appear very frequently as a most important problem may be important in another sense because it is frequently mentioned as an associated problem. In terms simply of frequency of mention, a background problem may achieve "importance" on the aggregate level, although it may not appear that "important" at the individual level. An important problem on the aggregate level may emerge from the associated problems on the individual level in different ways because conceptualization permits the kind of "importance" to be determined by the type of relationships involved.

Several issues in Table 1 also have mostly prominence relations (most often recorded as *important* problems), including the Democratic Landslide and Economic Change, a category which includes articles on the latest government indicators. Race shows an interesting pattern. Generally it is the most important or the isolated issue (both found 42.7% of the time), but rarely a background issue (14.4%). Race rarely forms the context—the background—for other issues.

Another form of standardization permits examination of the prominence or the contextual relation across issues for a particular problem code. These are instances of comparing two dyads which have a point in common. This is done by taking the data matrix and standardizing by row to look at the prominence relation or by column to look at the contextual relation.

In Figures 1 and 2, both using the prominence relation only, issues and relations were included only if at least 20% of an issue's relation existed with

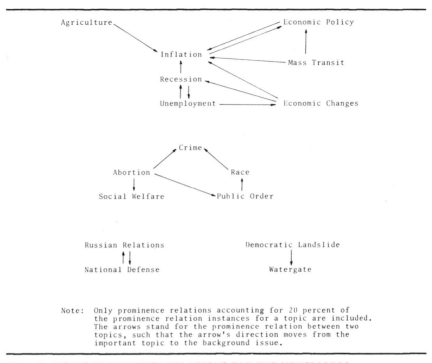

Note: Only prominence relations accounting for 20 percent of the prominence relation instances for a topic are included. The arrows stand for the prominence relation between two topics, such that the arrow's direction moves from the important topic to the background issue.

Figure 1: MAJOR PROMINENCE RELATIONS FOR THE NEWSPAPERS

one other issue. This definition is arbitrary. It generally would limit the number of issues and connections in any figure and hence makes the visual inspection easier. It systematically precludes study of certain data which may be of interest, however. Isolates are not included nor are issues which have many links, but none greater than 20% of the total number of contextual relations for that issue. How frequently a given issue was mentioned overall relative to the other issues also was not taken into account. Thus, an infrequently mentioned issue with a few strong relations may appear in a figure, while a frequently mentioned issue with many relations, none accounting for more than 20% of the total mentions, will not appear. This may have happened even though the actual number of instances of a relationship may be higher in the latter case than in the former. Other rules may be devised, but some simplification is necessary for heuristic purposes.

Figures 1 and 2 are illustrations of the prominence links found by the rules established above, the first for the respondents and the latter for the newspapers. The arrows stand only for the prominence relation, leading from the "most important" to the background or associated problem. The differences between the two maps are interesting. Watergate, for instance, serves only as a background problem for Democratic Landslide in the newspapers, but is a background problem for three categories pertaining to government among the

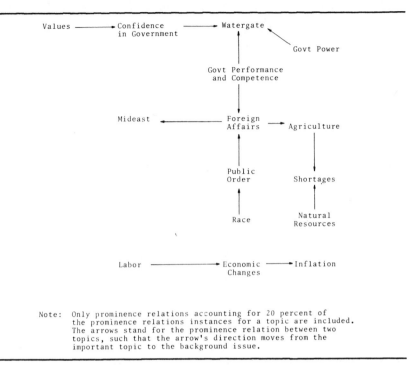

Note: Only prominence relations accounting for 20 percent of
the prominence relations instances for a topic are included.
The arrows stand for the prominence relation between two
topics, such that the arrow's direction moves from the
important topic to the background issue.

Figure 2: MAJOR PROMINENCE RELATIONS FOR THE PUBLIC

respondents and is indirectly related to a fourth, if Values is considered to be
linked also. Agriculture on the newspaper side is one of several issues that has
Inflation as the background issue. But respondents connect Agriculture not with
Inflation but with Shortages, which also serves as a background problem for
Natural Resources and Foreign Affairs. It is tempting to speculate about the
kinds of relations occurring here—newspapers were talking about the economics
behind farm production, but readers were recalling the famines, involved in
inflation, which were also in the news in 1974. Inflation, which was so pervasive
in the newspapers, being linked with five categories, is, on the respondents' side,
linked only to the important problem of Economic Change. As mentioned
before, this category refers to mentions of economic indicators, rather than
government Economic Policies, Recession, or other topics. It is important to
keep in mind that only certain aspects of the information in the matrices are
used in this comparison, but the differences between newspapers and respondents appear substantial. The differences might be interpreted as meaning that
issues, in the sense of the associations among problems, are quite different for
respondents and newspapers. Rank orders of problems (typically treated in
agenda-setting research) might be similar, yet differences appear quite large in
terms of agreement between newspaper articles and the public about how that
problem is defined in relation to others.

Other patterns are worth noting in the figures. While the economic issues are connected in the newspapers, as they were in the cluster analysis, noneconomic issues are also included. The links, however, give more information about the strongest connections between the economic issues using the prominence relation. Similar figures could, of course, be constructed using the contextual relation. There the strongest links for a given background issue across the other issues could be inspected. There are several examples of what might be termed reciprocal relations, including Russian Relations-National Defense on the newspaper data. These might be considered as co-occurring important problems, but only as aggregated across articles. Other reciprocal relations, but ones which also involve relations with other issues, are Inflation-Economic Policy and Recession-Unemployment.

It is tempting with figures such as these to study chains from issue to issue, but the rather complex conceptual framework should be kept in mind. The chains are *aggregates,* either across articles or across respondents. The connections through several issues were not made by individuals. But different kinds of radial patterns can be noted, those with a background and those with an important issue at the hub. In the respondents' figure, Watergate is a background hub and Foreign Affairs an "important" and a background hub.

DISCUSSION

We have tried to stake out some considerations which might lead to interesting and useful descriptions of content for use in mass communication and other substantive research. We focused on relationships, and attempted to lay out a strategy for better capturing what seems a common phenomenon in written messages: that ArB does not necessarily imply BrA. Further, if both exist, they may not be scaled in the sense of rank-ordering and one relation may not obviously imply the other. The sorts of comparisons possible using only descriptive content analysis have been expanded considerably. There seems no single best description; rather, we have attempted to outline a way of organizing materials and conceptualizing data. Borrowing from Coombs's theory of data, we gave two instances of conceptualizing the content analysis information, taking advantage of the *organization* in written and spoken material. No particular collection of observations need necessarily be interpreted as a particular type of data. The same type of organization we have described may be considered as entirely different data than the forms illustrated here.

From what we have outlined, a number of implications, directions, and problems emerge. The idea of directional relations implies that, in any form of questioning, the answers given will depend upon where the question effectively asks the respondent to start. Referring to the figure for the respondents, assume for a moment that the arrows are the only very likely connections respondents will give. If asked about Watergate, a respondent will not relate it to anything else because, if the respondent starts there, there is no arrow leading away from it. However, if the respondent is asked about Confidence in Government, Government Performance, or Government Power he may relate any of these to Watergate. Thus, if a question begins with a particular subject, the response and connections may be different than if the questions began with a different but related subject. Such problems, of course, may not so readily occur if the respondents are also given the issues for framing their answers. The alternative model, that the relationships are equally likely to emerge regardless of where the respondent is asked to start, in this conceptualization occurs only as a special case, as in Russian Relations and National Defense in the newspaper figure.

Differences between media messages and respondents' comments can be used to indicate the restructuring a respondent performed on the information given him, particularly if data on structure prior to the information exposure were gathered also. Differences can be noted in type and strength of relations among categories as well as which category is involved. Of course people may "think" extensively about a media structure and still retain the structure in the media message, a possibility which requires more complex experimenting to ferret out.

With a structural approach, agenda-setting hypotheses might be expanded to look at important relationships and types of issues—that is, which set they come from—rather than only the salience of a single issue. We can ask whether the media also tell the people what *relations* to use in thinking about issues as well as the issues themselves.

Differences in the structure of issues in the media could be traced over time as well. Comparisons could be made across media data-sets collected at different times. One type of difference that can be of interest is the emergence or filling of any empty cell in the data matrix. If the system of categories of major and auxiliary or background problems appears reasonably adequate across time, then some changes in issues, some changes in focus in the news, will be reflected in which cells in a data matrix are empty. For example, in 1974 there were no entries in the two cells generated by crossing the issues Russian Relations and Civil Liberties, each appearing in the important problem set and the background problem set. There probably would be a number of entries in both cells in 1977, while different cells would be empty. A zero in such a structure means that the relation has the potential of existing but has not occurred, which can be an important finding. The meaning of the empty cell comes from the structure in which it occurs: the Cartesian Product formed by crossing sets of issues. More complicated, but potentially useful, would be the tracing of issue definitions through the distribution of types of relations between one issue from one set and the issues in another set. More complicated changes could be traced as well.

The general organization permits a number of ways of aggregating the data. Aggregation across cases for both the symmetrical and directional relations resulted in moving from comparison of two points to comparison of two pairs of points. Only the relation between an important problem and a background problem was collected. At the individual level, an important problem was nominated and linked to another auxiliary or background problem. Respondents were not asked to nominate a background problem, then link it with an important problem. Nor, effectively, was this question addressed to the newspaper articles. The pattern of contextual and prominence relations between important and background problems can exist only at the aggregate level.

Finally, it is obvious that no sophisticated mathematical treatment was proposed or used in this paper. Quite simply, we do not find the techniques we know to be readily applicable, although uses certainly could be found. Some problems in this regard can be noted. First, isolates are treated as important and many techniques, such as those we have seen which are used in sociometric analyses, ignore or cannot use diagonal values. Second, methods generally assume that the nature of the relationship is the same in either direction, hence the property of direction is lost. Finally, it is not clear to us that reduction to underlying dimensions is necessarily the only way to use the data. What is needed is something which preserves the network. Perhaps by considering the network as it is, messages (perhaps stimuli in general) can be better specified, hence hypotheses more closely formulated and tested. Perhaps mass media researchers will make more use of the content of the media.

NOTE

1. By conceptually grouping the 284 problem categories, a reduced set of 28 content areas was established. Those issue areas are outlined below with some detail as to their specific content, excluding those that are self-evident (e.g., Abortion). Campaign Financing refers to the legal and ethical considerations of campaign contributions. Civil Liberties includes freedom of speech, rights of the accused, and women's rights. Confidence in Government refers to honesty and trust in the governmental system. Crime refers to law and order, violence, drugs, and guns. Democratic Landslide is specifically concerned with the overwhelming majority of Democratic victories in the 1974 congressional and state elections. Economic Changes refers to the fluctuation of economic indicators. Economic Policy encompasses specific policies such as Ford's WIN (Whip Inflation Now) program, monetary restraints, and taxes. Foreign Affairs deals with our relations with the rest of the world, excluding Russia, Israel, and the Arab counties. Government Performance and Competence covers the quality and efficiency of the government. Government Power concentrates on government control of business through regulation, government control of information, on the size of the federal bureaucracy and the power of each branch of the federal government. Inflation refers specifically to mentions of inflation, the high cost of living, or high prices. Labor refers to union-management relations. Mideast refers to the Arab-Israeli conflict. National Defense includes all references to the military, the arms race, the defense budget, veterans, and amnesty. Natural Resources covers both conservation and development of new resources. Public Order refers to protests, demonstrators, and terrorists. Race includes civil right problems, discrimination, and integration. Recession is limited to specific mentions of recession or depression. Russian Relations refers to United States-Soviet Union relations. Shortages refers to many kinds of deficiencies including food

shortages for economic reasons, famine, and the energy crisis. Social Welfare is a broad category including the social problems of education, the aged, health care, housing, and poverty. Unemployment refers directly to the mention of lack of jobs or attempts to remedy that situation. Values takes in references to moral decay, decadence among youth, and apathy.

REFERENCES

BERELSON, B. (1952). Content analysis in communication research. Glencoe, Ill.: Free Press.

CHAFFEE, S.H. (1975). Political communication. Beverly Hills, Calif.: Sage.

CLARKE, P., and KLINE, F.G. (1974). "Media effects reconsidered: Some new strategies for communication research." Communication Research, 1(2):224-240.

COOMBS, C. (1964). Theory of data. New York: John Wiley.

EDELSTEIN, A. (1973). "Decision-making and mass communication: A conceptual and methodological approach to public opinion." Pp. 81-118 in P. Clarke (ed.), New models for mass communication research. Beverly Hills, Calif.: Sage.

――― (1974). The uses of communication in decision-making: A comparative study of Yugoslavia and the United States. New York: Praeger.

HARARY, F., NORMAN, R.A., and CARTWRIGHT, D. (1965). Structural models: An introduction to the theory of directed graphs. New York: John Wiley.

LEWIN, K. (1951). "Problems of research in social psychology." Pp. 155-169 in D. Cartwright (ed.), Field theory in social science. New York: Harper and Row.

McLEOD, J.M., BECKER, L. B., and BYRNES, J.E. (1974). "Another look at the agenda-setting function of the press." Communication Research, 1(2):131-165.

McLEOD, J.M., BROWN, J.D., BECKER, L.B., and ZIEMKE, D.A. (1977). "Decline and fall at the White House: A longitudinal analysis of communication effects." Communication Research, 4(1):3-22.

MERTON, R.K., and LAZARSFELD, P.F. (1957). "Studies in radio and film propaganda." Pp. 509-528 in R.K. Merton, Social theory and social structure (revised ed.) Glencoe, Ill.: Free Press.

MITCHELL, R.E. (1967). "The use of content analysis for explanatory studies." Public Opinion Quarterly, 31(2):230-241.

PALMGREEN, P., KLINE, F.G., and CLARK, P. (1974). "Message discrimination and information holding about political affairs: A comparison of local and national issues." Paper presented at the annual meeting of the International Communication Association, New Orleans, April.

PART III

CONCEPTUALIZING TIME AND

TEMPORAL ORDER

Chapter 10

TIME IN COMMUNICATION RESEARCH

F. Gerald Kline

INTRODUCTION

TIME IN HiSTORY

TIME HAS A LONG and honorable history. And a controversial one as well. Despite the noble and extended philosophical treatment the study of time has received, our operational assumptions about it remain surprisingly simple. Most of us take for granted the notion that there are different rates of change through time for different objects, topics or outcomes. Yet we only have to eavesdrop on the current discussions about the theory of relativity, quantum theory, and wave mechanics to sense what precarious ground we are on. While the physical scientists often place time at the core of their theoretical debates, among social scientists conceptualizing about time has lagged far behind. It is odd that this should be the case since time surely is as much—or perhaps more— at issue in continuous, dynamic social processes as in the more phlegmatic physical processes.

The inseparability of the consciousness of time from that of change was not readily agreed upon in early periods. As space was difficult to separate conceptually from its concrete state, so time was similarly difficult to separate conceptually from changes and events "taking place" in it. Greek, medieval, and modern philosophy center on the contrast between the timeless realm of Being and the temporal realm of change. Thus for Plato the basic reality belongs to the timeless essence while the temporal realm is that of change. In our contemporary work we find that the concern with "truth" or true knowledge as opposed to mere opinion is the epistemological parallel.

One of the most difficult problems to be faced is the notion of time, and consequently change, being continuous. For the reality of our conceptualization is always linked to the character of the mathematics we bring to bear on the concept. For example, both Berkeley and Leibniz held that time is the order of succession of perceptions and as such it is inseparable from concrete infinite events. Therefore the flow of "empty time" had no meaning. Thus for Berkeley that infinite indivisibility of time and change (in the sense of the calculus) is a fiction since durational instants are not perceptible and therefore not real. Leibniz, however, believed that time and change consisted of ever-perishing instants—divisible ad infinitum.[1]

Developments in philosophy and psychology as to the indivisibility of psychological time and physical time have raised issues that need to be examined. Questions of minimal intervals of time, either physical that coincide with elemental events of nature, or psychological that have to do with the activities or capabilities of a person, need to be raised for future scrutiny. A modest beginning is offered with our discussions of time sampling and choosing a particular model, i.e., a Markov chain model, with particular assumptions that match conceptualizations by the user.

RESEARCH DESIGN CONSIDERATIONS

In chapters that follow this, time will not be considered substantively. There is, however, much in our literature concerned with time as a resource in the sense of its allocation to different activities. Much reliance also has been placed on the amount of time spent (with a particular medium, or talking to another, etc.) as a fundamental measure in communication research. The relative simplicity of "time spent with" as a concept has also made it popular among those who are not specialists. The most obvious, and often inane, example is the repeated use of the statistic of the number of hours a child spends with television compared with the number of hours attending school. Heavy viewers as opposed to light viewers of television is another current example. Of course these statements assume a great deal about the homogeneity of the content in a medium across time as well as the cognitive capabilities of the user.

A more sophisticated use of time spent with the media is found in comparative time budget studies (Szalai, 1973). Here, within time spans or across sites, the effects of different cultures and social structures on time use and displacement are analyzed. However, the implicit notions of time spent with a medium, and homogeneous content in that medium, still remain.

It is seldom in any communication behavior study that the notion of time is explicitly set aside. In a survey design the ordering of variables in the analysis strategy has some kind of time ordering or, if the researcher wants to make statements about relationships between variables without the time ordering, there is usually the underlying notion that the parameter estimates being made are constant over time.

The experimental mode explicitly takes time into account with a before and after measure of the effect of a particular manipulation. Here we find little consideration given to the length of the period before a pre- and a post-test except as it affects the face validity of the design. When dealing with repeated measures experiments (Winer, 1962) time is essential to the designer. There is the occasional situation, however, when the experimenter uses such a design to be efficient (in the pooling of error variance for example) rather than out of concern for the time factor. In any experimental situation the choice of when to measure (see Arundale's chapter) assumes an effect has had time to take place. Or in situations with two or more independent variables the time it takes for each to have their independent, or jointly simultaneous, effect is critical. This is an area not usually dealt with explicitly in most designs.

In approaches that attempt to use nonexperimentally manipulated changes, such as surveys with respondents empaneled for repeated interviewing, we usually see causal interpretations of turnover tables or cross-lagged correlations. As Heise (1970) indicates, the lags between measurement periods must be sufficiently long for effects to take place, all of the lags must have approximately the same time frame, the period in which the measurement is taking place must be shorter than the lag that is assumed to be operating, and the choice of measurement times must be about the same as the lag period. These are stringent constraints that are usually assumed away or, as in most instances, overlooked entirely. Of course the experimental design can be combined with the panel design for a field experimental approach that attempts to take into account more of the threats to validity than either one can separately.

Another approach is to collect, or assemble, series of data over a period of time. Although not fraught with the same number and kinds of assumptions listed above they do need a great deal more data over longer time periods. Krull and Paulson's chapter will deal extensively with this approach.

A variant of the latter approach, in the sense that a number of time points are needed, is the cohort analysis outlined by Danowski and Cutler in the next chapter. Here the age of respondents, a time-related concept, is the focus for assembling the data from cross-section surveys over a number of years. Their approach attempts to simulate the correlation that exists between respondents repeatedly measured in panel surveys or repeated measures experimental design.

Finally, the level of measurement chosen for time-based research designs can be an important factor. If we consider the various measurement periods as a nominal rather than ordinal or interval level of measurement, we are making theoretical decisions that need explication. This will be discussed shortly in greater detail.

APPROACHES TO TIME IN THE STUDY OF SOCIAL CHANGE

Heirich (1964) offers a useful typology of time use in social research. He examines the use of time "as an explanatory factor, a causal link between other variables, a quantitative measure of them and a qualitative measure of their interplay" (p. 386). Let us examine each of these and provide some examples appropriate to communication research.

TIME AS A SOCIAL FACTOR

The first way in which we can conceive of time as a social factor is as a resource that is expendable. The allocation of time to a particular behavior means making some kind of judgment as to the relative worth of competing behaviors. Secondly, attitudes toward time create their own dynamic.

Time as a Resource

There is a finite quantity of time, often thought of as the twenty-four-hour day, that once used is not easily regained. This is one way of classifying the classic time budget study. Thus allocating more time to television and away from certain traditional activities can be conceived of as indexing a major cultural shift across cultures or over time in the same culture. It is such a shift, simply conceived in most instances, that apparently motivates much of the antagonism toward TV.

In the realm of media economics the obvious resource that concerns the analyst is the amount of money a person is willing to spend for a particular product. In many instances, though, the cost of the media product is less of a reason for not purchasing than the lack of time to devote to using it (Becker, 1977). As Heirich notes, however, one must distinguish between relative time allocated and the input-output relationship. Spending less time, as an input activity, with the evening newspaper may not have diminished its importance if the same output of information gain, from reading it, is maintained. If TV use was responsible for such a shift in time away from newspaper reading it will have gained in relative importance. Studies in the elasticity of demand for time spent in different communication behaviors are needed in this field and, if undertaken, would shed light on this general approach to the concept of time in social research.

Some thought also must be given to the way in which time as a social factor is accounted for in different cultures. In certain Asian societies, such as Indonesia, time is not treated as a linear concept but as a circular concept in which the beginning is the end and the end is the beginning. Does the arrival of a fast-paced television program in a culture which does not cherish change for the sake of change meet with the same perceptions as in the producing culture? The exportation of "Anglo-American media" (Tunstall, 1977) to developing nations with potentially varying evaluations of time would certainly warrant investigation for this reason, as well as by those concerned over the impact of "cultural imperialism."

Time as a Social Meaning

A second way in which we can conceive of time as a social factor is through its social meaning. Attitudes toward time can have a dynamic character all their own. Thus Carey and Sims (n.d.) write:

> Looking back over his life from 1907, Henry Adams fixed the precise moment when the United States entered the modern world, the instant of the shift from the old universe of genteel New England to that of industrial America, in 1844: "the opening of the Boston and Albany Railroad; the appearance of the first Cunard steamers in the bay; and the telegraphic message which carried from Baltimore to Washington the news that Henry Clay and James K. Polk were nominated for the Presidency." The points of departure Adams chose to mark the old from the new universe were, significantly, three changes in communications technology.

Of course, one can choose other examples: The period in time when the printing press began to affect those who previously had control over information; the development of the high speed rotary press; the lifting of the FCC's license freeze on TV spectrum allocation in the U.S.; or the launching of the first communication satellite. Here we are dealing with attitudes toward such periods of time, regardless of the truth or falsity of their causal nature, which affect how we view the past. They acquire a social meaning all of their own that has a dynamic in its own right.

The social meaning of time can also be examined in the context of interpersonal communication behavior. Who talked to whom first? This question, having to do with sequence of time in particular behavior, may symbolize social grade, class or authority. Whether the person indexing the behavior is the researcher making a measurement of such a behavior difference, or whether the participants themselves are making the judgment is irrelevant for our purposes. The social meaning can affect subsequent actions. Thus either as a resource, or by having a social meaning, time can be considered as a social factor.

TIME AS A CAUSAL LINK

Since concern with causality is of such importance in theorizing we most often think of time as a way to help establish causal inference. That B follows A in time is not sufficient for the inference that A causes B. It does, if it happens consistently, rule out the reverse situation that B causes A. When one can manipulate postulated causal factor A to determine whether B is absent, there is greater confidence in the inference. There are two main ways, Heirich argues, that theorists have used time as a causal link. The first is when time is used as a setting. The second uses time as a sequence.

Time as a Setting

Temporally bounded structural patterns are often used in causal models as a configuration, either through lack of specific knowledge or inability to specify some part of a sequence operating. Take for example, the patterns found in Table 1. The data, taken from a survey reported by Kline (1972) and Kline et al. (1970), indicate a pattern of relationships for two different age groups. One can see that the pattern of relationships for each age group is quite different. Tension between the family and peers was much higher for young adolescents than for the older ones. It appears that as one progresses through adolescence, independence of both family and TV as sources of information and opinion becomes stronger. For peers and television, the case is reversed. Reliance on the family and on TV portrayals conflict with activities in the peer environment. Treating the three variables together in this fashion allows us to construct a configuration pointing to differential interaction of these socialization sources among time settings.

Evaluating individual events or relationships in relation to their larger pattern is often more useful than viewing them as items independent of setting. Thus the use of time, in this instance age or stage of adolescence, to segregate patterns of interactions is an important function for analysis in social research.

A second example of the configurational approach is the way in which a number of variables go together in a particular pattern at a point in time using factor analysis. Although seldom conceived as a causal model, and even less as time-related, we can view the typical factor analysis equation as follows:

$$z_j = a_{j1}F_1 + a_{j2}F_2 + ... + a_{jm}F_m + d_jU_j \text{ (where } j=1, 2, ..., n)$$

The z's represent sets of intercorrelated variables while the a's and F's represent the loadings and factors extracted. As a causal diagram it would look like Figure 1. We can conceive of factor analysis in terms of causal analysis if we assume no causal links among our indicator variables (z's) and that they are caused by some underlying pattern or factor. This pattern is conceived of as what caused respondents to answer the questions, or undertake the behavior measured by the z's. In the instance of TV independence noted in Table 1, the measure was

TABLE 1

INTERCORRELATIONS OF FAMILY AUTONOMY, PEER AUTONOMY
AND TELEVISION INDEPENDENCE FOR TWO AGE COHORTS[2]

	13-14 Year-olds	*18-19 Year-olds*
Family/Peer	−.45	−.05
Family/TV	+.21	+.38
Peer/TV	−.25	−.44

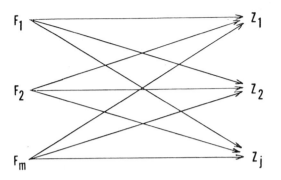

Figure 1.

derived from just such a causally conceived single factor model. Eight questions were administered to the adolescents, intercorrelated and factor analyzed. A one factor solution was derived with the factor loadings ranging from .11 to .57 while the items themselves intercorrelated over a range of −.36 to +.26 (see Kline, 1972, for further details and discussion).

Time as a Sequence

Another way to view time as a causal link is to examine relationships among variables where we can establish the sequence of events. If we have no knowledge about the time ordering of variables, or find that we cannot establish such an ordering, we cannot impute causality. Ordering on the other hand, can assist in this causal inference task.

Suppose we wish to determine whether the playing of a series of public service announcements on rock radio stations caused an awareness among adolescents that there was such a campaign going on. If we can establish the situation where in one location, or among one experimentally defined group, there is the potential to hear such a campaign, and if we can have a comparable group without such a campaign available, we should be able to make a reliable causal inference. Thus the playing of the material would cause those who heard it to discriminate messages while those that did not hear it, would not. Such a causal analysis—three field experiments that took account of the natural setting and the concomitant problems of audience interest, memory, or lack of hearing—was undertaken in Kline, Miller, and Morrison (1974) and Morrison, Kline and Miller (1976). Table 2 displays the data for experiments with messages concerning family planning, drug and alcohol use.

In each instance we had an appropriate design for making the time sequence operate on our behalf for the causal inference. We see the campaign was effective for family planning but had no impact for drugs and alcohol. Speculations

TABLE 2

MEAN CAMPAIGN MESSAGE DISCRIMINATION DIFFERENCES
AS A CONSEQUENCE OF RADIO ANNOUNCEMENT MANIPULATIONS

	Experimental City	*Control City*
Number of Messages Discriminated for:		
Family Planning	.72(N=90)	.18(N=95)
Drugs	.39(N=114)	.43(N=131)
Alcohol	.45(N=131)	.45(N=114)

concerning this lack of impact can range from the character of the stimulus presentation for each topic to the audience's interest in the topics at hand. For our present purposes this is a reasonable example of the classic causal analysis with a known time sequence. The next two examples will rest their interpretation on an assumed time sequence.

A configurational sequence is an elaboration of our last two examples. If we theorize that when we find A, B and C together we can expect to find D following from that pattern or configuration, we would expect a diagram such as that found in Figure 2. The coefficients shown in Table 3 are causal relationships estimated for young and old adolescents.

In this example it is clear that the family influence is predominant. The more autonomous adolescents are from their families, apparently the less they are socialized to give a positive evaluation of the institutions. The peers play a negligible role in the early period but, at a later age setting, the more one does rely on them, the more negative the institutional evaluation. And reliance on TV, although marginally important in the early teens, becomes negligible later on as a direct effect.[3]

Cycles are another aspect of time sequence that need to be considered. Here we are concerned with how A affects B which in turn affects A at a later time point. The most appropriate way to evaluate this kind of phenomenon is with measurement of the A's and B's at different time points. Krull and Paulson's chapter provides an insight into this issue for time series data.

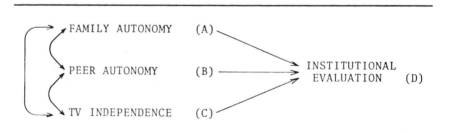

Figure 2.

TABLE 3

ESTIMATED CAUSAL RELATIONSHIPS FOR FAMILY
AUTONOMY, PEER AUTONOMY, AND TV INDEPENDENCE

Link	Age 13-14	Age 18-19
A ⟶ D	−.51 (−.57)	−.33 (−.36)
B ⟶ D	+.01 (−.01)	+.26 (+.21)
C ⟶ D	+.15 (+.15)	+.05 (+.04)
Variance Explained	34%	22%
A = Family Autonomy	C = TV Independence	
B = Peer Autonomy	D = Institutional Evaluation	

NOTE: Numbers in parentheses are understandardized path coefficients that allow comparisons across age groupings. The standardized coefficients with no parentheses should be compared only within age groupings.

Without time series or panel data, however, we are often forced to make certain conceptual assumptions that allow us to generate reciprocal causal parameter estimates using econometric techniques. In such a time-implicit analysis, we made the estimates shown in Figure 3 from data collected for a larger study in Minneapolis and St. Paul (Kline, 1969).

Here we see a mixture of uses of time for causal analysis. The demographics of income, age, education and occupation are all conceived as working together in a time setting, and as antecedent in time to the two dependent variables (in this instance time budget allocations). We postulated cyclical relationship between the use of time for TV viewing and newspaper reading. The finding that changes in TV time use dramatically affect newspaper reading time but not vice-versa needs close examination. And, the larger differences between income and age found in this analysis compared to Kline's earlier study (1969) reflect the greater number of influences controlled for in the latter paper. Although the relationship of the TV measure to that of newspaper time fits with perceptions by newspaper managements, it is only an example of how this kind of modeling can be done and should not be considered as definitive.

TIME AS A QUANTITATIVE RELATIONSHIP

Choosing the most appropriate time scale for the theoretical business at hand has been a neglected area in communication research. The length of time that a particular process operates will be importantly related to the consequences. Choice of time scale will also relate to the hypotheses being generated. If we use minutes, days, months, or years in our approach, such as the interval scale used in the Krull and Paulson chapter, there are quite different implications than if we choose to use a ordinal level of measurement as our time scale. And, as discussed earlier in our section on settings, we may be dealing at a nominal level.

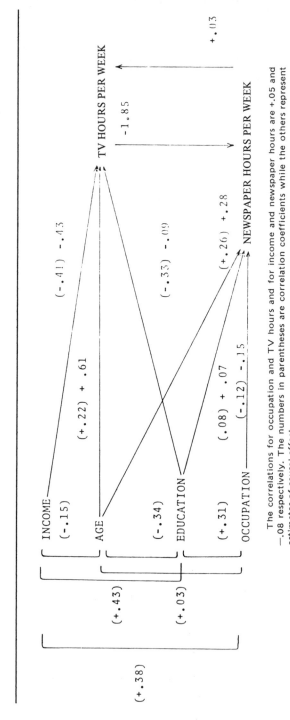

INCOME
(-.15)

AGE
(-.34)

EDUCATION
(+.31)

OCCUPATION

(+.43)

(+.03)

(+.38)

(-.41) -.43

(+.22) + .61

(-.33) -.09

(.08) + .07

(-.12) -.15

(+.26) +.28

TV HOURS PER WEEK

-1.85

+.03

NEWSPAPER HOURS PER WEEK

The correlations for occupation and TV hours and for income and newspaper hours are +.05 and −.08 respectively. The numbers in parentheses are correlation coefficients while the others represent estimates of causal effect.

Figure 3.

There are examples of the interval, ordinal, and nominal levels of time measurement to be found in our contemporary literature. Some obvious examples
are diffusion rates across time, conceived of as an interval measure; stages of
development such as those found in cognitive development and use of TV
content, where time is treated as an ordinal scale; and the use of such time-
related terms as stage of development found in comparisons of industrialized and
nonindustrialized parts of the world. Let's look briefly at each.

Time as an Interval Level Measurement

Diffusion research (Rogers and Shoemaker, 1971; Deutschmann and Danielson, 1960; Greenberg, 1964) concentrates on the speed with which a practice
has been adopted, or a news story has been heard, by a population of interest.
For our purpose here we can rely on Figure 4, adapted from Chaffee (1975; 89).
The abscissa is plotted in equal intervals of time and the major research concern
is the speed with which the particular phenomenon of interest diffuses to the
bulk of the population. Using notation found in Bartholomew (1973; 298-299)
we can examine the source-stimulation, random, and receiver-constraints models
found in Figure 4 as they relate to information diffusion.

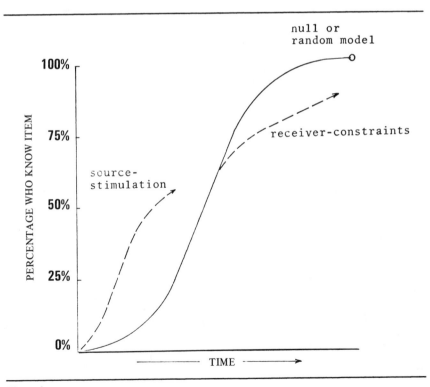

Figure 4.

Let E_s denote the transmission of the information from a source to any given member of the population. Assumed as a random event it would have the probability

$$Pr (E_s \text{ in } (T, T + \Delta T)) = \alpha \Delta T$$

This is the equivalent of saying the probability of transmission of information, E_s, to a random individual, from the news source, in the time period between T and some small increment of T, ΔT, is equal to the intensity of the source transmission, α, during that short period of time.

And, let us write the probability of the news, E_i, being communicated from one individual to another as

$$Pr (E_i \text{ in } (T, T + \Delta T)) = \beta \Delta T$$

Thus we can estimate α and β as the intensity of source and interpersonal transmission respectively. When exactly n people have received the information, the system is said to be in state n. We can write the probability of the system moving from state n to state n + 1 as follows:

$$Pr (n \rightarrow n + 1 \text{ in } (T, T + \Delta T)) = \lambda \Delta T$$

For our purposes the system can only move from n to n + 1 so it will be possible to express n in terms of the parameters α and β when the process is complete. As there are N - n persons who have not heard, the contribution to n from the source is $(N - n) \alpha \Delta T$. The contribution from the interpersonal communication will be $n(N - n) \beta \Delta T$, for all possible pairs of one "knower" and one "ignorant," and our interpersonal intensity parameter. Combining these results gives us an estimate of λ in terms of α, β and N.

$$\lambda_n = (N - n)(\alpha + \beta n)$$

Although we have talked of the above as a diffusion process it is directly comparable to a pure stochastic birth process model for a population. And in diffusion, as in birth processes, we are particularly interested in the distribution of n(T), the number of hearers at time T, or in T_n, the time it takes to reach n people. A mathematical expression of n(T) is found in Bartholomew (1973; 300).

$$Pr (n(T) = 0) = e^{-\lambda_o T}$$

Since we can write λ in terms of α, β and N, as indicated above, the problem is solved in principle.

The practical problems of calculating the distribution, even for small N's, is formidable however. Bartholomew (1973; 302-306) shows how making assumptions about large N's can throw light on the process. Although further explication is beyond the scope of this chapter it is worth noting that we can obtain estimates of α, β, T_n, and n(T). T_n is a measure of the *duration* of the news diffusion process, while λ and β play a role in the *rate* process. From Figure 4 we would expect that there would be a different T_n to reach asymptote for each of the curves; α would be relatively larger for a source-stimulation curve, while β would be a more important parameter to examine for the receiver-constraint curve.

The advantage of treating time as an interval level concept as we have done in this example is in being able to pick up on the conceptually powerful notions of *rate* and *duration*. Additionally we can evaluate the *changes in rates* of change, such as those found at the inflections in our curves in Figure 4. To explore why such changes take place when they do, we can look for additional variables, or structural features (c.f. Chaffee, 1975) for a more complete explanation.

Time as an Ordinal Level Measurement

The widespread interest in cognitive development and comprehension of TV programming offers us an opportunity to examine the use of time as an ordinal level of measurement. Following work by Piaget (1954), Ward, Wackman, and Wartella (1977) examine the levels of comprehension of TV advertising by children at different age levels. The use of age in their research is a surrogate for the more ephemeral notions of stages of development in cognitive processing by children. Although age is used as an estimate of the isomorphism between chronological development and cognitive development, it is used as ordinal level measurement. The major premise is that the level of development of a four-year-old is less than, and prior to, the developmental level of a seven-year-old. And, in turn, the seven-year-old's level of development is less advanced than, and prior to, a nine-year-old's.[4] In effect, there is the equivalent of an ordinal scale (Schuessler and Strauss, 1950) underlying the conceptual notion of levels of cognitive development. A child must pass through stages of development that have an ordering and these stages are on a time dimension but are not necessarily equally spaced for all children. These stages have major implications for the cognitive differentiation, specification, and organization of media content.

Time as a Nominal Level Measurement

The debate over the last few decades as to the role of mass media in national development (Rogers, 1976) highlights certain mixed measurement perspectives on time. Some argue (Lerner and Schramm, 1967) for a stages of growth point of view in which stage one (whatever that might be) is a necessary condition for movement to stage two. Others argue (Bendix, 1967; Schramm and Lerner, 1976) that with the rapid development and dissemination of advanced communication technology there are opportunities for nation states to hurdle stages and move to advanced development without the painfully slow transitions from oral to print to electronic based societal information systems. Here we can see that some conceptual schemes would argue that if the stages can be hurdled then time is being treated nominally.

If we wish to argue that the widespread dissemination of advanced communication technology to less advanced parts of the world took place at different points in time than in the rest of the world, then we should be able to examine the mean incidence of media penetration among the population for major differences. Suppose for example we chose those countries that gained their political independence at different time periods. The argument that might support such a conceptual distinction would have to hinge on the cohesive political forces that provide for stable and sustained growth of the communication infrastructure along with the need for such communication to sustain continued stability. A second approach places these countries on a methodologically more attractive ordinal political modernization time scale. Let us examine Table 4a and b to see how the first nominal time measure contrasts with the latter ordinal approach.

The data in Table 4a, taken from Kline, Kent, and Davis (1970) indicate that choice of any of the nominal time periods prior to 1946 would not sustain the notion that the longer the period of political independence the more advanced the infrastructure and thus greater penetration. Rather, it appears that lumping the countries with political independence prior to 1946 and contrasting them with all others in the later time period would capture the relationship sought. The similarity among the first three time periods would seem to indicate that whatever penetration took place, did so independently of early political development. A reasonable guess would be that the countries that gained their independence subsequent to 1945 were former colonies of European nations and thus their lack of independence was correlated with lack of other elements that are necessary for media penetration.

The data in Table 4b show a strong relationship between development, media penetration measures and the ordinal time scale. With the possible exception of radio set use in the early and midtransitional stages it appears that the ordinal approach is quite appropriate. The data, however, are not complete, in the sense of newer communication technology such as TV and satellite developments. We would need that to determine whether the stages can be hurdled. If, for example, early transitional countries could obtain such developments, and support their effective use, whereas some or all of the midtransitional countries could not, we would have to question the ordinal level of our time measure.

This last section has outlined the interval, ordinal, and nominal use of time as

TABLE 4a

AVERAGE MEDIA PENETRATION AND DEVELOPMENT
SCORES BY DATE OF POLITICAL INDEPENDENCE

	Before 19th Century	1800-1913	1914-1945	After 1945
	(N=21)	(N=29)	(N=13)	(N=37)
Literacy	71%	63%	62%	32%
Newspapers	4.7	3.9	4.5	1.8
Radios	2.6	2.4	2.7	1.6
Cinema	3.8	3.5	4.1	2.1
Urbanization	11%	16%	15%	15%

TABLE 4b

AVERAGE MEDIA PENETRATION AND
DEVELOPMENT SCORES BY POLITICAL MODERNIZATION

	Modern	Mid-Transitional	Transitional
	(N=58)	(N=16)	(N=30)
Literacy	72%	46%	27%
Newspapers	4.6	2.8	1.8
Radios	2.6	1.9	1.7
Cinema	3.7	2.9	2.0
Urbanization	17%	12%	9%

a quantitative relationship. Other aspects must be kept in mind when using each of these approaches. Comparisons of rates of change in different cultures raise the question of whether intercultural or cross-polity comparisons will be valid if we do not have an understanding of how time and change are valued. In a society like the U.S., change is often valued for its own sake. Can we expect to find little impact of a particular rate of change in such a society, whereas in a more traditional situation the same rate of change would produce major dislocations? We are a long way from adequately handling such questions at present. To deal with such questions we will have to develop conceptual strategies for dealing with time as a quantitative measure.

TIME AS A QUALITATIVE MEASURE

We must distinguish between social processes and social change. In many instances social processes are part of an equilibrium phase of a stable situation. Tichenor and his colleagues (Donohue, Tichenor, and Olien, forthcoming) represent a school of thought that takes this viewpoint. And Kline (1972) has outlined the way in which this equilibrating process has played a major role in mass communication research theorizing. Social change, on the other hand, implies a qualitative difference as an outcome.

Suppose a person with a particular set of cognitions is confronted with a quite different social context; a situation in which the incoming persuasive messages are powerfully different from ones usually confronted. Heirich (1964: 389) argues that at least four outcomes are possible; suppression, routinization, adaptation or revolution. As the last term is not appropriate for our example a comparable term might be conversion. Let's examine them one at a time.

The literature on selective exposure and acceptance provides some rationale for the way in which incoming messages might be *suppressed. Routinization* might allow us to select those portions of the message that seem to fit with preexisting perspectives and thus treat the incoming messages, and perhaps even the producers of the messages, as if they were part of the previous situation. *Adaptation* is the more likely outcome. Here, those parts that could be exchanged for previous cognitions would be accepted with a new organizational outcome as a consequence. Finally, the recipient of the messages might be *converted.* Each of the four alternative outcomes represent a qualitative change of increasing effect.

With the realization that there are varieties of outcomes there must come the awareness of the role time plays. Time is relevant to the interplay of the dimensions already discussed. How long, for example, does the particular set of interacting measures of family and peer autonomy and TV independence remain in equilibrium in early adolescence before shifting to the new equilibrium found later? What set of political modernization characteristics go together during the early and mid-transitional periods and how does media penetration relate to such changes? What are the causal factors that produce qualitative shifts in the diffusion curve asymptote when we treat time as an interval measure? In short, the conjoint relationship between causal linkage and time as a quantitative measure can often be used to describe or explain qualitative outcomes of the process of change. Questions such as these need to be asked as we gain sophistication in handling time in our research conceptualizations and designs.

CONCLUSION

This has been a long and wide-ranging discussion of how the concept of time has been used, abused, and avoided in communication theory and research. Continued calls for process models of both mass and interpersonal communication alert us to inadequacies in our traditional research designs. But making the calls, hearing the calls, and acknowledging them are no excuses for inaction. Historians in our field claim time as their major stock in trade—but as Carey and Sims (n.d.) have pointed out we have a legacy of biographical studies which treat time even more casually than those whose research draws on the cross-sectional, descriptive survey. The experimental tradition inherited from the social psychologists of the 1940s and 1950s used time as a basis for causal imputation but seldom went further to explicate the conceptual question of when post measures are to be taken. Nor has this been addressed in more recent analyses. In recent years there have been a number of attempts to use survey panel designs to examine shifts in communication behavior outcomes, but these suffer from the same kind of conceptual poverty that plagued the earlier laboratory experiments. Choosing the next time class meets, the next election, or when the money for experimental manipulation will run out, are not conceptually appropriate ways of defining when the T_1, T_2, or T_n measures are to be taken.

The following three chapters represent a healthy step in the direction of tackling some of these issues head-on. Each presents an original contribution to the topic of constructing time based designs in communication research.

NOTES

1. I am indebted to Milic Capek's essay on Time in *Dictionary of the History of Ideas.*
2. Family autonomy deals with the self-determination of the child living at home. Peer autonomy is conceived of as the independence an adolescent has vis-à-vis the peer group he or she is embedded in. Both of these concepts were operationalized by a number of items that related to each concept. A factor analysis procedure provided evidence of a simple structure for each concept. Factor scores were then generated for each respondent for each concept. Television independence was conceptualized as the manner in which content viewed on TV was considered real and useful. A similar factor analysis strategy was used to develop respondent scores from a battery of items. A person who is considered TV dependent is one who treats content on television as real and useful for everyday life and relies on it for information.
3. Not shown in this analysis, but reported earlier (Kline, 1972), independence does play a strong indirect role due to the configurational pattern found in late adolescence.
4. Misspecification is possible using this approach where one might find a child who has developed slowly yet placed in a stage category with other children of the same chronological age.

REFERENCES

BARTHOLOMEW, D.J. (1973). Stochastic models for social processes (2nd ed.). London: John Wiley.
BECKER, G. (1977). The economic approach to human behavior. Chicago: University of Chicago Press.
BENDIX, R. (1967). "Tradition and modernity reconsidered." Comparative Studies in Society and History, 9 (April): 292-346.
CAPEK, M. (1973). "Time." Pp. 389-398 in Dictionary of the history of ideas. New York: Charles Scribner.

CAREY, J.W., and SIMS, N. (n.d.). The telegraph and the news report. Unpublished manuscript from the Institute of Communications Research, University of Illinois.

CHAFFEE, S.H. (1975). "The diffusion of information." In S.H. Chaffee (ed.), Political communication: Issues and strategies for research. Beverly Hills, Calif.: Sage.

DEUTSCHMANN, P.J., and DANIELSON, W.A. (1960). "Diffusion of knowledge of the major news story." Journalism Quarterly, 37(summer):345-355.

DONOHUE, G.A., TICHENOR, P.J., and OLIEN, C.N. (forthcoming). Mass communication, policy, and community decisions. Beverly Hills, Calif.: Sage.

GREENBERG, B.S. (1964). "Person-to-person communication in the diffusion of news events." Journalism Quarterly, 41(autumn):489-494.

HEIRICH, M. (1964). "The use of time in the study of social change." American Sociological Review, 29(2):386-397.

HEISE, P.R. (1970). "Causal inference from panel data." In E.F. Borgatta (ed.), Sociological methodology. San Francisco: Jossey-Bass.

KLINE, F.G. (1969). Urban-suburban family structure and media use. Ph.D. dissertation, University of Minnesota.

――― (1971). "Media time budgeting as a function of demographics and life style." Journalism Quarterly, 48(summer):211-221.

――― (1972). "Theory in mass communication research." In F.G. Kline and P.J. Tichenor (eds.), Current perspectives in mass communication research. Beverly Hills, Calif.: Sage.

――― (1972a). Cross-sectional designs for communication research: path analysis. Invited paper for a symposium on advanced methodology at the meetings of the Association for Educational in Journalism.

KLINE, F.G., DAVIS, D.K., OSTMAN, R. VUORI, L., CHRISTIANSEN, N., GUNARATNE, S., and KIVENS, L. (1970). "Family and peer socialization and autonomy related to mass media use, mass institution evaluation and radical political activism: A descriptive analysis." Paper presented to the International Association for Mass Communication Research, Constance, Germany.

KLINE, F.G., KENT, D., and DAVIS, D.K. (1970). "Problems in causal analysis of aggregate data with applications to political instability," in J.V. Gillespie and B.A. Nesvold (eds.), Macro-quantitative cross-national analysis. Bevery Hills, Calif.: Sage.

KLINE, F.G., MILLER, P.V., and MORRISON, A.J. (1974). "Adolescents and family planning information: an exploration of audience needs and media effects," in J.G. Blumler and E. Katz (eds.), The uses of mass communications: current perspectives on gratification research. Beverly Hills, Calif.: Sage.

LERNER, D., and SCHRAMM, W. (1967). Communication and change in the developing countries. Honolulu: University of Hawaii—East-West Center Press.

MORRISON, A.J., KLINE, F.G., and MILLER, P.V. (1976). "Aspects of adolescent information acquisition about drugs and alcohol topics," in R.E. Ostman (ed.), Communication research and drug education. Beverly Hills, Calif.: Sage.

PIAGET, J. (1954). The construction of reality in the child. New York: Basic Books.

ROGERS, E.M. (1976). Communication and development: critical perspectives. Beverly Hills, Calif.: Sage.

ROGERS, E., and SHOEMAKER, F. (1971). Communication of innovations. New York: Free Press.

SCHRAMM, W., and LERNER, D. (1976). Communication and change: the last ten years— and the next. Honolulu: University of Hawaii—East-West Center Press.

SCHUESSLER, K., and STRAUSS, A. (1950). "A study of concept learning by scale analysis." American Sociological Review, 15:752-762.

SZALAI, A. (1973). The use of time: Daily activities of urban and suburban populations in twelve countries. The Hague: Mouton.

TUNSTALL, J. (1977). The media are American. London: Constable.

WARD, S., WACKMAN, D.B., and WARTELLA, E. (1977). How children learn to buy: the development of consumer information-processing skills. Beverly Hills, Calif.: Sage.

WINER, B.J. (1962). Statistical principles in experimental designs. New York: McGraw-Hill.

Chapter 11

POLITICAL INFORMATION, MASS MEDIA USE IN EARLY ADULTHOOD, AND POLITICAL SOCIALIZATION: SEEKING CLARITY THROUGH COHORT CURVES

James Danowski and Neal E. Cutler

INTRODUCTION: THE RESEARCH CONTEXT

EARLY WORK IN THE AREA OF POLITICAL SOCIALIZATION is notably deficient in its treatment of the role of mass communication in the development of the individual's orientations to the political system. As Chaffee, Ward, and Tipton (1973) point out, these deficiencies in the efforts of some political scientists may be summarized as a lack of direct empirical research on the impact of mass communication on political socialization. Political socialization investigators have acknowledged that political information is indeed received from these sources, yet have been quick to dismiss the importance of mass communication. The basis for this dismissal seems to have derived from three sources: (1) questionable assumptions about the nature of the mass communication process; (2) the inappropriate use of existing data; and/or (3) apprehension about the complexity of the process.

An example of the first basis of dismissal is the view that mass media are mere antiseptic conveyors of messages generated by other agents of socialization, most notably government agencies and officials, and political interest groups (Dawson and Prewitt, 1969). This assumption about the operation of the mass communication systems is questionable in light of the "gatekeeping" function of mass communication organizations (Dimmick, 1974) and the recent trend in journalism toward greater reporter-initiated political information.

AUTHOR'S NOTE: This paper is part of a larger research project examining age differences in orientations toward politics and communication, partially supported by Administration on Aging grant 93-P-57621/9. The authors acknowledge the assistance of Barbara Eisenstock in the preparation of this paper. The data used in the analysis were originally collected by the Institute for Social Research at the University of Michigan, and were made available for the present analysis through the Inter-University Consortium for Political Research.

An earlier version of this paper was presented to Annual Meetings of the International Communication Association, Political Communication Division, Chicago, April, 1975.

A second example of the first basis of dismissal lies in the assumed relationship between interpersonal communication networks and mass communication use patterns. The assumption is that because mediated political information is received and interpreted in the context of the interpersonal communication networks in which media users are imbedded, these networks and not mass communication messages are of primary importance in the socialization process (Jaros, 1973). However, a systemic view of communication processes would suggest that there is a mutually reciprocal relationship between the information individuals seek in the media and the information they discuss in interpersonal communication networks (Atkin, 1972; Chaffee and McLeod, 1967; and Chaffee, 1972); the topics of discussion shape message selection patterns, while the incidental acquisition of other messages changes subsequent topics of discussion. Thus, the recognition that mass communication messages are processed within a social context need not suggest that media use functions only as a dependent variable in the political socialization process.

The second major justification for dismissing the importance of mass communication in the political socialization process, the inappropriate use of existing data, links directly to the point made above regarding interpersonal communication networks. Political scientists have tended to assume that peer networks are important in the political socialization process, merely based upon generalizations from studies in other areas (Jaros, 1973). For example, Dawson and Prewitt (1969:129) state:

> In pointing out the growing significance of peer groups, these studies do not deal with the specific issue of political socialization. However, inasmuch as the form and process of political learning parallel other forms of social learning, these patterns can be assumed to hold for political socialization. Peer groups are important agencies through which political orientations are transmitted, nurtured, and altered.

It is questionable whether such generalizations can be made without regard to the salience of the topics of interpersonal communication around which peer groups are formed and maintained. Intuitively it would seem that adolescents would form peer groups less around shared political views than around shared views in such areas as social activities, academic interests, sexual interests, and the use of consciousness-altering substances. In fact, Atkin and Greenberg (1974) state that peer groups seem to have little influence on political socialization.

A further example of the inappropriate use of existing data merits only brief mention, since it represents a similar process to that highlighted above. This is the use of the two-step flow hypothesis. It has been argued that since research shows that mass media messages reach only a small number of attentive opinion leaders who then pass on these messages along with interpretation and influence to their constituent groups, then these groups and their opinion leaders are of much greater importance than mass media in the political socialization process

(Dawson and Prewitt, 1969). An important factor left unconsidered by this analysis is that such research has been conducted with adults rather than adolescents. Perhaps more importantly, more recent research and thinking have moved toward a multi-step flow model with the recognition that the two-step flow hypothesis itself has a weak basis of support (e.g., Troldahl and Van Dam, 1965; Troldahl, 1966-1967; Lin, 1971).

Perhaps the major inappropriate use of data and generalizations derived from other contexts, and directly transferred to the context of political socialization, has been skillfully argued by Chaffee, Ward, and Tipton (1973). These researchers point out that political scientists use Klapper's (1960) work to suggest that mass media messages act primarily to reinforce the existing attitudes and orientations of the user. The flaw in this transfer to the political socialization context is the failure to recognize that Klapper's view is predicated on the condition that the individual already has well-formed cognitions which can be reinforced. Chaffee et al., propose that in the pre-adult such well-formed political cognitions do not exist. Moreover, recent research shows that individuals' exposure to political media messages begins in primary school (Atkin and Gantz, 1975) at a period when they appear to have only very weak affective orientations to political figures and minimal cognitive patterning of the political environment (Greenstein, 1968).

The third source for dismissing the importance of mass communication in the political socialization process is exemplified by a statement made by Jaros (1973:125):

> Indeed mass communication and its impact on political behavior must be investigated thoroughly. However, perhaps precisely because of the great breadth of its possible effects, it has not been dealt with in a political socialization context. Accordingly, it is appropriate to leave this field to more explicit treatment by specialists in political communications.

Although Jaros made these judgments in 1973, this more explicit treatment by political communication specialists had already begun. Since about 1970 political communication researchers had initiated direct investigation of mass communication's role in the political socialization process (McLeod, O'Keefe, and Wackman, 1969; Byrne, 1969; Hollander, 1971; McLeod, Atkin, and Chaffee, 1972; Dominick, 1972; Chaffee, Ward, and Tipton, 1973; Atkin, Crouch, and Troldahl, 1973; Atkin and Gantz, 1975; Atkin et al., in press). The general thrust of this research has been to examine political mass communication use as an *independent* variable rather than as a dependent variable. Research results have tended to support the view that mediated political information can serve as a causal predictor of other political orientation variables. Atkin and Greenberg (1974:7) aptly review this research and conclude:

> In sum, these studies show that mass communication contributes substantially to the political socialization process during adolescence. Most young

people attend to political stimuli in the mass media, beginning with television news viewing in elementary school and later newspaper reading. The weight of the evidence from the research literature indicates that this informal media use produces major effects on political knowledge; it also appears to influence political attitudes and participation, although to a lesser extent.

Recent major reviews of the literature on mass media and political behavior have been completed by Kraus and Davis (1976), Atkin (in press), and Chaffee (1977).

Our own view is that communication and political socialization are probably best conceptualized as primarily a mutually reciprocal causal system, and hence not causally linked in the classical sense. The roots of this assumption lie in a systemic, "infographic" view (Danowski, 1976) of human behavioral processes. As with other perspectives loosely tied under the umbrella of "systems theory," this infographics view contains a cybernetic model of the over-time connections between the structure of environment and the structure of the internal system. The environment exerts primary influence at certain times, while the internal system exerts primary influence at yet other times, in a sort of cyclical pattern over time. Thus, at specifiable points in the political socialization system, communication variables operate as causal agents. At other times, of course, the communication behavior variables are to be explained by other elements within the socialization model.

THE FOCUS OF THE PRESENT RESEARCH

Nearly all political socialization research in general, and political communication socialization in particular, is focused on pre-adults. However, a *process* view of human behavior suggests that socialization is a set of relatively continuous life-cycle phenomena (e.g., Inkeles, 1969); changes may occur over time in the uses and impact of political information throughout the life experience. Nevertheless, nearly all researchers have tended to focus on the pre-adult life stage and to assume that orientations toward the political environment developed in this period persist throughout the life span. There is, however, little empirical foundation for this view. Only a few scholars have given attention to the inadequacies of a general socialization perspective which is limited to this narrow segment of the life span (Brim and Wheeler, 1966; Riley, Foner, Hess, and Toby, 1969; Prewitt, Eulau, and Zisk, 1966-1967). Still fewer scholars have recognized the potential importance of a life-span perspective in the context of communication and political socialization (McLeod and O'Keefe, 1972). The present research addresses itself to this deficiency in current knowledge about the political socialization process through more extended portions of the life span.

In examining the role of mass communication in the political socialization process, three basic areas may be focused upon: exposure patterns, uses and gratifications, and effects. Since other research cited earlier has demonstrated the importance of mass communication about politics as an independent variable, it is important to explore the changes over time that occur in media users' patterns of exposure to political information. Consequently, the scope of the present paper is limited to exposure patterns. If variations are found in exposure patterns through the life cycle, the next logical step for research is to examine the associations of exposure with gratifications and effects variables.

The present research focuses on the adult life stage from the early twenties to the early thirties. The mediated political information use of individuals is examined as they formally enter the political system and participate for the first decade. Examination of older life stage periods is left to future research (e.g., Cutler and Danowski, 1975).

RELATED RESEARCH

Previous research directly related to the focus of this paper is minimal. Some research has examined age and media use, but has used the entire age range in linear correlation/regression models (e.g., Samuelson, Carter, and Ruggels, 1963; Kline, 1971). This prevents the detection of life-span variations that are non-linear, and in particular provides no basis for specific attention to the early adult life stage. It appears that the only major work which gives empirical attention to mediated political information use in early adulthood is that of Jennings and Niemi (1968; 1974; 1975). While their research primarily revolves around parent/child political behaviors, they also examine maturational changes in political media use through the life span. In their 1968 research they examine cross-sectional national election surveys from 1964 and 1966 gathered by the Survey Research Center of the University of Michigan. Although data are unreported, the conclusion reached is that the period of early adulthood shows "rapid growth" (p. 451) in the use of media for political information. In 1974, based on the 1964 SRC data, they present a table (mean number of media by age) and draw a similar conclusion: "The process [of increasing media use] continues after high school, so that regular media usage continues to climb well into the adult years" (p. 259).

Although cross-sectional data may have value in suggesting maturational propositions, the validity of conclusions based merely on this evidence is questionable. As Riley (1973) has clearly pointed out, cross-sectional data confound three competing explanations of change in a particular variable. Maturational or aging effects, generational or cohort effects, and secular or period effects are inseparable in cross-sectional data. Change may be accounted for in part by processes of aging which transcend the particular socialization experiences of individuals, in part by the relatively unique historical experiences which a particular birth cohort has undergone, and in part by the transitory events of a period within which the data were gathered. Cohort analysis, a general technique employing the secondary analysis of a series of existing cross-sectional surveys (Cutler, 1968,1976; Hyman, 1972), offers a basis for separating out these competing explanations.

Essentially cohort analysis involves the examination of a series of representative samples of the same population. Within each survey one or more distinct age cohorts can be defined, such that the behaviors of these cohorts can be traced through the series of cross-sectional measurements. Thus, for example, the 25-year-olds in a 1950 survey represent the birth cohort of 1925; in turn, this cohort is represented by the 35-year-olds in a 1960 survey, and the 45 year-olds in a 1970 survey. Any sequence of age gradations can be employed as long as one or more birth cohorts can unambiguously be identified in the series of available surveys. While cohort analysis using series of cross-sectional surveys does not enable the examination of the same individuals over time, it does enable the longitudinal study of population aggregates grouped by age.

Before proceeding with the cohort analyses of the present research, Jennings and Niemi's (1975) follow-up study merits discussion. In this study the authors show an improvement over simple cross-section analysis, by reporting the results of their national panel study of high school seniors and their parents in 1965, and later in 1973. This is a different sample than that used in deriving the socialization conclusion from the 1964 presidential election study of adults. Among the analyses is a two-point-in-time trend analysis of media exposure from 1965 to 1973 for both parents and offspring. The results for offspring are most germane here.

Reporting only "raw" media exposure, unadjusted for overall period effects on the population, the authors show newspaper reading as stable over the eight-year interval, television use as increasing rather substantially, and radio and magazine use as declining slightly.

In the research reported below, the cohort analysis will be used to test the Jennings and Niemi findings. However, at this point it should be kept in mind that while Jennings and Niemi improved upon the earlier cross-sectional analysis, the two-point trend analysis suffers from the following basic methodological limitations: (1) general media use is apparently measured, and use for political information is not isolated in the analysis; (2) period effects go uncontrolled, except that the comparison with parent media behavior provides a minimal but significant degree of control; and (3) most importantly, only a single birth cohort of young adults is examined, leaving open the possibility that other birth cohorts, examined in different eight-year periods of contemporary history but during the same life-cycle stage (roughly age 18 to age 26), might behave quite differently.

RESEARCH HYPOTHESIS

The present research tests the basic proposition set forth by Jennings and Niemi, based on the 1964 survey analysis: *As individuals mature through early adulthood, exposure to political campaign information increases.* However, as they later report (1975), their further test of this proposition shows only an increase for television.

In addition to this hypothesis regarding changes in amount of exposure to political media messages, the present research explores patterns of usage across a set of four media. This second investigation seeks to provide answers to the question: Is there increasing convergence of usage patterns across media as individuals mature through early adulthood? That is, is there increasing consistency in the use of alternative sources of political information?

RESEARCH METHODS AND RESULTS

The data used in this analysis were originally collected by the Institute for Social Research of the University of Michigan in conjunction with the presidential election campaigns from 1952 through 1972. Thus, the results are derived from six representative samples of the national population. Each survey asked respondents to report on their use of mass media for information about the election campaigns. For each medium, mean scores were computed for each age group. The questions asked and the response alternatives were highly consistent across the six points in time and, aside from minor variations, read as follows: [1]

(1) We are interested in this interview in finding out whether people paid much attention to the election campaign this year. Take newspapers for instance—did you read about the campaign in any newspaper? (If yes) How much did you read newspaper articles about the election—regularly, often, from time to time, or just once in a great while?

(2) How about radio—did you listen to any speeches or discussions about the campaign on the radio? (If yes) How many programs about the campaign did you listen to on the radio—a good many, several, or just one or two?

(3) How about television—did you watch any programs about the campaign on television? (If yes) How many television programs about the campaign would you say you watched—a good many, several, or just one or two?

(4) How about magazines—did you read about the campaign in any magazines? (If yes) How many magazine articles about the campaign would you say you read—a good many, several, or just one or two?

TABLE 1

AGE BY EXPOSURE TO POLITICAL MEDIA MESSAGES:
A CROSS-SECTIONAL LOOK AT 1964

Age Group	TV	Radio	Newspapers	Magazines	Total
21-24	1.63	0.57	1.25	0.46	3.91
25-28	1.67	0.73	1.42	0.64	4.47
29-32	1.77	0.87	1.76	0.85	5.25

A CROSS-SECTIONAL LOOK AT 1964

Before presenting the data longitudinally, let us reconsider the cross-sectional 1964 findings that were used by Jennings and Niemi in arriving at their conclusions regarding increasing use of political messages through the period of early adulthood. Examination of the data they appear to have used, as well as other data, shows that television, radio, newspapers, magazines, and total media exposure each increase with increased age in the 1964 survey (see Table 1). Thus it can be seen how, using these data, Jennings and Niemi arrived at their conclusion of increasing use of media for political information through early adulthood. However, as has been pointed out earlier, cross-sectional data can neither confirm nor deny a developmental relationship.

THE PRESENTATION OF COHORT DATA

As pointed out earlier, cohort analysis provides a means for separating three competing explanations for change in a variable in relation to age—generational, maturational, and period effects. In the present research one variant of cohort analysis is used. To structure the data for the cohort analysis, each cross-sectional survey has been sorted into a series of four-year age groups. Since the age interval (four years) is the same, patterns of cohort aging across the twenty-year period are presented in their least scientifically ambiguous form.

In deciding the cutoff point for early adulthood, we wished to have the capability of detecting nonlinear trends, while having the greatest number of replications of the same life stage. Obviously, at least three points in time are needed to detect nonlinear trends. If the cutoff were made between the ages of 32 and 33, then four complete early adult cohorts would be available for analysis (see tables in Appendix). On the other hand, if we moved to four points in time, cutting between ages 36 and 37, only three full cohorts would be available. Thus, to maximize the number of available cohorts and still retain capabilities for detecting nonlinear trends, the current analysis defines early adulthood as the period between the ages of 21 and 32.

Changes in exposure values for each medium will be examined as the four separate age cohorts formally enter the political system and develop over two distinct four-year life-stage intervals (21-24 to 25-28 and 25-28 to 29-32). Cohort data on the raw exposure means will not be extensively treated in this analysis; however, Table B, which appears in the Appendix, presents these values for reference. The reason for not using the raw means is that the values for these variables may be influenced by period effects operating within a given cross-section. Perhaps most important, our preliminary investigation has shown a general decline in media use across most period to period intervals. Another major set of period effects is likely to be the differential availability of the media over the twenty-year period, e.g., the increasing saturation of television from 1952 through 1972. Another major set of period effects are the differential political environments within each cross-section that are created by varying factors operating within a particular presidential election campaign. Exemplifying these possible effects are the large margins for the victor in the elections of 1956, 1964, and 1972, and the relatively close elections of 1952, 1960, and 1968. Also, the elections of 1960 and 1964 represented Democratic victories, while 1952, 1956, 1968, and 1972 yielded Republican winners. Such manifestly political attributes may differentially influence aggregate levels of political interest in general, and use of mass media in particular.

Because the primary concern of the present paper is with testing the developmental hypothesis that exposure to political media messages increases through early adulthood, these period effects should be controlled in the analysis. Thus, the distribution of exposure values for all age groups within each survey have been standardized to a mean of zero (0) and a standard deviation of one (1). The bulk of the analysis will center on changes in these Z-scores for the exposure variables for each of the four birth cohorts.[2] The change in exposure for each cohort as it matures will be measured by the specific cohort scores *relative* to the scores of the other age groups in the sample year. This controls for the period effects operating upon each respective survey. Thus, for example, if use for the whole sample of age groups decreases at a faster rate than for an early adult age group, then the latter will show a *relative increase.*

In evaluating the hypothesis, the following criteria will be used. If all four cohorts show the expected trends, then the hypothesis is considered fully supported by the data. In the case that three of the four cohorts conform to the hypothesized pattern, then weak evidence for support will be concluded. When two or fewer cohorts show the expected trends, then the hypothesis will be considered rejected.

REPLICATING THE 2-POINT PANEL STUDY

Before moving to the full cohort analysis of the present research, it is appropriate to replicate the analysis of the single birth cohort presented by Jennings and Niemi (1975). Keeping in mind that different samples are being used, we

TABLE 2
USE OF TELEVISION FOR POLITICAL CAMPAIGN INFORMATION:
COHORT MATRIX OF Z-SCORES*

Age Group	1952	1956	1960	1964	1968	1972
21-24	+0.39	−0.02	−0.32	−1.39	−2.31	−1.52
25-28	+0.53	+0.82	−0.03	−1.73	−0.21	−0.41
29-32	+0.71	+0.74	+0.62	−1.21	−0.21	−0.71

*Scores in addition to those for the four complete cohorts are included to allow more complete examination of these patterns. In each figure, the cohorts are labelled according to the year in which the cohort was age 21-24.

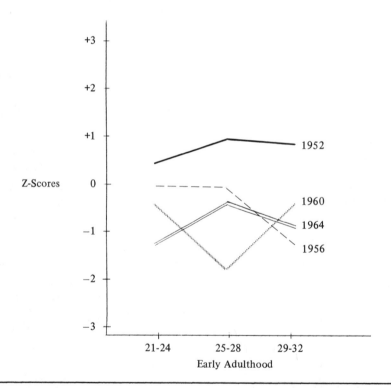

Figure 1: USE OF TELEVISION FOR POLITICAL CAMPAIGN INFORMATION:
COHORT TRENDS

examined the closest birth cohort in our own data (ages 21-24 in 1968; 25-29 in 1972) and replicated the analysis. Using raw media exposure, the same patterns as reported by Jennings and Niemi were found. However, by using the Z-score transformation noted above, the media behavior of the young cohort is examined relative to changes that occurred for the samples as a whole in 1968 and 1972. This more controlled analysis shows that for the young cohort, newspaper reading declined *less* than for other age groups, resulting in a relative increase in newspaper use for this younger group.

The same analysis for television shows a more rapid increase in television viewing for the young cohort relative to the full sample. This yields an even larger relative increase in television viewing than reported by the other authors. The patterns Jennings and Niemi report for radio and magazines are essentially replicated by our analysis.

THE CURRENT COHORT ANALYSIS

Table 2 shows the Z-scores for exposure to campaign politics on television of each cohort at three points in time. By following the diagonal lines through each of the surveys, the changes in relative exposure can be tracked.[3] Figure 1 graphically portrays changes over time in television exposure for each of the four cohorts. As can be seen, the 1952, 1956, and 1964 cohorts tend to behave in a similar pattern of non-linearity. The cohorts of 1952 and 1964 show a slight increase from the early twenties to the mid-twenties, and a slight decrease from the mid-twenties to the early thirties. The 1956 cohort is stable from the early to the mid-twenties, and shows a somewhat larger decline from the mid-twenties to the early thirties. The 1960 cohort shows an opposite pattern to the other three cohorts. There is a substantial decline in television exposure from the early to mid-twenties, and a comparable increase from the mid-twenties to the early thirties. Thus, these data suggest that the hypothesis is not supported for television.

Relative changes in newspaper exposure are found in Figure 2. Here the cohorts tend to show a somewhat linear increase in exposure through early adulthood, although the 1960 cohort deviates slightly in exhibiting a small dip in reported exposure from the early to mid-twenties, and a subsequent increase from mid-twenties to the early thirties. Thus, for the newspaper medium, there appears to be support for the hypothesis in that relative media use for political information increases through early adulthood.

Relative changes in radio exposure for each of the four cohorts are displayed in Figure 3. Only the 1964 cohort shows an increase across the three points in time. The remaining cohorts all show a decline from early to mid-twenties. The 1960 cohort continues to decrease from mid-twenties to early thirties, while the 1952 and 1956 cohorts increase moderately in this life-stage. These highly mixed patterns do not support the hypothesized increases in political media exposure through early adulthood.

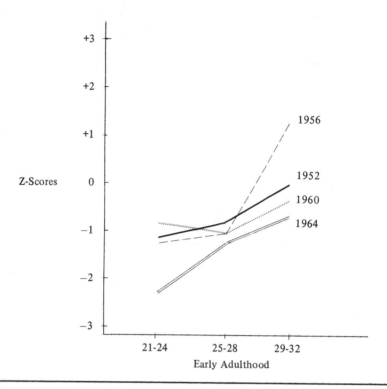

Figure 2: USE OF NEWSPAPER FOR POLITICAL CAMPAIGN INFORMATION: COHORT TRENDS

The cohort values for relative magazine exposure shown in Figure 4 reveal an increase across the three life-stage points for the 1956 cohort. The 1964 cohort strongly increases in magazine reading for political information from the early to mid-twenties, but decreases almost 50% from mid-twenties to early thirties. The 1952 and 1960 cohorts show virtually no change through early adulthood, having relatively horizontal lines. Considering these patterns, there is little basis for support of the maturational hypothesis in the context of magazine use for political information.

To summarize at this point, this series of four cohort analyses has shown that the hypothesis suggested by the conclusion of Jennings and Neimi—that of increasing exposure to media political information through the early adulthood years—gains little support when period effects are controlled, and four birth cohorts are tracked through three time points, representing eight years of development. Only in the context of newspaper use, and not for any other medium, is there evidence that relative exposure to political information increases through early adulthood.

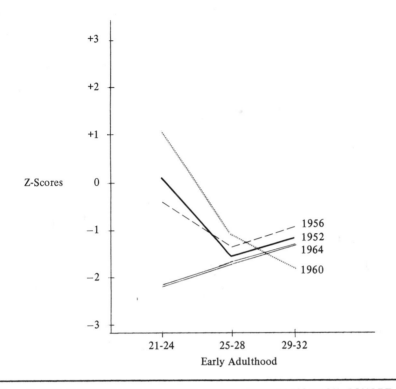

Figure 3: USE OF RADIO FOR POLITICAL CAMPAIGN INFORMATION: COHORT TRENDS

ENTROPY IN USE OF MEDIA

The over-time rates of media exposure for cohorts, taking one medium at a time, sheds light only on the features of the *particular* medium use situation. Granted that these characteristics are of interest to students of certain media, these asynchronous analyses of media use are inadequate for those interested primarily in the *information user* and not a particular information medium. If the objective of interest is the mapping of systemic user information processing characteristics, as should be the case in the study of political socialization, then the *structure* or *pattern* of media use, across all appropriate media, becomes important.

This type of analysis requires a measure of *variance* across media use distributions for the set of media. However, because media are essentially *nominal,* (i.e., unordered) in their typically perceived form, not usually being viewed with respect to any pervasive metric standard, then usual measures of dispersion such as standard deviation are clearly inappropriate. What is called for is

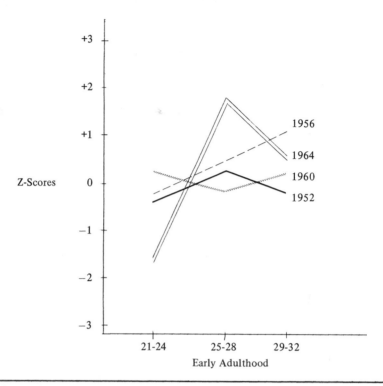

Figure 4: USE OF MAGAZINES FOR POLITICAL CAMPAIGN INFORMATION:
COHORT TRENDS

a dispersion metric compatible with unordered alternatives. Information theoretic measures of entropy provide a convenient metric, also facilitating cross-discipline theoretic integration.

In the present analysis, the question of interest is: To what extent are there early adulthood maturational trends in the structuration of individual exposure to the mass media for political information? To measure patterning of use in this way, an information theoretic measure of relative uncertainty is used. Media channel entropy indexes the degree of rectangularity in the distribution of an individual's exposure to television, radio, newspapers, and magazines, relative to the maximal amount of rectangularity possible. The more the distribution is rectangular, the more exposure is allocated equally across media; media channel entropy increases as the allocation of units of exposure becomes more equal (see Danowski, 1974a, 1974b).

Indexing of media channel entropy is created by the function:

$$\frac{\Sigma \; p_i \; \log_2 \; 1/p_i}{\log_2 \; N}$$

where p_i is the proportion of media exposure allocated to a particular medium, relative to total media use,[4] and N is the number of media. The resulting values range from 0.0 to 1.0; as the values approach 1.0, entropy, or similarity of use across media, increases. Computations for the index were made through SPSS software with the appropriate log base transformations.

As with the earlier exposure variables, media channel entropy was averaged for each age group within the six cross-sectional surveys, and each age group was then treated as the unit of analysis. Z-scores were computed for each of the sixteen age groups within the six surveys to control for the possible period effects within the respective cross-sections. As with the earlier analysis, this enables the maturational effects relative to generational or cohort effects to be more clearly identifiable.

Figure 5 shows the relative changes in media channel entropy for each of the

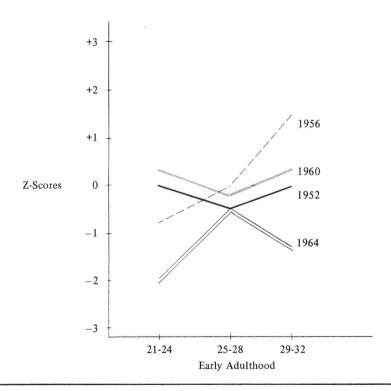

Figure 5: CHANNEL ENTROPY OF MEDIA USE FOR POLITICAL CAMPAIGN INFORMATION: COHORT TRENDS

four cohorts as they develop through early adulthood. The graphic portrayal readily shows the extent to which the cohorts behave differently. The 1952 and 1960 cohorts remain relatively stable in media channel entropy from the early twenties through to the early thirties. On the other hand, both the 1956 and the 1964 cohort show a relative increase from the early to the mid-twenties, but from the mid-twenties to early thirties the 1956 cohort continues to increase while the 1964 cohort decreases at about the same rate. Thus, there is no basis for concluding that there is a general overall developmental effect as individuals move through the early adult life stage. Change over time in media channel entropy appears to be attributable to unique cohort differences rather than a developmental socialization sequence.

SUMMARY AND DISCUSSION

Studies of political socialization have almost universally focused on children, adolescents, and teenagers—life stages prior to the individual's formalized or legal entrance to membership in the political system. Following from the traditional way in which political socialization has been approached, communication researchers have primarily examined the pre-adult patterns of media use and without empirical justification have then implicitly or explicitly extrapolated to adult (or at least young adult) patterns of political communication behavior.

The work of Jennings and Niemi, while focused largely on pre-adult political socialization, has given some empirical attention to socialization and political communication in adulthood. Their examination of cross-sectional national election data for adults from 1964 and also 1966 leads them to conclude that the socialization patterns of higher media use in adolescence (found by them and a number of communication researchers) continue through early format citizen participation and well into the later years. However, since cross-sectional data do not provide evidence for the developmental or maturational patterns of individuals, studies based on cross-sectional designs can only be suggestive of a life-stage hypothesis. Indeed, such an hypothesis is quite plausible since initial participation in a new complex social experience is likely to represent a time when adaptation to the norms of that system occurs most rapidly. The Jennings and Niemi (1975) follow-up, a two-point panel study, improves the ability to isolate maturational processes, but is relatively limited.

The purpose of the present research, therefore, has been to apply the analytic model of cohort analysis to the examination of early adulthood patterns of political information-seeking through the mass media. The application of cohort analysis to the problem has directed our attention to evidence for increases in media political information-seeking as a correlate of the maturational process within identifiable cohorts of citizens. In the longitudinal data of this paper, changes in early adulthood have been measured as the developmental changes in four different birth cohorts observed at three different periods in the early life-cycle: 21-24, 25-28, and 29-32.

The analysis examined five different variables measuring media usage in political campaign contexts: frequency of use of television, radio, newspapers, and magazines, and a measure of entropy of media channel use indicating the distributional profile across the four media. With a single notable exception, the hypothesized pattern of increased exposure to the media from age 21 through age 32 failed to appear. Thus, *the basic hypothesis of increased media use for political information in the early years of formal political participation must be rejected.*

The only context in which the socialization-linked hypothesis can be said to be supported is in exposure to newspapers. Across each of the four cohorts examined in Figure 2 a general relative increase is seen in newspaper usage in the early years of adult political maturation. The cohorts do not all exhibit the same level of newspaper usage, nor are the slopes of the curves uniform for all cohorts. Nevertheless, the hypothesized pattern does occur, and it is replicated by each of the four cohorts.

The basic hypothesis suggested by Jennings and Niemi, therefore, can be accepted only in the case of political information-seeking through newspapers. Students of political socialization, political science, and communication are thus challenged to seek an understanding of this relationship. Further analysis should consider at least the following issues, which speak not only to the explanation of the observed newspaper pattern, but also to the more general issues of socialization and media consumption.

First, investigation should be made of the extent to which a range of components of the high school and college experience emphasizes—in a manifest or latent way—the greater legitimacy of newspapers as a source of political information. For example, even though television has now saturated its potential set ownership market, and although television networks spend large sums to produce news, public affairs, and election results coverage, the standard high school civics text and introductory American politics text typically emphasize the traditional role of newspapers in democratic information systems. Thus, the patterns of increasing information-seeking through newspapers found for those at the youngest stages of the political life cycle might be a consequence of the particular kind of orientation found in the materials and practices of civic education.

Second, perhaps the nature of newspaper content is such that the medium offers increasing adaptive utility to young adults as they mature through the early political life cycle. The normative structure of political democracy has traditionally emphasized the importance of the informed citizen who processes information so that policy alternatives can be fully known, outcomes sufficiently analyzed, and decisions rationally made. Indeed, critics and journalists alike have noted that while television can provide the immediacy of news, newspapers provide the details and the background analyses. Thus, it may be the case that young adults increasingly perceive newspapers as enabling their more effective adaptation to the normative expectations for adequate participation in political democracy.

Third, the form or structure of newspapers as an information delivery and storage medium may be associated with its increased use for political information through early adulthood. The newspaper user can be more selective of specific message components and can more easily store and retrieve information than the consumer of broadcast media. Thus, newspapers offer the user a greater degree of control over the information environment. Perhaps along the lines of the adaptive utility notion suggested above, as individuals mature through early participation in the political system, adjustment to its normative structure can be more effectively accomplished by increasing the use of media over which the individual has greater informational control. In so doing, adaptive efficiency may be increased.

Finally, it may be speculated that as an individual matures through early adulthood there may be physiologically linked changes in individual information processing characteristics that increase the correspondence between the individual's cumulative "internal" information processing structures and the newspaper medium's particular structural characteristics. However, this suggestion is offered merely for heuristic purposes, since specific concepts and measurement procedures to effectively deal with the structure of each of these components (the user and the medium) in this manner are only recently beginning to be developed.

A more general challenge for explanation is the development of logics to understand why in the case of most other media the birth cohorts behave very differently. The strong implication of the current analysis is that researchers must increasingly look to historical perspectives and methodologies in order to adequately understand the phenomena they observe at the moment. Indeed, not only the content, but the nature and process of socialization have been shown to be affected by historical and generational influences (Bengtson and Cutler, 1976; Cutler, 1975, 1977).

Moving lastly to questions about the information processing structures of users, another pattern found among the cohort data suggests a direction for future research linking communication and socialization. The graphic depictions of the cohort data for three of the four media variables indicate a distinct pattern of convergence. For newspapers, radio, and channel entropy there is a substantial convergence of the standardized values for the cohorts in the middle portion of the early adult life stage, i.e., the 25-28 interval. In other words, there is greater variance in these measures in the first and third life-stage intervals than there is in the mid-twenties.

The data for these three variables suggest that no matter what the level of media use in the first national election after formal entry into the political system, each cohort shows adjustments in aggregate media use so that by the second election campaign the relative use of these media becomes very similar across all the cohorts. The consistency with which this pattern occurs across the cohorts, each of which enters the political system experiencing a different first election campaign, suggests that this homogenizing process occurs regardless of the political climate of a particular election campaign.

It is interesting to examine this pattern in light of McLeod and O'Keefe's (1972) suggestion that the immediate post-high school years represent a key point of discontinuity in the socialization process. In the present data the wide variation across different cohorts in the levels of these particular media variables during the first election campaign may be a result of this discontinuity. However, the continuity of socialization to the political system may be re-established after the experience of the first election campaign. That is, by the second election campaign the cohorts are using some media for political information at about the same level.

The follow-up phenomenon is also interesting. After this convergence during the time of the second election, these same cohorts, for the same three media variables mentioned above, again move to more widely varied levels of media usage in their third election campaign. This suggests that the patterns of variation associated with maturation within identifiable cohorts may reflect the unique characteristics of the cohort, but at certain points in the early adult years there may be particularly strong socialization effects. In this case, it appears that the experience of the first election campaign may be a forceful socializing influence on political communication behaviors.

These suggestions regarding the socialization-linked convergence of media use patterns are, of course, only speculative. Nonetheless, the patterns suggest that one measure of the strength of a socialization agency or experience is the degree to which it produces patterns of homogeneity, or a reduction of variance, in behaviors over time—and that these effects can be observed in the developmental patterns of different birth cohorts.

In conclusion, this research concerning communication and political socialization has indicated that *the experiences of pre-adulthood do not generally produce an orientation toward political information-seeking in which all media are attended to with increasing frequency in the early years of adulthood.* Only newspaper use shows the pattern of increase through the early adult life stage. Future research should explore further the system-level and individual-level importance of this difference between the use of newspapers and other information media. In addition, the socializing impact of the experience of the first presidential election campaign merits more careful attention. More generally, the cohort patterns across media have suggested that analyses of the communication behaviors of maturing birth cohorts offers a fruitful context for the development of both communication and socialization theory. Increased attention to communication and socialization over the life span offers promise for the formulation of more comprehensive understanding of the processes of human behavior.

NOTES

1. The major exception to this pattern of response alternatives occurred in 1956, in which the alternative responses were dichotomously coded as "yes" or "no." With respect to coding, across all surveys the "no" responses were coded as zero (0); the minimal responses were coded as one (1); the moderate responses were coded as two (2); and the maximum responses were coded as three (3). Although it is recognized that these are ordinal data, means have been computed to maximize the use of information contained in the data in performing analysis on the media use variables, and in computing and analyzing the channel entropy variable.

2. In computing Z-scores, each survey was stratified into 16 age groups, each of which was defined on an interval of four years (except for the upper age group, 80+). Each age group was treated as an equal element in a distribution of mean exposure scores. Thus, Z-scores within each survey for a particular variable are based on the mean of these means and the standard deviation of the distribution of these means, i.e., each survey represents a 16-element vector for which a Z-transformation was carried out.

3. Complete Z-score matrices will not be presented for the remaining analyses, which only present the cohort patterns of maturational development. Complete data tables appear in the Appendix; see Table C.

4. It should be recognized that these p values are computed from ordinal component scores, and thus the analysis to follow should only be taken as illustrative and suggestive.

APPENDIX

TABLE A
CELL SIZES OF AGE GROUPS BY SURVEY*

Age Group	1952	1956	1960	1964	1968	1972
21-24	64	105	48	121	105	107
25-28	99	146	152	133	127	102
29-32	85	177	144	131	97	86

*Numbers represent respondents having complete media use data.

TABLE B

USE OF MEDIA FOR POLITICAL CAMPAIGN INFORMATION:
COHORT MATRIX OF RAW MEAN SCORES*

Age Group	1952	1956	1960	1964	1968	1972

A. TELEVISION

Age Group	1952	1956	1960	1964	1968	1972
21-24	1.33	2.04	1.88	1.62	1.71	1.67
25-28	1.37	2.37	2.00	1.67	2.01	1.86
29-32	1.42	2.34	2.20	1.77	2.01	1.81

B. NEWSPAPERS

Age Group	1952	1956	1960	1964	1968	1972
21-24	1.85	1.81	1.58	1.25	1.10	.87
25-28	1.96	1.86	1.51	1.42	1.33	1.04
29-32	2.05	2.08	1.82	1.76	1.55	1.12

C. RADIO

Age Group	1952	1956	1960	1964	1968	1972
21-24	1.78	1.33	1.29	.57	.69	.61
25-28	1.54	1.03	.65	.73	.54	.72
29-32	1.60	1.14	.71	.87	.54	.49

D. MAGAZINES

Age Group	1952	1956	1960	1964	1968	1972
21-24	.92	.77	.79	.46	.63	.67
25-28	1.10	.86	.83	.64	.74	.60
29-32	.98	1.02	.69	.85	.60	.63

E. CHANNEL ENTROPY OF MEDIA USE

Age Group	1952	1956	1960	1964	1968	1972
21-24	.57	.44	.60	.44	.48	.43
25-28	.58	.46	.58	.53	.52	.49
29-32	.62	.51	.58	.62	.55	.44

*Scores in addition to those for the four complete cohorts are included to allow more complete examination of these patterns.

TABLE C

COHORT MATRIX OF Z-SCORES FOR FIVE MEDIA BEHAVIORS

Age Group	1952	1956	1960	1964	1968	1972

A. TELEVISION (see Table 2, Figure 1)

B. NEWSPAPERS (see Figure 2)

Age Group	1952	1956	1960	1964	1968	1972
21-24	−1.14	−1.25	−0.87	−2.35	−2.40	−2.00
25-28	−0.34	−0.93	−1.17	−1.14	−1.25	−1.10
29-32	+0.29	+0.43	+0.17	+1.28	−0.15	−0.68

C. RADIO (see Figure 3)

Age Group	1952	1956	1960	1964	1968	1972
21-24	+0.07	−0.51	+1.60	−2.11	−0.89	−0.93
25-28	−1.64	−1.37	−1.20	−1.17	−1.58	−0.58
29-32	−1.21	−1.08	−1.00	−0.35	−1.58	−1.32

D. MAZAGINES (see Figure 4)

Age Group	1952	1956	1960	1964	1968	1972
21-24	−0.40	−0.37	+0.05	−1.40	+0.37	+0.85
25-28	+1.40	+0.18	+0.28	−0.20	+1.75	+0.35
29-32	+0.20	+1.18	−0.05	+1.20	0.00	+0.57

F. CHANNEL ENTROPY OF MEDIA USE (see Figure 5)

Age Group	1952	1956	1960	1964	1968	1972
21-24	0.00	−0.74	+0.27	−1.92	−1.33	−1.40
25-28	0.00	−0.44	0.00	−0.19	−0.44	−0.19
29-32	+1.25	+0.29	0.00	+1.54	+0.22	−1.15

REFERENCES

ATKIN, C. (1972). "Anticipated communication and mass media information seeking." Public Opinion Quarterly, 36:188-199.

――― (in press). "Television news and political socialization." Public Opinion Quarterly.

ATKIN, C., CROUCH, W., and TROLDAHL, V. (1973). "The role of the campus newspaper in the new youth vote." Paper presented to the Association for Education in Journalism, Ft. Collins, Colorado.

ATKIN, C., GALLOWAY, J., and NAYMAN, O. (1976). "News media exposure, political knowledge and campaign interest." Journalism Quarterly, 53:231-237.

ATKIN, C.,and GANTZ, W. (1975). "The role of television in the political socialization of children." Paper presented to the International Communication Association.

ATKIN, C., and GREENBERG, B. (1974). "Mass communication and political socialization." East Lansing, Mich.: Michigan State University, Department of Communication, (mimeo).

ATKIN, C., LYLE, J., LeROY, D., WOTRING, C., and GREENBERG, B. (in press). Government in the sunshine. Tallahassee: Florida State University Press.

BENGSTON, V., and CUTLER, N. (1976). "Generations and intergenerational relations: Perspectives on age groups and social change." In R. Binstock and E. Shanas (eds.), Handbook of aging and the social sciences. New York: Van Nostrand Reinhold Company.

BRIM, O., and WHEELER, S. (1966). Socialization after childhood: Two essays. New York: John Wiley.

BYRNE, G. (1969). "Mass media and political socialization of children and pre-adults," Journalism Quarterly, 46:40-42.

CHAFFEE, S., JACKSON-BUCK, M., LEWIN, J., and WILSON, D. (1972). "The interpersonal context of mass communication." In F.G. Kline and P.J. Tichenor (eds.), Current perspectives in mass communication research. Beverly Hills, Calif.: Sage.

――― et al. (1977). "Mass communication and political socialization." In S. Renshon (ed.), Handbook of political socialization: Theory and research. New York: Free Press.

CHAFFEE, S., and McLEOD, J. (1967). "Communication as coorientation: Two studies." Paper presented to annual meetings of the Association for Education in Journalism, Boulder, Colo.

CHAFFEE, S., WARD, S., and TIPTON, L. (1973). "Mass communication and political socialization." In J. Dennis (ed.), Socialization to politics. New York: John Wiley.

CUTLER, N. (1968). The alternative effects of generations and aging upon political behavior: A cohort analysis of American attitudes toward foreign policy, 1946-1966. Oak Ridge: Oak Ridge National Laboratory.

――― (1975). "Toward a generational conception of political socialization." In D.C. Schwartz and S.K. Schwartz (eds.), New directions in political socialization. New York: Free Press.

――― (1976). "Generational approaches to political socialization." Youth & Society, 8:175-207.

――― (1977). "Generational analysis and political socialization." In S. Renshon (ed.), Handbook of political socialization: Theory and research. New York: Free Press.

CUTLER, N., and DANOWSKI, J. (1975). "Process gratification vs. content gratification in mass communication behavior: A cohort analysis of age changes in political information-seeking." Paper presented at the annual meeting of the Pacific Chapter of the American Association for Public Opinion Research, Los Angeles.

DANOWSKI, J. (1974a). "An uncertainty model: Friendship communication networks and media related behaviors." Paper presented to the International Communication Association, New Orleans.

––– (1974b). "Alternative information theoretic measures of television messages: an empirical test." Paper presented to the Association for Education in Journalism, San Diego.

––– (1976). "Environmental uncertainty and communication network complexity: a cross-system, cross-cultural test." Paper presented to annual meetings of the International Communication Association, Portland, Oregon.

DAWSON, R., and PREWITT, K. (1969). Political socialization. Boston: Little, Brown and Co.

DIMMICK, J. (1974). "The gate-keeper: An uncertainty theory." Journalism Monographs, 37:1-38.

DOMINICK, J. (1972). "Television and political socialization." Educational Broadcasting Review, 6:48-56.

GP.EENSTEIN, F. (1968). "Political socialization," International Encyclopedia of the Social Sciences, 14:551-555. New York: Macmillan.

HOLLANDER, N. (1971). "Adolescents and the war: The sources of socialization." Journalism Quarterly, 48:472-479.

HYMAN, H. (1972). "Cohort analysis." In H. Hyman (ed.), Secondary analysis of sample surveys: Principles, procedures, and potentialities. New York: John Wiley.

INKELES, A. (1969). "Social structure and socialization." In David Goslin (ed.), Handbook of socialization theory and research, pp. 613-632. Chicago: Rand McNally.

JAROS, D. (1973). Socialization to politics. New York: Praeger.

JENNINGS, M. and NIEMI, R. (1968). "Patterns of political learning." Harvard Educational Review, 38:443-467.

––– (1974). The Political character of adolescence. Princeton, N.J.: Princeton University Press.

––– (1975). "Continuity and change in political orientations: A longitudinal study of two generations." American Political Science Review, 48:1316-1335.

KLAPPER, J. (1960). The effects of mass communication. New York: Free Press.

KLINE, F.G. (1971). "Media time budgeting as a function of demographics and life style," Journalism Quarterly, 48:211-221.

KRAUS, S., and DAVIS, D. (1976). The effects of mass communication on political behavior. University Park, Pa.: Penn State University Press.

LIN, N. (1971). "Information flow, influence flow, and decision-making process," Journalism Quarterly, 48:38-40.

McLEOD, J., ATKIN, C., and CHAFFEE, S. (1972). "Adolescents, parents, and television use." In G. Comstock and E. Rubinstein (eds.), Television and social behavior: Television and adolescent aggressiveness. Washington, D.C.: U.S. Government Printing Office.

McLEOD, J. and O'KEEFE, G. (1972). "The socialization perspective and communication behavior." In F. Kline and J. Tichenor (eds.), Current Perspectives in Mass Communication Research. Beverly Hills, Calif.: Sage.

McLEOD, J., O'KEEFE, G., and WACKMAN, D. (1969). "Communication and political socialization during the adolescent years." Paper presented to the Association for Education in Journalism, Berkeley, Calif.

PREWITT, K., EULAU, H., and ZISK, B. (1966-1967). "Political socialization and political roles," Public Opinion Quarterly, 30:569-582.

RILEY, M. (1973). "Aging and cohort succession: interpretations and misinterpretations," Public Opinion Quarterly, 37:147-152.

RILEY, M., FONER, A., HESS, B., and TOBY, M. (1969). "Socialization for the middle and late years." Pp. 951-983 in D. Goslin (ed.), Handbook of socialization theory and research. Chicago: Rand McNally.

SAMUELSON, M., CARTER, R., and RUGGELS, W. (1963). "Education, available time and use of the mass media." Journalism Quarterly. 40:491-496.

TROLDAHL, V. (1966-1967). "A field test of a modified 'two-step flow of communication' model." Public Opinion Quarterly, 30:609-623.

TROLDAHL, V., and VAN DAM, R. (1965). "Face-to-face communication about major topics in the news." Public Opinion Quarterly. 29:626-634.

Chapter 12

TIME SERIES ANALYSIS
IN COMMUNICATION RESEARCH

Robert Krull and Albert S. Paulson

TIME IS AN IMPLICIT FACTOR in behavioral studies of every type. In survey designs time appears in two ways. First, when causal arguments are made, time order among the variables is assumed. Second, when variables are balanced against one another in multivariate analysis, the paths among variables are assumed to be constant over time. The validity of popular analytical tools, such as path analysis, is threatened if these assumptions are not warranted.

Time is explicitly involved in behavioral experiments, but assumptions about the response rates of the variables are often hidden. In one of the simplest designs, an independent variable is controlled at a time specified by the experimenter and the situation is observed for effects on the dependent variable. It is assumed that the time frame chosen for the experiment is sufficiently long for effects to be observable, but not so long that effects have decayed. In more complicated analyses involving a number of independent variables, it is assumed that all the effects on the dependent variable appear at about the same time. If this were not the case, statistical interpretation of the relative strengths of the causal links would be misleading.

Research designs which utilize a small number of time frames also make rather strong assumptions. Heise (1970) points out that among the assumptions made in cross-lagged analysis of panel data are the following about time: that causal lags are sufficiently long to assess effects, that all causal lags operate in the same time frame, that the measurement period is shorter than the causal lag and that the time between measurements of the variables is about the same as the causal lag period.

Time series analysis requires few of the assumptions described for the three preceding settings and allows the statistical examination of time order and length

AUTHORS' NOTE: We would like to express our thanks to the Children's Television Workshop for providing some of the data analyzed in this paper.

of causal lags among variables. Time series analysis does require measurement of the independent and dependent variables at a fairly large number of time points. The statistics used also do not determine causality, although they give more information about causal relationships than may be obtained by other methods.

Time series techniques were developed largely for analysis of economic data but their applicability is much wider. They may be used for a variety of social science problems, one example of which will be developed at length. Examples of other potential applications will be given towards the end of the paper. A glossary of the key terms employed appears as an appendix to this paper.

A Communications Sample Problem. We shall employ an example which motivated the use of time series analysis and in describing the example we shall discuss the relevant concepts of the method. The problem itself dictated the method's application since the length of causal lags was a primary theoretical concern and since a large number of time-sequenced data points was already available.

Specifically, we are concerned with the relationship between characteristics of television programs and the attention of the children viewing them. The problem is to determine how the characteristics of programs *transfer* to children's attention and includes such aspects as the delay before children react to programs, the size of their reaction, and the duration of the reaction. In most approaches to this issue it has been necessary to assume that children react to programs almost immediately and that the duration of their reaction was about as long as the sampling interval. These conditions were necessary for simple correlations between program attributes and attention to be meaningful. In this paper, we will attempt to examine the issue, making as few assumptions as possible.

SIMPLE TYPES OF TIME SERIES

Simple time series generally are considered to consist of four components: trend, cycle, seasonal, and random components. A trend is a change in overall level from the start to the end of the series. The trend could be a linear increase or decrease in level over time, or could take a more complicated curvilinear form. Cycles and seasonal components are both regular periodic movements of approximately sinusoidal shape. But while the seasonal components are natural and short term, cycles may be of varying length and need not be grounded in any obvious natural aspect of the series described. Random components may be viewed as variation in the series due to many uncontrolled disturbances. These components appear to have no regular pattern and in some fields of study are called white noise. Not all of these components are necessarily present in a series.

The object of time series analysis of simple series is to separate the major trend, cyclical, and seasonal components to leave just white noise. Limitations and complications of the data are sometimes such that this cannot be done

(Kendall and Stuart, 1968, Chaps. 45-50; Malinvaud, 1970; Box and Jenkins, 1970, Chap. 2). Let us now look at our research example.

Figure 1 depicts the time path, or *realization*, of the average percent attention paid by ten children to a 19-minute test version of the television show, The Electric Company. The time series was obtained by measuring the attention, averaging over the ten children and then plotting the values. The series is short as time series go, containing only 38 points. Although such short series have been successfully analyzed (Draper and Smith, 1972), a longer series of about 100 points would be preferable for more reliable results (see Box and Jenkins, 1970, Chap. 2). This is because the measurements over time in this methodology correspond to measurements of individuals at a single time point in cross-sectional analysis and similar sampling rules apply. However, it is still possible to ascertain a few characteristics of this series.

First, the beginning of the series is different in character from the end of the series and this may indicate that it is not generated by a single process throughout. Consequently, the series is said to be *nonstationary*. Second, there appears to be a slight downward *trend* in percent attention during the program. Third, there also appears to be a distinct, regular oscillation or periodicity in the last half of the series.

The first general characteristic, the nonstationarity, makes it difficult to fit a statistical model to the data. This behavior of the series may be due to averaging, since each point represents a weighted sum. Some children in the sample may be behaving very differently from others and these sub-groups may be dominating different parts of the series. Before aggregating the ten series, a check should have been made that the data for the sub-groupings were roughly homogeneous. From here on we will assume that the attention data is really stationary to simplify the illustration of analytical procedures. We will point out problems in the statistics used which may be due to nonstationarity where this occurs. The other two characteristics, trend and periodicity, will be discussed next.

The slight trend shown in Figure 1 might be due to children's being bored with viewing during a long period and gradually becoming inattentive. In future studies it might be advantageous to correct for children's fatigue before attempting to assess the attention-getting power of television program variables. Periodic oscillations of the cyclical and seasonal kind could be considered together in this instance. Long cycles of attention during a program could be produced by satiation with program material presented in the different segments of a show. Short cycles of attention could be produced by children's shifting back and forth between the television screen and things occurring in the room in which the set is located. Separation of the underlying components of this and other series requires the set of procedures described in a following section. Before we do that, let us compare the children's attention series to that of the one program complexity variable in the show they are watching.

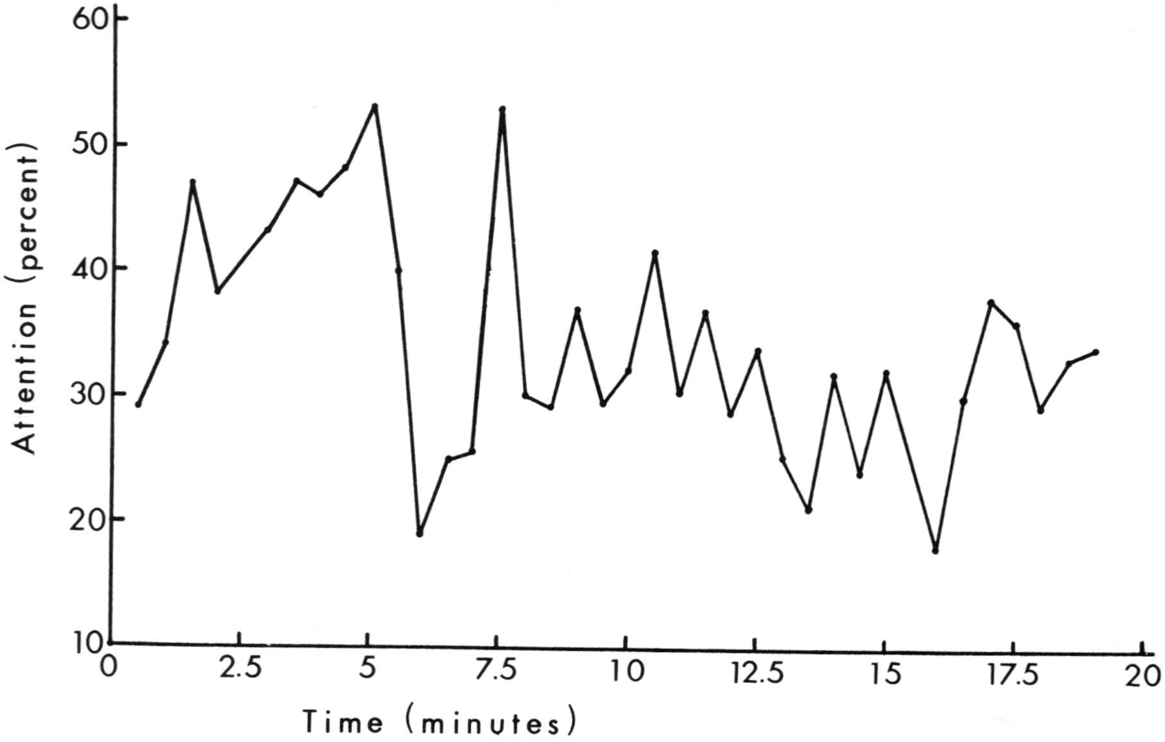

Figure 1: CHILDREN'S ATTENTION TO A VERSION OF THE ELECTRIC COMPANY

When one examines the children's attention data in Figure 1 and then the television program complexity data in Figure 2, it is evident that time series may vary substantially in appearance. The set entropy measure in Figure 2 is a weighted average of the number of scene locations appearing in each 30-second interval of the program. A full description of the variable is available elsewhere (Watt and Krull, 1974). The path of the variable is less regular than that of children's attention, going from zero to near maximal values within four measurement points on several occasions. However, it appears to behave consistently throughout the sample television program and this may make it easier to handle statistically.

PROCEDURAL STATISTICS

In discussing these procedures we will assume that the series under analysis does not show the apparent nonstationarity of the children's TV attention data. More specifically, we will assume that the series is *covariance stationary*. That is, if we let $x_t, x_t, \ldots x_t, x_{t+1}, \ldots, x_n$ be a set of observations which constitute a time series, then the covariance between any pair of observations x_t depends only on the time difference. Thus x_1 and x_2 have the same covariance as x_t and x_{t+1}, $t = 2, 3, \ldots, N$. If the series examined is not stationary, as may be the case for children's attention given in Figure 1, we assume it is possible to make the series stationary through some transformation although it will not be done here.

The Autocorrelation Coefficient. The autocorrelation coefficient is one tool for describing the smoothness of a time series. If a series is very smooth, the data points near one another in time would have similar values. Figure 1 shows that, particularly for the beginning of the television show, children's attention changes rather slowly from one 30-second interval to the next. If the series is very rough, the data points near one another in time have very different values. Figure 2 shows that the adjacent values of the set entropy variable are relatively wide apart.

The autocorrelation can show these differences in the behavior of the series by correlating adjacent data points with one another. One autocorrelation coefficient can be obtained by correlating each data point with the one ahead of it. A second coefficient can be obtained by correlating values two time periods apart, and so on. The sizes of the autocorrelations can then be plotted against the distance between the points, or the *lags*. The graph is called the *correlogram*.

The sample autocorrelations are defined mathematically by:

$$r_k = \frac{c_k}{c_o} \tag{1}$$

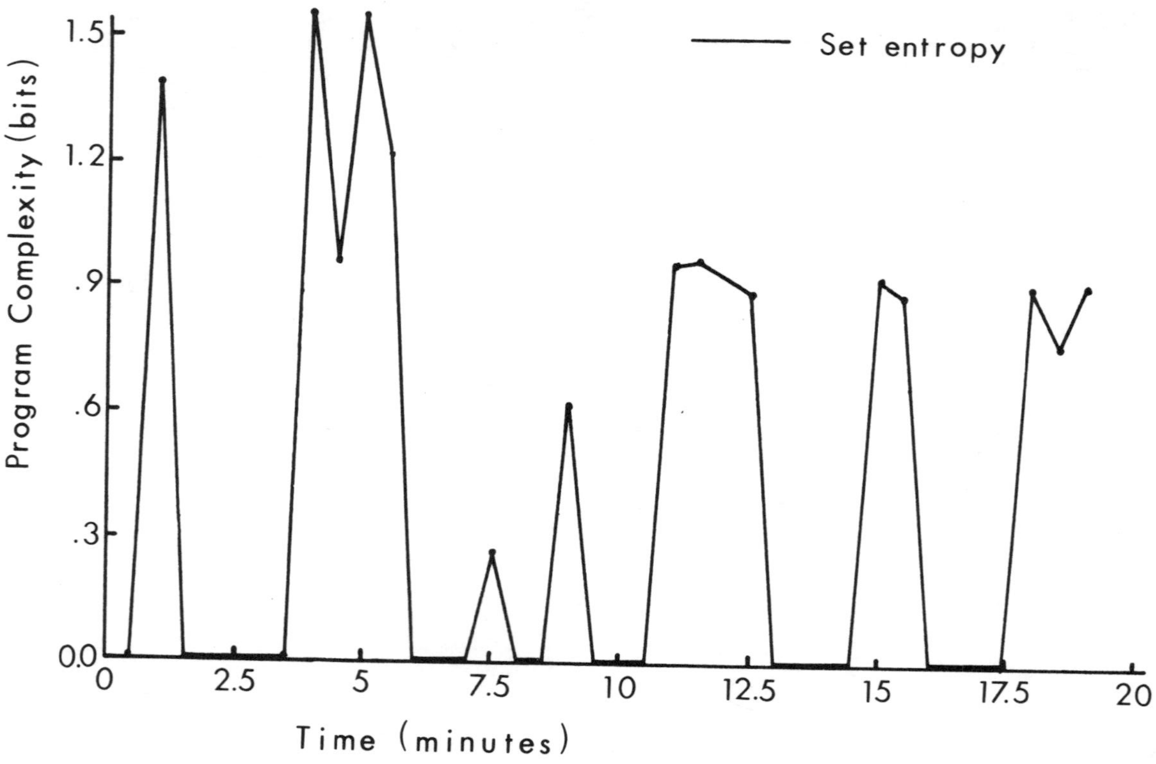

Figure 2: TELEVISION PROGRAM COMPLEXITY OF A VERSION OF THE ELECTRIC COMPANY

where

$$c_k = \frac{1}{N-k} \sum_{t=1}^{N-k} (x_t - \bar{x})(x_{t+k} - \bar{x}) \qquad [2]$$

and

$$\bar{x} = \frac{\Sigma x_t}{N}$$

Note that c_0 is just the variance of the x's and that the c_k's are cross-covariances between lagged data points.

Figure 3 gives the autocorrelations, r_k, for the children's attention series shown in Figure 1. One can see that the autocoorelation declines as the points correlated get farther apart. That is, as one moves away from any point in the series, the attention levels become less similar.

One can also interpret the autocorrelation in terms of the predictability of the series. For example, as one moves either forward or backward in time from any point in the series, the information about where attention was at the point chosen becomes less and less useful. One can predict less on the basis of the information one has and this is reflected in the decreasing autocorrelations. In the case of children's attention, the autocorrelation drops to .40 by moving 30 seconds, one measurement interval. This indicates that one can predict attention with 16% precision on the average (in terms of variance-accounted-for) at a lag of 30 seconds.

The smoother the series, the slower the autocorrelation drops to zero. Very jagged series are likely to produce autocorrelations which drop rapidly into negative values. The autocorrelations in Figure 3 indicate there are not likely to be sudden reversals in level of children's attention. The spike around 150 seconds would lead one to expect low or high values of attention at roughly 150 second intervals. The behavior of the series in Figure 1 seems to support this expectation, especially in the second half of the graph. On the other hand, the autocorrelations (for set entropy) in Figure 4 are very negative within 120 seconds, leading one to expect a large number of reversals from high to low complexity values in the series. The behavior of the latter series in Figure 2 seems to correspond to this behavior of the autocorrelations.

The Power Spectrum. The autocorrelation function contains a good deal of information concerning the time series (x_t). Sometimes, however, this information is difficult to extract because sampling variability may introduce misleading patterns into the autocorrelations. Another, mathematically equivalent, way of looking at this information often proves useful. This different perspective comes from a field called *Fourier analysis* or *spectral analysis* and is provided by the

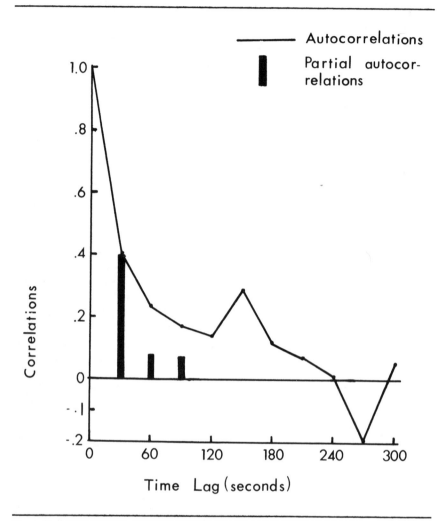

Figure 3: AUTOCORRELATIONS AND PARTIAL AUTOCORRELATIONS OF CHILDREN'S ATTENTION TO THE ELECTRIC COMPANY (test version)

Fourier cosine transform of either the autocovariance or the autocorrelation function.

This device is used to transform information about the series in the time domain into the,so-called, frequency domain with the hope that new facets of the time series will become evident. While the autocorrelation represents the relationship among parts of the series in terms of time lags, the object of this technique is to describe a series in terms of its dominant cyclical components. Interested readers should refer to other papers for the more elegant, but more

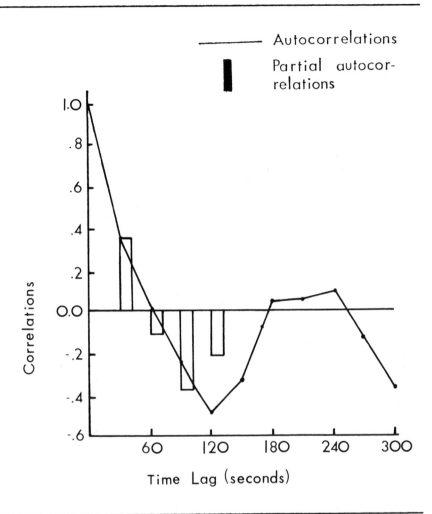

**Figure 4: AUTOCORRELATIONS AND PARTIAL AUTOCORRELATIONS OF TELE-
VISION PROGRAM COMPLEXITY**

complicated, solutions obtained through spectral analysis (Granger and Hatanaka, 1964; Jenkins and Watts, 1968; Bloomfield, 1976).

MODEL BUILDING

Model building in time series analysis is a complex process of comparing several alternate formulations which may fit the data nearly equally well. The purpose of model building is to explain the largest amount of variance in the series with the fewest possible coefficients. Parsimony is a particularly acute problem in time series analysis because one has to explain the interdependence among data points in simple series; and for transfer function models one has to add lags to explain the interdependence among independent variable data points and co-efficients explaining the relationship between the independent and dependent variables.

If an impelling theoretical model were available, the question of parsimony would generally be of marginal interest unless the theoretical model was dependent on a (relatively) large number of parameters. In the latter case the utilization of the model may be operationally unattractive and computationally intractable. The sensitivity of theoretical models to the number of parameters incorporated in these models and the agreement of them vis-à-vis empirical data also generates a concern for parsimony. Since the application of time series analysis to communications problems is so new, few theoretical guidelines for model building are available. An essentially empirical procedure is likely, therefore, to provide useful information and perhaps lead to development of theoretical models. Fortunately, judicious experimentation with independent and dependent variable coefficients usually provides a reasonable empirical solution with a small number of coefficients (Box and Jenkins, 1970).

Models may be built using either the time domain or frequency domain. The results are mathematically related, but some readers find one form easier to interpret than the other. This paper will concentrate on the time rather than frequency domain solutions.

In the following section we will discuss model building for single series. This is necessary before we can treat the more complicated independent-dependent variable models. The single variable formulations have become known as *ARIMA* models through the popularity of a particular text in the area (see Box and Jenkins, 1970). Models which relate dependent variables to one or more independent variables are called *Transfer Function* models. It should be noted that there are marked similarities between the ARIMA and Transfer Function models to be pointed out later.

ARIMA MODELS

ARIMA models (Auto-Regressive Integrated Moving Average Models) attempt to separate out trends and oscillatory components of a series so that only white noise remains. These models usually provide a good fit to the data with one, or generally not more than two, time lags taken into consideration. Determination of the optimum model involves examination of the autocorrelations, partial autocorrelations, the power spectrum, and the residuals left after the statistical model fitted is removed. In building up to ARIMA models we shall discuss autoregressive, moving average, and mixed models.

Autoregressive Models of Order p, AR(p). Autoregressive models describe the behavior of time series in terms of the interdependence between adjacent data points. In doing so they relate each data point to weighted functions of data points at preceding lags. The two quantities required to construct an autoregressive model are the number of lags to be included and the weights to be assigned. Choice of the appropriate number of lags, called the *order "p"* of the model, is suggested by the pattern of the autocorrelations and partial autocorrelations. An autoregressive model is of the form:

$$z_t = \phi_1 z_{t-1} + \phi_2 z_{t-2} + \ldots + \phi_p z_{t-p} \tag{3}$$

where: ϕ's are the autoregressive coefficients, z's are the observed values of the series as deviations from the mean of the series.

Partial autocorrelations in time series analysis correspond to ordinary partial correlations in cross-sectional analysis. A partial autocorrelation gives the correlation between two time points with the correlation among intermediate time points held constant. Partial autocorrelations are useful because they indicate which kind of model is likely to best fit the data. Whereas an AR(p) process has an autocorrelation function which is infinite in length, but which dies off exponentially to zero, the partial autocorrelations will be nonzero up to a point $(k \leqslant p)$ and then will be zero beyond that point $(k > p)$.

The formulas for obtaining the best estimates of the partial autocorrelations are complicated; the solution involves iterative determination of the optimal combination of coefficients. These formulas will not be given here (see Kendall and Stuart, 1968, and Box and Jenkins, 1970). However, computational formulas of low efficiency are essentially the same as those for the cross-sectional case except for some notational differences. These simpler versions have been used to compute the values given in the figures.

In Figure 3 the vertical black bars represent the first, second, and third partial autocorrelations of children's attention. The first partial matches the first lag autocorrelation because there are no intermediate correlations to hold constant. The second and third partials are both less than .10 and are not significantly larger than zero. This pattern indicates that the autocorrelations for lags greater than 30 seconds are spurious and the result of the decaying effect of the first lag autocorrelation. These results conform to requirements for data best fitted by an AR(p) model. The autocorrelations die off and the partial autocorrelations cut off after a first significant one. Now we know that the variable should be fitted with an AR model, but we do not know which one.

The number of lags included in an AR model corresponds to the number of non-zero partial autocorrelations. Children's attention would require one lag and would be called an AR(1) process. AR(1) processes are also called Markov processes. The value of the autoregression coefficient is very simple to determine for an AR(1) model, since it is equal to the first lag autocorrelation. A reasonable model for children's attention is as follows:

$$z_t = .40z_{t-1} + a_t$$

where a_t represents random error.

We can now summarize what this model tells us. We had outlined trends, two types of periodic functions, and white noise as components of time series. The AR model assumes there to be no trends in the data and expresses the dependency between adjacent data points produced by periodic functions through the correlation between time lags. In the case of children's attention, we have assumed the slight trend in the data to be of negligible significance and have fitted a model involving one time lag, an AR(1) model. This model says that each data point is dependent on only one preceding point and that the correlation between the points is .40. Although this correlation leaves a good deal of the variability in the variable unexplained, it also indicates some constraint on the amount of change in children's attention which could be produced by television program variables. Not taking this kind of constraint into account might lead one to misinterpret program effectiveness (see Carlsson, 1972, for a discussion of dependent variable causal lags and their effect on causal interpretations in general).

Moving Average Models of Order q, MA(q). Moving average models relate each data point to disturbances or errors. Recall that autoregression models relate each data point for a variable to previous values of the variable. The moving average process is defined as:

$$z_t = a_t - \theta_1 a_{t-1} - \ldots - \theta_q a_{t-q} \qquad [4]$$

where θ's are moving average coefficients, and a's are errors or random shocks.

Conceptually the moving average process is one which behaves such that the values of a variable at a point in time are a weighted average of a finite number of disturbances. As for the autoregressive process, one has to determine the number of lags needed and the weights to be assigned; but in this case, it is the number of disturbances and weights for the disturbances which have to be determined. The autocorrelations and their partials are used again. The computation of the weighted coefficients is more complex than for AR models, so only the results of the computations will be discussed here.

One should first discriminate here between a simple moving average and a moving average process. A simple moving average, or rolling average, is one of a set of techniques for removing random disturbances from data. If disturbances in a series are truly random they will probably have a mean of zero and will, therefore, average out over the whole series. However, the disturbances will introduce noise into the data and may make interpretation difficult. It is often advantageous in such cases to filter disturbances out.

Simple moving averages attempt to smooth data by using several adjacent data points to represent each point. The average value of each data point plus one, or more, to either side of it is taken to represent the point. It is expected that since the random disturbances average to zero over the series as a whole, some averaging out of the disturbances in each interval can occur and leave the series smoother.

A moving average model of a series operates in a related way. The model can be seen as a filter which operates on random disturbances by taking a weighted average of a finite number of adjacent disturbances. In other words, it produces smoothing by working more directly with the disturbances in a statistical way.

As before, the autocorrelations and partial autocorrelations provide information about whether or not a moving average process of order q, MA(q), would provide a good fit to the data. In general, the autocorrelations of MA processes cut off to zero at some point ($k \geqslant q$), and the partial autocorrelations die off smoothly. This pattern is the reverse of that shown by series fitted efficiently by AR models. Neither of the two series we have used as examples fits with the MA pattern. The set entropy television program variable has autocorrelations and partial autocorrelations which both die off. A model for data of this sort will be described in the next section on mixed models.

It should be noted that AR and MA models of time series are complementary. Series could be fitted with either model, but the choice of the wrong model will produce a very inefficient fit requiring a very large number of coefficients (see Box and Jenkins, 1970, for a full discussion of this point).

Autoregressive Moving Average Models, ARMA (p,q). As we mentioned, the set entropy television program variable did not conform to either of the models described so far. The variable's autocorrelations dropped exponentially like those of an AR process; and the partial autocorrelations dropped exponentially like those of an MA process. Although data such as these can be approximated inefficiently by either model, a more parsimonious method is to combine the AR(p) and MA(q) models into one ARMA (p,q) model. The ARMA model has the following form:

$$z_t = \phi_1 z_{t-1} + \phi_2 z_{t-2} + \ldots + \phi_p z_{t-p} - \theta_1 a_{t-1} - \ldots - \theta_q a_{t-q} \qquad [5]$$

where: the ϕ's, θ's, z's and a's are defined as before.

Both the autocorrelations and partial autocorrelations of such a process tail off, and the set entropy series would, therefore, be more efficiently fitted with this model. Several ARMA models were fitted to the data, but none of them explained much variance. A closer examination showed a strong cyclical trend of about 210 seconds. It was necessary to remove this cycle before a model could be fitted. This procedure is described in the next section.

The Integrated Autoregressive Moving Average Model, ARIMA (p,d,q). It is possible to reduce many types of nonstationary time series to stationary ones by transforming the series. Trends can be seen as a simple form of nonstationarity and sometimes can be removed from the data by differencing the series. An ARMA (p,q) model becomes an ARIMA (p,d,q) model when the data modeled is differenced to order "d". More complicated forms of nonstationarity, such as the changes in character of the children's attention series in Figure 1, are not possible to remove through differencing.

If the nonstationarity is due to a linear trend, then a first difference suffices. For quadratic trends, second differences effect stationarity, and so on. First differencing involves subtracting each data point from the one ahead of it and produces a series $\Delta x_t = x_t - x_{t-1}, t = 2, 3, \ldots, N$; where the x's are data points and N is the number of observations. Second differences are formed from the x_t's in the same way to yield a series $\Delta(\Delta x) = \Delta^2 x_t = x_t - 2x_{t-1} + x_{t-2}$. The ARIMA (p,d,q) process may be written in terms of the ARMA (p,q) process as follows:

$$\Delta^d(z_t - \phi_1 z_{t-1} - \phi_2 z_{t-2} - \cdots - \phi_p z_{t-p})$$
$$= a_t - \theta_1 a_{t-1} -, \ldots - \theta_q a_{t-q}$$

[6]

It is possible to handle a wide variety of time series with this general model with relatively small values of p,d, and q. ARIMA models are important for our purposes because any covariance stationary process can be approximated arbitrarily closely by either an AR(p) or MA(q) process, provided p and q are sufficiently large (Anderson, 1971). The ARMA process adds parsimony because it is more flexible than the AR or MA processes; and the differencing of order d in ARIMA models allows handling of certain kinds of nonstationarity.

We found that differencing was ineffective in removing the effects of a 210 second (7 lag) cycle from the set entropy data. This may have been due, in part, to the high degree of differencing required combined with the shortness of the series available, 38 points. A solution to the problem was to fit an estimate of the cycle to the data using Fourier methods, remove the fitted curve, and then find an ARIMA model for the residuals.

We found that the cycle of 210 seconds accounted for 39% of the variance in set entropy. When this cycle was removed, an ARMA(1,1) model accounting for an additional 24% of the variance was fitted. In total this rather unorthodox "ARIMA" model accounted for 63% of the variance in set entropy. The equation for the model, with J_7 representing the contribution of the cycle, is

$$X_t = .63J_7 - .80X_{t-1} + 1.23a_{t-1} + a_t$$

We have not described procedures by which the parameters in standard ARIMA models are estimated. There is a general computational procedure (Box and Jenkins, 1970, Chaps. 6-9), but its description is beyond the scope of this article. Packaged computing routines providing estimates of the parameters are readily available. The reader should be aware, however, that to a degree the determination of the best parameter values is as yet a combination of art and science.

Although these models are essentially single variable models, the effects of causal variables appear by affecting the AR correlations between observations and the MA correlations between disturbance terms. Therefore, these models can encompass external influences implicitly without requiring their measurement or explicit inclusion through causal links in a model. There are some situations in which this would be advantageous because measurement is very difficult or because causal links may be very complicated. This would be a weakness in other situations where one wanted to examine causal relationships between independent and dependent variables directly. As mentioned previously, models including both independent and dependent variable terms are called transfer function models. We shall now describe transfer function models and show their relationship to ARIMA models.

TRANSFER FUNCTION MODELS

Transfer function models do require adding independent variable terms to the models we have discussed so far; but, fortunately, the additional terms can be seen as merely an extension of earlier models. The ARIMA model, given in equation 6, can be re-written as an infinite weighted sum of disturbance terms:

$$z_t = \sum_{j=0}^{\infty} \psi_j a_{t-j} \qquad [7]$$

Here the input is white noise, a_t, and is related to the variable, z_t, by the transfer function with coefficient ψ_j. The coefficients in the transfer function are called the impulse response function. The function (7) describes the response of the dependent variable to input which occurs randomly without any dependencies of its own. For more general input, the transfer function will have to take account of the interdependency between lags of the independent variable.

An equation for the case of a single independent variable (X_t) and a single dependent variable (Y_t) can be written in a form analogous to equation 6 as:

$$Y_t - \delta_1 Y_{t-1} - \dots - \delta_r Y_{t-r} = \omega_b X_{t-b}$$
$$+ \omega_1 X_{t-b-1} + \dots + \omega_s X_{t-b-s} \qquad [8]$$

Here the Y_t are analogous to the autoregressive lags of the ARMA model and the X_t are analogous to the random a_t disturbances of the moving average lags of the ARMA model. The subscript "b" in the equation refers to the delay between the action of the independent variable and the response of the dependent variable. Equation 8 can also be written in the same form as equation 7 under some rather mild assumptions (Box and Jenkins, 1970, pp. 345 et seq.):

$$Y_t = \sum_{j=0}^{\infty} \lambda_j X_{t-j-b} \qquad [9]$$

where the λ_j may be determined from equation 8.

As before, the coefficients λ_j are called the impulse response function and the whole equation is called the transfer function. Random error can be entered into the equation as a white noise term N_t (or in a more complicated form if one has additional information). The equation then becomes:

$$Y_t = \sum_{j=0}^{\infty} \lambda_j X_{t-j-b} + N_t \qquad [10]$$

Because equation 10 requires an infinite number of coefficients, it is not as convenient to use as a transfer function model as is equation 8. Computational packages for estimating coefficients for equation 8 are available, but a detailed description of the procedures is beyond this paper.

A spectral approach may also be useful in assessing the relationships between independent and dependent variables, but its application is more difficult and also requires a larger number of data points than we have available for the example problem. Further discussion of spectral methods for this purpose can be found in Jenkins and Watts (1968), Granger and Hatanaka (1964) and Hannan (1970).

Procedural Statistics. The autocorrelation coefficients used in identifying ARIMA models will also be used to identify transfer function models. In addition to the autocorrelations we will make use of the cross-correlation function. The cross-correlation is simply the ordinary cross-sectional correlation between the independent and dependent variables computed at different time lags. This can be seen by examining the following.

The cross-covariance coefficient at lag k is given by

$$c_{xy}(k) = \frac{1}{n-k} \sum_{n-k}^{N-k} (x_t - \bar{x})(y_{t+k} - \bar{y}) \qquad [11]$$

for $k = 0, 1, 2, \ldots,$ or

$$c_{xy}(k) = \frac{1}{n-k} \sum_{t=1}^{N-k} (y_t - \bar{y})(x_{t-k} - \bar{x}) \qquad [12]$$

for $k = 0, -1, -2, \ldots$.

Dividing the cross-covariance by the standard deviations of the variables X_t and Y_t provides the cross-correlation coefficient.

$$r_{xy}(k) = \frac{c_{xy}(k)}{S_x S_y}, \quad k = 0, \pm 1, \ldots$$

It should be noted that the correlations at positive (k) and negative lags (−k) are generally not equal.

The cross-correlation can be used to give information about the amount of delay between changes in the independent variable and changes in the dependent variable, the strength of the relationship between the two variables and the duration of the causal effect. However, the cross-correlation cannot provide all of this information by itself. It is necessary to take into account the autocorrelations of the independent and dependent variables. We will discuss how this is done in the section on model building. Let us look more closely at the cross-correlation by examining the relationship between children's attention to the television screen and television program complexity.

The pattern one would typically expect for an unambiguous set of cross-correlations is given in Figure 5. The abscissa in the graph gives the lag between the independent and dependent variables; the ordinate gives the magnitude of the correlation at a given lag. The correlations are nonsignificant (close to zero except for sampling variability) up to a point. Then the correlations show a significant negative or positive peak, followed by nonsignificant correlations. The time period between zero lag and the correlation peak is indicative of the causal lag between the independent and dependent variables. The spread of the peak is indicative of the duration of the effect.

Figure 6 shows the graph of the cross-correlations between program set entropy, and children's attention. The figure also shows the cross-correlations between another program variable called nonverbal dependence entropy and attention. This program variable and its cross-correlations will be described in a following section. At negative time lags, set entropy is negatively correlated with children's attention. At positive time lags, the program variable is positively correlated with children's attention. This set of correlations is somewhat at variance with the expected pattern described for cross-correlations above.

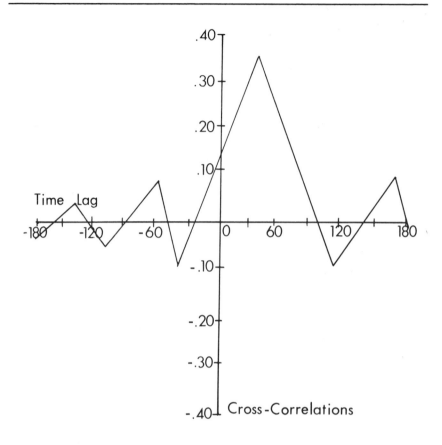

Figure 5: CROSS-CORRELATIONS EXPECTED FOR A CLEAN CAUSAL RELATION-SHIP

We had expected that the cross-correlations would be near zero until a certain time interval and that they would then become either strongly positive or strongly negative, and that they would then again be near zero. Instead we have significant negative correlations at negative lags and significant positive correlations at positive time lags. The positive lag correlations are fairly easy to explain. Since the cross-correlations from the zero lag to the 90 second lag are all positively significant for the relationship between set entropy and attention, it appears that as set entropy increase children's attention increases almost immediately and remains high for about 90 seconds.

The correlations at the negative time lags are somewhat more difficult to explain. Correlations at negative lags indicate that changes in the dependent variable precede in time changes in the independent variable. This can indicate

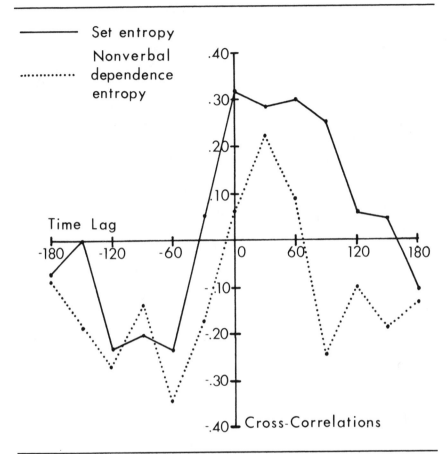

**Figure 6: CROSS-CORRELATIONS BETWEEN CHILDREN'S ATTENTION AND TELE-
VISION PROGRAM COMPLEXITY**

that the causal order between the independent and dependent variables is the reverse of that expected. In our example, if the correlations at positive time lags were zero, the negative time lag correlations would seem to indicate that increases in children's attention produced decreases in set entropy. That is, the correlations would indicate that children's attention was really the causal variable and the television program complexity is really the effect. This can hardly be the case. The existence of the positive correlations at positive lags makes the situation even more complicated.

Jenkins and Watts (1968) argue that this pattern of cross-correlations can be produced by either mutual causation of the variables or by a causal factor outside the model causing changes in both variables. The second explanation would simply mean that we have left out some relevant television situation variable, possibly a program variable. The first of Jenkins and Watts's explanations extends rather interestingly to television viewing. One might well argue that when television program complexity increases, children respond relatively rapidly to the change by increasing their attention to the set. Before program complexity increases (at negative time lags), children pay low levels of attention. For children to be able to do this they must know the show sufficiently well to be able to anticipate changes in program complexity. In a way they "make" the program higher in complexity by ignoring (paying less attention to) the show during low complexity intervals in anticipation of higher complexity segments to follow. A good deal of research would be required to validate this hypothesis.

TRANSFER FUNCTION MODEL BUILDING

Two procedural statistics, the autocorrelations and the cross-correlations, are used to construct equations for transfer functions in the time domain. In addition, the residuals are examined to determine how well the model used fits the data. In some cases, the models to be fitted are rather simple, and ordinary regression may be used once the model is identified. When the models are more complex, especially in the error structure, the procedures of Box and Jenkins are preferable.

Several models for the relationship between set entropy and children's attention were examined. We assumed that the cross-correlations at negative lags, indicating some anticipation by children, could be ignored in searching for a simple, but not optimal, model. For each case we used ordinary multiple regression and examined the residuals to detect departures from randomness. The best transfer function found was

$$Y_t = .29Y_{t-1} + .39X_t + .27X_{t-3} + e_t$$

where Y_t is children's attention and X_t is set entropy. One could diagram this relationship in path analysis form as in Figure 7, although the procedure is not generally used in the time series literature.

This model was surprisingly good in a number of respects. First, given the difficulty of fitting an ARIMA model to the set entropy data, obtaining a good simple fit here was unexpected. Second, the model fitted accounts for a good deal of variance in children's attention as indicated by the multiple correlation of .56 ($F = 4.68$; $p < .01$; d.f. = 3,31). Third, the residuals are not severely disturbed.

Taken together, these results seem to indicate that, for this test version of The Electric Company, children's attention depends on both previous attention and on two different time lags of set entropy. The advantages gained by using time series methodology in this instance were a three-fold increase in variance-accounted-for in children's attention over the simple cross-sectional correlation

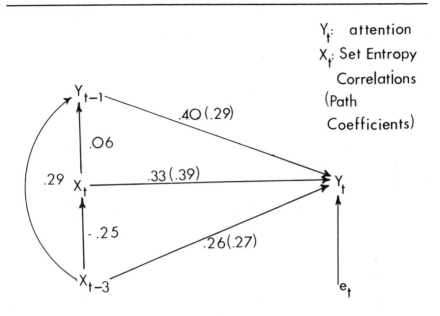

Figure 7: PATH MODEL OF TRANSFER FUNCTION BETWEEN SET ENTROPY AND ATTENTION

and the information that about three time periods (about 90 seconds total lag) of the television program ought to be taken into consideration. More complicated fitting procedures could have been used to obtain coefficients explaining more variance, but this seemed unnecessary for the purposes of this paper. If empirical models of this form were found to hold for a larger sample of programs in this series, one would have a strong basis for the development of a theoretical model.

The set entropy program variable behaves in a rather complicated way, but there is some indication that this may not be typical of television program variables in general. For example, nonverbal dependence entropy, a measure of the degree to which both visual and verbal parts of a program are used to convey information, was found to be an AR(1) process from data on the sample program (see Watt and Krull, 1974, for a description of this variable). The cross-correlation for this variable was given in Figure 6.

Although there was some indication of anticipation in the relationship between children's attention and nonverbal dependence entropy, a simple regression transfer function with the program variable as a predictor was obtained when anticipation was handled in the same way as before

$$Y_t = .40Y_{t-1} + .23X_{t-1} + e_t$$

where Y_t is children's attention and X_t is nonverbal dependence entropy. A path diagram is given in Figure 8.

The multiple correlation of the variables in the equation and attention is .46. The more usual procedure, using cross-sectional rather than time series techniques, would have been to correlate children's attention scores with nonverbal dependence entropy scores for the same time interval. That would yield a correlation of .08. The improvement of the time series procedure over the usual one is a 33-fold increase in the amount of variance accounted for in attention. However, nonverbal dependence entropy is still not a powerful predictor of attention even in the time series setting. A sample size of 75 time points would be needed to make the path coefficient of .23 significant at .05 level.

Since this relationship was so simple we attempted to reverse the theoretical causal order to see how that transfer function would turn out. This analogous procedure for the prediction of nonverbal dependence entropy from children's attention yields the following equation

$$X_t = .20X_{t-1} - .34Y_{t-2} + e_t$$

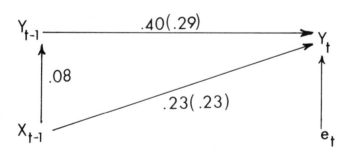

Y_t: attention

X_t: Nonverbal Dependence

Correlations (Path Coefficients)

Figure 8: PATH MODEL OF TRANSFER FUNCTION FOR NONVERBAL DEPENDENCE AND ATTENTION

In words, this program complexity variable is positively correlated with itself at the preceding time period and negatively correlated with the children's attention at two preceding time periods. This relationship would not have been examined at all without time series analysis. What it means is a theoretical problem which goes beyond the technique that revealed it.

OTHER RESEARCH APPLICATIONS OF TIME SERIES

At the beginning of this paper we indicated that we would describe a technique allowing an assessment of the time order of variables, and the lag, the size, and the duration of causal relationships in communication research. We have used the example from television viewing research to illustrate the statistics and modeling procedures needed. The example has shown some of the problems typically encountered in attempting to use this method—shortness of series, non-stationarity of processes, and possible mutual causation. However, the example has also shown that the more usual methods of assessing relationships may underestimate the strength of causal links and that marked increases in explanatory power may be obtained by use of time series analysis. To illustrate how time series methods could be used to treat different communications problems, we will briefly describe potential research projects from three additional areas— nonverbal communication, small group communication and persuasion.

One issue frequently treated in nonverbal behavioral research is the relationship of nonverbal cues to the perception of emotions by observers. Related issues include the determination of which cues are relevant, the size of the relationship between cues, and the perception in time. This kind of problem would be amenable to time series analysis because a fairly large number of data points should be obtainable in a running interaction.

A study design could involve the coding of nonverbal behavior over time, the assessment by observers (subjects) of the emotions displayed, and statistical analysis by time series methods. The autocorrelations, spectra and ARIMA models could give information about interdependencies and cycles in nonverbal behavior. For example, are there cycles in smiling? Transfer functions could be used to determine the lead or lag of, for example, smiling with respect to the perception of the smiler's being friendly. Is smiling a behavior which follows a person's being perceived as friendly on other bases, or is it actually the cause of one's being perceived as friendly at that moment?

One could use time series analysis in small group research to see the effect of communication content on interaction patterns. One issue in this area might be how the proportion of task related comments made by members affected the rate of interaction. Again, data could probably be generated relatively rapidly over a short period of time so that a sufficient number of points for time series analysis would be available.

A study design for this topic could include the coding of comments for their task relatedness and coding of interaction for the number of comments made by each individual over time. Time series statistical analysis could include assessment of interdependence and cycles in both task related comments and rate of interaction by autocorrelations, spectra and ARIMA models; and transfer functions could be used to determine how long changes in the interaction rate took to appear after comments by group members became more or less task related.

Time series analysis could be used to assess the effect of mass media content on public opinion. One could determine whether mass media content lagged or led changes in public opinion, and which media were more in step than others with public opinion. The difficulty with running such a study would be scoring public opinion over a long period of time. Fortunately, if sample groups of respondents could be taken as fairly equivalent, different individuals could be used at different time points and inter-sample differences would probably appear as high frequency noise which could be filtered out by methods described in a preceding section.

A study design in this area could involve coding of media content on a particular topic and assessment of public opinion on the same issue (probably through existing records), both done over time. Time series statistics could be used to show the pattern in mass media content and public opinion individually over time. Are there cycles in public opinion, for example? Then one could attempt to find a transfer function between media content and opinion to show how much content leads or lags opinion. One could also see if certain media move with public opinion relatively closely, while other media are more strongly related to public opinion although they operate at greater lag periods.

We hope that these examples and the discussion of time series methods in this paper have provided an appreciation of the value of these techniques. Working with them may appear more complicated than it really is because of the amount of unfamiliar terminology (see appended Glossary). We expect that with increased use of these methods the terminology will become more familiar to most researchers through exposure to the literature and that a coherent set of mathematical notation will be developed which is more closely aligned with that used in communication research.

APPENDIX:

A GLOSSARY OF TIME SERIES TERMINOLOGY

Autocorrelation Coefficient. An analog of correlation which assesses the dependence between all the corresponding values of a single variable separated by a given time period, or lag. It is the representation of interdependence among all values of the output variable separated by time lag k.

Autoregressive Process (AR). A time series where previous values of the output variable enter into the determination of the current value.

Autoregressive/Moving Average Process (ARMA). A time series where previous values of the output variables (observable) in combination with current and previous values of the input variable (non-observable) enter into the determinattion of the current value of the output series.

Continuous Time Series. The output variable is a continuous function of time and hence may be sampled at *any* set of distinct time points (no matter how close together).

Cross-Correlation Coefficient. An analog of correlation which assesses the dependence between two variables whose values are measured at time periods separated by a given lag.

Cyclical Models. Values of the variable are expressed as functions of the strengths of theoretically underlying cycles in the process.

Delay. Time difference, or lag, between the action of the independent variable and the response of the dependent variable.

Differencing. A procedure for removing long-term trends from a variable by subtracting the preceding value from each current value of the variable.

Discrete Time Series. Values of the variable are available at separate, usually equally spaced, intervals only.

Fourier Analysis. Decomposition of the values of a variable into weighted sums of the sines and cosines of cycles representing the series.

Identification. The process of using statistical and visual properties of time series in both the time and frequency domains to arrive at a hypothetical model which will adequately and efficiently represent the series of interest.

Impulse Response Function. The set of coefficients in a transfer function specifying the reaction of a variable to a change in an input variable.

Integrated Autoregressive/Moving Average Process (ARIMA). A time series where previous values of the output variables (observable) in combination with current and previous values of the input variable (non-observable) enter into the determination of the current value of the output series after differencing the series to produce stationarity.

Lag. The time difference of two values of a variable (or variables) considered together.

Moving Average. Current values of a variable are expressed as a mathematical combination of past, current and future values of the variables. The simplest combination is the mean of adjacent values, but a variety of weighting combinations can also be used.

Moving Average Processes. A time series where current and previous values of the input variables enter into the determination of the current value of the output variable.

Partial Autocorrelations. An analog of partial correlation which assesses the dependence of values of a variable separated at fixed lag with the effect of an intervening lag held constant.

Spectrum. Or power spectrum, assesses the strength of cycles underlying the time series of a variable. It is the Fourier cosine transform of the autocovariance function, and is the representation of interdependence among adjacent values of a variable in the frequency domain.

Stationary. A time series is stationary if any translation of the time origin leaves its statistical properties unaffected.

Time Series. A set of data, usually measured at equispaced points in time.

Transfer Function. The set of coefficients linking current values of a dependent variable to past values of the dependent variable and current and past values of one or more independent variables.

Trend. A long-term movement of data points to either side of the mean of the series.

REFERENCES

ANDERSON, T.W. (1971). The statistical analysis of time series. New York: John Wiley.

BLACKMAN, R.B., and TUKEY, J.W. (1958). The measurement of power spectra. New York: Dover.

BLOOMFIELD, P. (1976). Fourier analysis of time series: An introduction. New York: John Wiley.

BOX, G.E.P., and JENKINS, G.M. (1970). Time series analysis: Forecasting and control. San Francisco: Holden-Day.

CARLSSON, G. (1972). "Lagged structures and cross-sectional methods." Acta Sociologica, 15:323-341.

DRAPER, N.R., and SMITH, H. (1972). Applied regression analysis. New York: John Wiley.

GRANGER, C.W.J., and HATANAKA, M. (1964). Spectral analysis of economic timer series. Princeton, N.J.: Princeton University Press.

HANNAN, E.J. (1970). Multiple time series. New York: John Wiley.

HEISE, D.R. (1970). "Causal inference from panel data." Pp. 3-27 in E.F. Borgatta (ed.), Sociological methodology. San Francisco: Jossey-Bass.

JENKINS, G.M., and WATTS, D.G. (1968). Spectral analysis and its applications. San Francisco: Holden-Day.

KENDALL, M.G., and STUART, A. (1968). Advanced theory of statistics, Vol. III. New York: Hafner.

MALINVAUD, E. (1970). Statistical methods of econometrics. New York: American Elsevier.

WATT, J.H., and KRULL, R. (1974). " information theory measure for television programming." Communication Research, 1(1):44-68.

WONNACOTT, R.J., and WONNACOTT, T.H. (1970). Econometrics. New York: John Wiley.

Chapter 13

SAMPLING ACROSS TIME FOR COMMUNICATION RESEARCH: A SIMULATION

Robert B. Arundale

IN 1970 JAFFE AND FELDSTEIN reported the results of a series of studies on "speaker switching" in dyadic communication. Among many findings on the patterns of speech and silence in dialogue, they demonstrated (1970:4) "the utility of a rule . . . which specifies the *interdependence* of the participants in a dialogue" (emphasis mine). That is, within the time sampling framework they employed, they found that the probability of a participant's being in a state of, say, silence, at one time point depended upon the state occupied by the *dyad* at the immediately preceding point.

Concurrent and similar research by Hayes, Meltzer, and Wolf (1970:267) yielded conflicting results. Their data favored "an *independence* model [which] postulates that each interactor's behavior is independent of the previous acts of other group members, but rather is dependent only upon *one's own* previous acts" (emphasis mine). Hayes et al. explained the strikingly different conclusions from these quite similar studies by noting that in indexing the states of each ongoing dyadic conversation, they had sampled across time almost twice as frequently as Jaffe and Feldstein. Hayes et al. (1970:268) concluded that the decision regarding how frequently to sample "may have profound effects on the conclusions drawn from the data," but they did not pursue the issue.

The conflicting conclusions of these two speaker switching studies highlight a much more general principle in communication research: In studies of change over time, a close relationship exists between how one samples across time and the validity of the conclusions one can draw from the data. More specifically, in the absence of representative sampling across time, the data simply do not contain the information one needs to draw valid conclusions about change over time.[1] This article provides not only a general guideline for designing research that achieves representative sampling across time, but also a study of the effects that following or ignoring that guideline can have on research results. Three issues must be clarified before the guideline can be developed.

SAMPLING ACROSS TIME

First, the term "sampling" as in "sampling across time" has three possible senses: (1) sampling from a population of persons or events at two or more points in time, as in a panel study or in taking two random samples from a city to assess attitudes before and after a campaign (see McCombs, Becker, and Weaver, 1975); (2) sampling from a set of time-ordered measurements on some variable, as in taking a sample totaling one hour from an interaction analysis of a three-hour discussion (see Stech and Goldberg, 1972); or (3) sampling or indexing the value of a variable at each of a series of time-ordered points, as in categorizing the type of student-teacher interaction taking place once every three seconds. In this article, "sampling across time" refers exclusively to sense (3), and it will become apparent that representative sampling in this sense is a prerequisite to valid results in frameworks (1) and (2).

Second, a brief consideration of the concept of a "state space" will provide the means for clarifying the key concepts of "communication variable" and "time." Briefly, the "state" of some variable, like the *location* of an aircraft or the *attitude* held on an issue, can be described only in reference to the "space" defined by some dimension or set of dimensions like latitude, longitude, altitude, or the evaluative dimension of a semantic differential. Within such a "state space" one can readily conceptualize and measure the *difference* between two distinct locations or attitudes. But one cannot describe the *change* in a location or an attitude without simultaneously referring to the separate dimension of time. Such change is often of interest, not in and of itself, but as it relates to another variable in a different state space—whether that variable is time-independent (as, for example, aircraft weight or message intensity) or is itself time-referenced (e.g., a sequence of direction changes or of persuasive messages). In short, in discussions of change over time, *"time" is not a variable with explanatory force.* "Time" is, instead, "clock time" or the referent dimension that enables one to conceptualize and describe the change over time in communication variables that do have explanatory force.[2]

Third, by applying the distinction between "continuous" and "discrete" quantities both to the state of a variable and to time, one creates a four-part classification of processes useful at several points in the article:

(a) continuous state—continuous time process

(b) continuous state—discrete time process

(c) discrete state—continuous time process

(d) discrete state—discrete time process

This classification may be applied to a given process (1) as it is theoretically conceptualized, (2) as it has been indexed by a measurement procedure, and (3) as it is treated by an analytic technique. One may thus *conceptualize* "attitude" as a continuous variable that changes across continuous time; one may *measure* a particular attitude on a continuous scale (like a semantic differential), but in discrete time (before and after some event); and one may treat this same attitude in *analysis* in terms of both discrete states (pro, neutral, and con) and discrete time. If a variable is conceptualized as discrete, it will be clearly inappropriate to measure or analyze it as continuous, just as it is inappropriate to apply analysis techniques assuming continuous data (ratio or interval) to discrete data (ordinal or nominal).

Classifying time as continuous or discrete is basic to another important and closely related distinction—one that is often overlooked. When time is used as a referent dimension for studying change, it is almost always conceptualized as continuous, and is frequently measured accordingly. But there are two approaches to continuous measurement of time: *analog* measurement, as in the moving paper tape of a chart recorder; or *digital* measurement, as in the recording of a sequence of times like 0.0, 2.5, 5.0, 7.5 seconds, and so on. Note that digital measurement does not necessarily render the time dimension discrete, nor does it necessitate the use of a discrete time analytic technique, because the requirements of continuous measurement are usually met. (Truly discrete measurement of time, as in "before and after" or "trial number 8," will thus be considered only briefly here.)

Separating the analog versus digital distinction from the continuous versus discrete time classification makes it clear that virtually all study of change over time in communication research involves not only digital measurement, but also digital analysis of time. In other words, it involves both data and analyses keyed to a series of distinct points in time—"sampling across time" for short. But digital treatment of time has one potentially serious drawback not present in analog measurement and analysis. If one indexes the state of a variable at each point in a series of time points, the resulting data will not always accurately represent the change in that variable. Indeed, there is an identifiable sampling interval beyond which digital sampling across time fails to produce a complete representation of the change in the variable under study. Because most communication research into change over time involves the digital treatment of time, a guideline that specifies this critical sampling interval is important.[3]

A GUIDELINE

Adequate sampling across time of a communication variable requires a researcher to evaluate the relationship between the interval at which sampling occurs and certain time-linked characteristics of the change in that variable.

Alternatively, the choice of a sampling interval along the time dimension determines the degree to which the data on change over time represent the information potentially available in the state space. An analogy may help: The effect of the sampling interval on the information contained in one's data in many ways resembles the capability of a given microscope to resolve objects in its field. An optical microscope has a lower limit on its ability to resolve or to distinguish among small features determined in part by the wavelength of visible light. An electron microscope has a considerably greater resolving power and can therefore distinguish among much smaller features, in large part because the wavelength of its electron beam is much shorter than the wavelength of visible light.

The parallel to the resolution phenomenon in communications engineering has been known for three decades and is embodied in the Sampling Theorem (Cherry, 1957:140-143; Gabor, 1946). This theorem applies to all continuous state—continuous time variables. It holds that as long as a variable contains no component frequency higher than a given frequency, f, that variable (or "signal") will be specified *completely* by distinct (or digital) measurements spaced at intervals of 1/2f. Because the wavelength, w, of a given frequency equals 1/f, the sampling interval becomes w/2 or one half the wavelength of f, the highest frequency. In other words, given an arbitrary sampling interval, Δt, the data produced by separate measurements made at this interval will *not* provide complete information on those components of the signal under study with a wavelength (or "cycle length") less than 2Δt.

The Sampling Theorem forms the basis for the guidance available in the communications engineering literature on how frequently one should sample across time to obtain representative data. Unfortunately, this guidance has had little direct value for researchers in human communication, both because it has not been widely available and because it exists in a form directly applicable only to continuous state—continuous time variables.[4] A researcher who can obtain continuous measurement of the state of a communication variable may choose from a broad range of techniques for analyzing change over time. But it is not always possible to meet the requirements of interval or ratio measurement in human communication research. More importantly, there exists a large class of communication variables that are conceptualized as discrete, as for example, the states of a dyadic conversation or one's knowledge of a particular news event. Because the available guidance on sampling across time does not cover the important case of discrete state variables, the guideline developed in this article focuses on choosing a sampling interval when the communication variable is conceptualized or measured as discrete.

The guideline for sampling across time from a discrete state variable can be formulated most directly by constructing an analogy to the continuous state case considered in the Sampling Theorem. (The guideline can be developed formally, as well.) If a discrete state variable has two possible states, x and z, one can define its "cycle length" as a time period that begins as the variable enters state x, continues while it remains in state x, moves to and remains in state z, and ends as it exits from state z. If the minimum time the variable can remain in state x equals the time for state z, then the cycle length is twice this shortest "sojourn time" for x and z. But because in the more general case a variable may have one state or component with a minimum sojourn time less than that for any other state, one must define the "*minimum* cycle length" as twice the shortest time interval for which the variable can remain in any one of its states. The Sampling Theorem suggests, then, that for one's data to represent all states or components *completely*, one must index the variable at intervals equal to or less than half this minimum cycle length. The guideline for complete resolution when sampling across time from a discrete state variable follows directly: *The sampling interval must be equal to (or shorter than) the shortest time interval for which the variable under study can remain in any one of its states.*[5]

This key guideline may appear at first to be "intuitively obvious." It is less obvious that given a specific sampling interval, Δt, the data that result cannot provide fully accurate information on any variable having a state with a minimum sojourn time of less than Δt. Nor will the data completely represent any cycle length that is less than $2\Delta t$. To the extent that the theoretical conclusions drawn from a study depend on information about states with minimum sojourn times shorter than Δt, those conclusions will be either unwarranted or invalid because the data simply do not fully represent the occurrence of the states.

In actual practice, achieving adequate sampling across time means choosing an appropriate sampling interval in the planning stages of a study. The choice depends on the characteristics of the variable under study, just as one chooses to use an electron microscope if the structures are too small to be resolved optically. Alternately, if a particular sampling interval has already been employed, one knows both the size of the smallest intervals that can be resolved and the limits that must be placed on the theoretical conclusions. The guideline may be used both in this *a priori* or prospective sense, and in this *post hoc* or retrospective sense. The study described in this article provides the basis for considering both uses.

DESIGN

The guideline just developed is widely applicable: It provides a standard for sampling across time from any discrete state variable in a variety of research contexts, including interaction analyses, cross-sectional studies, and multiple time point experimental or quasi-experimental designs. The data such sampling produces may be analyzed using a number of techniques, including Markov chain analysis, constraint analysis (Ashby, 1958), and Krippendorff's (1971) categorical equivalent to analysis of variance.

Any study of how sampling across time affects research results must focus on one such research context. This study focused on the interaction analysis of speaker switching, coupled with Markov chain analysis, first, because speaker switching is a fundamental property of dyads which has recently attracted researchers (e.g., Wiemann and Knapp, 1975) interested in discovering the rules governing this basic social communication context. Second, speaker switching is conceptualized as discrete, but is relatively manageable, being typically studied using four states: (1) silence, (2) person A talking, (3) person B talking, and (4) simultaneous speech. Third, speaker switching is susceptible to interaction analysis, which makes the study representative of the use of this general approach. Fourth, the phenomenon can be described by and analyzed as a Markov chain because it meets the assumptions inherent in the use of this technique (Jaffe and Feldstein, 1970: 51-95). Markov chain analysis is particularly appropriate given its increasingly wide use as an analytic tool in human communication research in the last few years, as for example in Cappella (1976), Hawes and Foley (1973, 1974), Hewes (1975a,b), and Hewes and Evans-Hewes (1974). Finally, while Hayes et al. (1970), Jaffe and Feldstein (1970), and Scheidel (1974) have all studied various aspects of the problem of choosing a sampling interval in the context of speaker switching studies, none has considered the more general issues it raises.

DATA AND PROCEDURES

The author chose a simulation approach to produce the speaker switching data, both to avoid potential instrumentation problems and to assure that the data met the assumptions required for the use of Markov chain analysis. Jaffe and Feldstein (1970:116-117, 123-130) discuss the problems and variables in the laboratory instrumentation used to study speaker switching, and suggest how these factors both may vary with researchers and their equipment, and may interact differentially with the sampling interval, especially at short intervals. Generating the data by simulation avoids these problems, and affords precise, a priori knowledge of the information actually contained in the variable under study—a necessary referent for examining how well various sampling intervals resolve that information.

Furthermore, because it is difficult to assess differences in resolution except as some analytic technique is applied, the assumptions underlying the technique must be met. While speaker switching data generally meet the assumptions for Markov chain analysis, there is no assurance that the data gathered in actual observational contexts will always do so. Producing data by simulation assures that the generative mechanism meets the required assumptions and that no measurement effects intervene to alter these characteristics. Similar problems of meeting assumptions and of instrumentation led Tick and Shaman (1966) to adopt a simulation approach in generating the data in their study of sampling effects in continuous state variables.

Following the simulation method described by Halperin and Lissitz (1971), the author generated nine separate series of speaker switching states from the empirically derived transition probability matrices provided by Jaffe and Feldstein (1970:73) and by Scheidel (1974:5). The method of generating these (basic series of 512 states assured that (1) each series represented the observed series from which Jaffe and Feldstein and Scheidel derived their matrices; (2) each series was statistically independent from all other series generated from the same matrix; (3) all series generated from the same matrix were homogeneous (i.e., they were governed by the same transition probabilities); (4) all series were stationary (i.e., the transition probabilities did not change over time); (5) the series were first order (i.e., the probability of being in a state at t_1 depended only on the state at t_0); and (6) the distributions of sojourn times for the four states were exponential. Items (1) and (2) are useful in characterizing the data, but items (3), (4), and (5) are the most important, since they represent the three basic assumptions underlying Markov chain analysis. Item (6) follows as a direct consequence of the order assumption when time is treated as continuous (Bartholomew, 1967; Cane, 1959; Singer and Spilerman, 1974).

These basic series of 512 states were then transformed into the "time sequences" or "signals" that were subjected to sampling. Two transformations were applied, the first producing signals in which the *minimum sojourn time* (MST) for each state was equal. Here each state in each basic sequence was given a time value of 5 "time units," thereby converting the basic series, for example the states 21334, into a time sequence having the same underlying states, i.e., 2222211111333333333344444. The resulting signals were each 2560 time units long, with each state having an MST of 5 units. The more general case is, of course, a signal in which each state has a different MST. A second transformation provided signals with the following MSTs: 6 units for state 1, 11 units for state 2, 8 units for state 3, and 5 units for state 4 (the shortest MST). This transformation also provided a more variable signal in that the sojourn times in each state were not simply multiples of the MST. Specifically, each state in each of the basic series was given a time value equal to its MST, plus several additional time units, determined in each case by multiplying the "standard deviation" value established for each state, times a random integer from zero to four. The resulting signals were truncated at 2560 time units to provide comparability.

Of the two transformations, the first provided signals most like those observed by Scheidel and by Jaffe and Feldstein. That is, because both studies utilized equal interval sampling to derive transition probabilities, generating a signal by restoring those equal time intervals created the most highly accurate reproduction. Accordingly, the second transformation did not produce a replica of the observed signals, but represented instead the more general case of a generative mechanism with different parameters for each of its states.

To simplify the discussion, only a subset of the signals generated by these techniques is presented here. One of these (signal J) was derived from the Jaffe and Feldstein matrix, and two (signals S1 and S2) stem from the Scheidel matrix. These three signals are considered in both their "equal MST" and their "different MST" transforms. The results for all other signals generated from these matrices were the same as for these three. This choice illustrates the results for two quite different signal types (J and S) and for two independent but similar signals (S1 and S2). Table 1 presents the means and standard deviations for the sojourn times in all states of each signal. (Note that the underlying distributions are exponential, not normal.) The "%T" row shows the total percentage of the signal time spent in that state. Each time unit was considered to have a value of 0.05 seconds in generating these signals, and multiplying the mean and SD by this constant produced durations consistent with those observed by Jaffe and Feldstein (1970:137-142).[6] The time constant is arbitrary, however, and all subsequent discussion is phrased in terms of "time units." Tests of the stationarity assumption (4) and of the order and distribution assumptions (5 and 6) provided independent confirmation that the procedures for deriving each of the final signals from its respective basic series retained its conformance with the Markov chain assumptions. Because there was no need to combine signals in this study to achieve stable transition frequencies, the homogeneity assumption (3) was not directly relevant, though it did assure that signals S1 and S2 were comparable.

TABLE 1
BASIC STATISTICS FOR SIGNAL STATES (IN TIME UNITS)

	Equal MST Signals[a]			Different MST Signals[b]		
	S1	S2	J	S1	S2	J
State 1						
MEAN	13.1	12.8	16.2	22.1	19.9	33.3
SD	10.2	9.3	11.6	16.5	15.1	29.0
%T	52.7	53.3	26.0	39.7	37.3	14.3
State 2						
MEAN	7.2	7.6	45.7	24.8	34.3	180.2
SD	6.0	3.9	38.6	12.8	21.7	181.7
%T	10.7	13.1	60.7	19.3	32.1	70.4
State 3						
MEAN	8.6	8.3	25.0	29.1	24.8	76.2
SD	5.7	5.3	10.3	21.6	17.1	37.4
%T	18.6	16.6	12.7	31.8	21.3	14.9
State 4						
MEAN	9.6	7.9	5.0	11.2	9.5	5.5
SD	6.5	4.0	0.0	7.1	5.1	0.7
%T	18.0	17.0	0.6	9.2	9.3	0.4

a: MST for all four states is 5 units.
b: MST for State 1 = 6; State 2 = 11; State 3 = 8; State 4 = 5.

A three step procedure was applied to each of the signals to determine how sampling at different intervals affected the ability of the sampled data to represent or resolve the information in the original signals. First, a set of equal interval samples was taken from each signal at intervals of 1 through 15 units, as well as at 20 units. Second, each of the 16 samples resulting from each signal was cast into a transition frequency matrix, and was then converted to a transition probability matrix by dividing each entry by the row total. Finally, each of the 16 transition frequency matrices was compared with its respective "standard information matrix," a matrix whose transition frequencies represented the information actually contained in the original signal. A parallel procedure was followed for each transition probability matrix. "Information actually contained" was operationalized as the exact frequency (and hence probability) of transitions in the original signal, both to different states and to the same state. Because same state transitions are the primary component in indicating the distribution of time actually spent in each state, all such transitions were recorded with the same time scale.

Exact data were obtainable in this study because the basic series underlying each signal and the method of transformation to the final signal were known. Comparisons of the transition *frequencies* for each sample with those in the standard information matrix were made by subtracting the two matrices and examining the absolute differences. The parallel comparisons of transition *probabilities* used the goodness-of-fit and likelihood ratio tests developed for Markov chain analysis (Anderson and Goodman, 1957).[7] Unlike the transition frequencies from which they are derived, transition probabilities are linked closely to Markov chain analysis. The choice of a different analytic technique might then permit another approach to this aspect of the operationalization. Transition frequencies, on the other hand, are not linked to a specific analytic technique and represent a highly general and accurate means for both describing and analyzing change in any discrete state variable.

SAMPLE TYPES AND ANALYTIC TECHNIQUES

Transition frequencies also provide the basis for a distinction among the three types of samples from discrete state variables. It will be useful in considering the results of the analyses just described to identify both the properties of these types of samples and their interrelationships. The distinction among the samples also forms the basis for a fairly general classification of the analytic techniques applicable to each type.

A *time sequence* sample results when the state of a signal is indexed at equal time intervals, so that if a variable remains in a given state for 11 seconds, and the sampling interval is four seconds, the variable will be indexed in that state three consecutive times. Time sequence sampling is uniformly employed in speaker switching research, and underlies many interaction analysis procedures.

In a *state switch* sample, the state is indexed each time and only when the state changes, hence a signal with the sequence 22214444 would result in a state switch sample of 214. Such samples are useful in communication research when one is interested only on what class of events follows or precedes another class. Finally, in an *event sequence* sample, the state of a signal is indexed each time and only when some previously defined "event" occurs. The event is usually an observational or theoretical unit like a "trial" or "a single complete statement uttered by one person." Given the latter definition of an event, if one observed Fred ask a question, Joe and Mary each answer, and Fred make two separate supportive statements, the event sequence sample might be QAASS. (If the event were a "change in state," this event sequence sample would reduce to the state switch sample QAS.) Event sequence sampling is also found in a number of interaction analysis procedures utilized in communication research.

The general properties of and relationships among these types of samples are most apparent when one examines their respective transition frequency matrices. Time sequence sampling produces a *transition frequency matrix* (TFM) like that illustrated in Table 2. The diagonal in this matrix shows the frequencies of transitions to the same state, while the off diagonals show the frequencies of transitions between all possible pairs of different states. A state switch sample, by definition, has no transitions to the same state, thus its TFM has a diagonal which always consists of zeros. The off diagonals show the frequencies of "state switches" and consequently are identical to the off diagonals of any time sequence sample of the signal that falls within the guideline. Because the 5 unit sampling interval which produced the matrix in Table 2 is equal to the shortest MST in the signal, the state switch sample for the equal MST version of signal S1 can be obtained directly from Table 2 by substituting zeros on the diagonal. The same relationship holds for any time sequence sample whose sampling interval is consistent with the guideline.

Unlike a state switch sample, an event sequence sample does have transitions to the same state. But the frequencies on the diagonal of the TFM are generally somewhat smaller than those for a time sequence sample of the same signal

TABLE 2
TRANSITION FREQUENCY MATRIX FOR 5 UNIT SAMPLE
FROM EQUAL MINIMUM SOJOURN TIME VERSION OF SIGNAL S1

	STATE	t_1				ROW TOTAL
		1	*2*	*3*	*4*	
	1	167	25	44	34	270
t_0	*2*	14	17	11	13	55
	3	47	7	40	1	95
	4	41	6	0	44	91

constructed within the guideline. The event sequence sample is thus intermediate between the time sequence and the state switch sample. But because of its situation-specific definition of the sampled event, it bears no formal relationship to either type, despite the fact that an event sequence sample has the same off diagonals as an adequate time sequence or state switch sample, assuming the event sequence sampling defines each state consistently

The distinctions among the three sample types are especially critical because the different samples may be analyzed using only certain techniques. While the examples of techniques used here involve the Markov chain model, the restrictions involved in treating time as either continuous or discrete are general to other analytic techniques. *Time sequence samples* of a discrete state variable permit a broader range of analytic techniques than either of the other two types, as these three cases illustrate:

(1) Because the sampling points are equally spaced, time sequence sampling constitutes interval, and hence continuous measurement of time, even though the measurement is digital. Time sequence samples can therefore be analyzed using continuous time analytic techniques like the continuous time Markov chain model (which requires that sojourn times be exponentially distributed) or the semi-Markov chain model (which relaxes the distribution assumption). Both permit certain violations of the homogeneity assumption, but both are more complicated than the next two cases. Neither model seems to have been employed in communication research, although both have been productively applied in related fields, as suggested by Jaeckel (1971) and Singer and Spilerman (1974).

(2) Although some information would be lost, time sequence samples may also be analyzed using discrete time analytic techniques. In this case, time is measured at the ordinal level: thus the conclusions must be limited to statements regarding an ordered sequence of points. The discrete time Markov chain model exemplifies an analytic technique applicable in this case, although it is not applied as often here as in case 3 because of the information loss.[8]

(3) Because time sequence sampling provides continuous measurement of time, a discrete time technique can often be used to model a continuous time analysis. The result is usually a simpler analysis that nevertheless retains the conceptualization of time as continuous. The conclusions drawn in this case are restricted by the analytic technique to statements regarding distinct points in time, but these points are separated by a known interval, so that it is possible, for example, to make predictions to specific future time points. Much of the development of the discrete time Markov chain model has been oriented toward the modeling of continuous time analyses. But again, treating time as continuous also requires, as in case 1, that the distribution of sojourn times in each state be exponential. Failure to meet this requirement usually forces a shift to the more general continuous time semi-Markov model (Bartholomew, 1967:45-46; Singer and Spilerman, 1974:383).

State switch and *event sequence samples* permit a smaller set of analytic techniques than time sequence samples. Of the two, event sequence sampling is often particularly attractive because it avoids some of the problems of obtaining complete resolution addressed by this article. That is, a researcher can normally define an event in such a way that even its shortest occurrence can be identified and recorded. But this capability of completely resolving comes at some cost because the subsequent analysis must utilize either a continuous time technique (case 1) or a discrete time technique (case 2).

In cases where a researcher constructs a state switch or an event sequence sample with no record of the times at which each state switch or event boundary occurred, the result is ordinal measurement of time, requiring a discrete time analytic technique, as in case 2. Because many applications of state switch or event sequence samples occur in contexts where time is conceptualized as discrete, this restriction poses no problem (e.g., Lewis, 1970; or Suppes and Atkinson, 1960). Where time is conceptualized as continuous, however, the failure to measure time points precludes maintaining the conceptualization in the analysis and interpretation.

Where the researcher conceptualizes time as continuous and does measure state switch or event boundary times, the result is continuous (though still digital) measurement of time. But because the time intervals are *not equal,* the data can be analyzed only with a continuous time technique. The unequal time intervals preclude using a discrete time technique to model a continuous time analysis, as case 3, unless one makes the untenable assumption that the events are implicitly equal in length. A continuous time analytic technique is required to accommodate the unequal intervals, but unfortunately the development of these techniques has been oriented almost entirely toward equal interval sampling, as in case 1. Little or no attention has been paid to the difficulties of performing an analysis utilizing unequal time intervals, even in the more highly developed case of continuous state—continuous time techniques (Freeman proved in 1965:77-89 that analyses based on unequal intervals were possible, but none has yet been implemented).

In short, time sequence, event sequence, and state switch samples may all be analyzed with discrete time techniques, as in case 2. These analyses present few difficulties, but they restrict one's conclusions (and hence conceptualization) to statements regarding an ordered sequence of points. Thus "change over time" can be treated only as "change over sequence." But it is both common and highly desirable in communication theory to conceptualize times as continuous—a point Coleman (1964) has strongly emphasized regarding social phenomena in general (Jaeckel, 1971, summarizes these arguments). Because continuous measurement of time is straightforward, the main hindrance in developing continuous time conceptualizations lies in applying continuous time anaytic techniques to these three types of samples. (Recall that sampling cannot be avoided except by analog measurement of time.)

Neither event sequence nor state switch samples can be analyzed readily with continuous time techniques, and applying them to time sequence samples is fairly complex. A much less complex alternative is to use a discrete time analysis of a time sequence sample to model a continuous time analysis, as in case 3. Most researchers interested in a continuous time conceptualization have taken this approach in applying Markov chain analysis to human communication behavior. The studies of Cappella (1976), Hewes and Evans-Hewes (1974), Jaffe and Feldstein (1970), and Scheidel (1974) all provide examples. As a result, this article focuses on time sequence sampling, not only because of its past use in studying discrete state variables, but also because of its potential in developing continuous time conceptualizations of communication phenomena. Using a time sequence sample in research, however, raises the added question of how well the sample resolves the information in the signal under study. The next section addresses that question.

RESULTS

EQUAL MST SIGNALS

Figure 1 shows the results of comparing the transition probabilities for the time sequence samples from each of the equal MST signals, with the probabilities in the standard information matrix for that signal. The vertical axis is the chi-square value for the goodness-of-fit statistic, and values not presented on the graph are very large. For example, at a sampling interval of 2 units, signal S1 = 465, signal S2 = 517, and signal J = 104.[9] The values below the lines indicating the p = .05 level indicate sampling intervals whose transition probabilities show no statistically important difference from the transition probabilities for the original signal. (A zero value indicates identity.) The results show that sampling intervals from 5 to 8 units for signals S1 and S2, and from 4 to 8 for signal J, adequately resolve the information in the signal, while other intervals do not. To assess how these results square with the guideline, one must consider two factors: first, the type of resolution produced by each sampling interval; and second, the power of the test.

The most general and most accurate indicator of how well a given sampling interval resolves a signal is the absolute difference between the TFM for the sample and for the standard matrix. As noted earlier, any sampling interval within the guideline indexes exactly all transitions to *different* states—the off-diagonals of the TFM. Because the equal MST signals have an MST of 5 units for all states, samples taken at intervals from 1 through 5 units show zero differences from the standard information matrix for transitions to different states. At intervals of 6 units and above, the off diagonals do show differences from the standard matrix, because intervals greater than the MST fail to index some transitions to different states. The magnitude of these differences increases with the sampling interval.

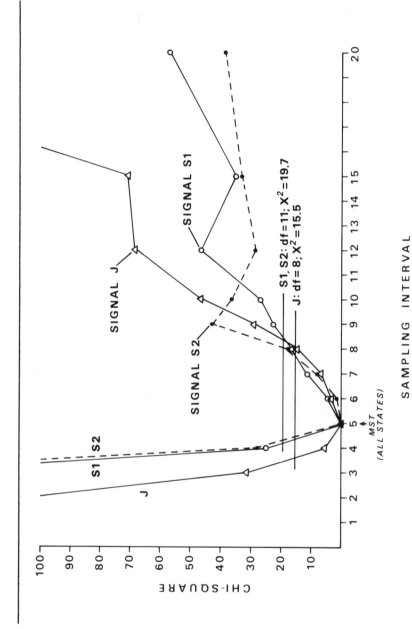

Figure 1: GOODNESS-OF-FIT (RESOLUTION) versus SAMPLING INTERVAL FOR EQUAL MST SIGNALS

A modified pattern holds for the absolute differences in transitions to the *same* state—the diagonal of the TFM. Here, sampling intervals from 1 through 4 units show large differences from the standard matrix for each signal. These differences decrease to zero for the sample taken at the MST of 5 units. In effect then, sampling intervals less than the MST collect more information than necessary on the sojourns in each state. At intervals of 6 units and above, the diagonal also shows differences from the standard matrix, which increase fairly rapidly as the sampling interval increases. Intervals longer than the MST completely overlook some sojourns, particularly those equal to or close to the MST value.

In terms of transition frequencies, then, the analysis can be summarized this way: Sampling intervals below the MST *over resolve* (or index too frequently) transitions to the same state, even though they *exactly resolve* (index with zero difference) transitions to different states. A sampling interval equal to the MST exactly resolves both the same state and different state transitions, while intervals above the MST *under resolve* both types (fail to index some transitions). Under resolution is the more serious problem, for once information has been lost in sampling, it cannot be regained. The guideline developed in this article notes that for *complete resolution,* the sampling interval must be equal to or less than the shortest MST. From this analysis, then, it is evident that complete resolution encompasses not only exact resolution of different state transitions, but also either exact or over resolution of same state transitions. But more importantly, the guideline *precludes* under resolution of the signal.

Unfortunately there is a cost involved in gaining the accuracy and generality of a transition frequency analysis of the effects of sampling on resolution. The analysis is not restricted by the assumptions of a particular analytic technique, but it also provides no criterion for a "significant" departure from exact resolution. The analysis of sampling effects based on transition probabilities presented in Figure 1 provides the needed criterion. Because a *transition probability matrix* (TPM) results from dividing the entries in each row of a TFM by the row total, the presence of an over resolved same state transition frequency both raises the probability for that transition, and correspondingly lowers each of the different state transition probabilities in that row. Thus, despite the fact that the different state transition frequencies remain constant through the 5 unit sampling interval, sampling at intervals from 1 through 4 units (3 units for signal J) produces TPMs that are statistically different from the TPM for the standard information matrix. Sampling intervals from 5 through 8 units (4 for signal J), *adequately resolve* the information present in a signal, in the sense that these intervals index both the same and the different state transitions in a manner sufficiently close to exact resolution to produce TPMs that are statistically similar to the standard matrix. For sampling intervals of 9 units and above, the under resolution of transitions to the same state and to different states is sufficiently high that the TPMs for these samples again become statistically different. Intervals above the MST (6 to 8 units here) always under re-solve the signal to some degree. But whether the statistically insignificant loss of information occurring at these intervals is a matter of concern can be decided only in the context of a particular investigation.

The range of sampling intervals that provides adequate resolution will vary from study to study because it depends in part on the power of the test for resolution. In this case, power varies most directly with the number of obser-vations, as indicated in the following brief analysis: Because the probabilities in each row of a TPM total 1.0, they are independent of the probabilities in all other rows. The chi-square statistic is thus computed for each separate row by evaluating the expression,

$$\chi^2_{row} = n \sum_{j=1}^{m} [(o_j - e_j)^2 / e_j]$$

where m is the number of states, n is the TFM *row* total (and the sum of the n's across rows equals the total N), and o_j and e_j are, respectively, the observed and expected *probabilities* in the given row. The total χ^2 is then the sum of the independent χ^2s for each row. The power of a chi-square test depends on four variables: the significance level (here p = .05); the degrees of freedom (m − 1); the number of observations n; and the "effect size," which in this case is the value in brackets (Cohen, 1969:209-265). Given a fixed significance level and degrees of freedom, increasing the total number of observations, N, in this study both increases n for each row and brings the observed probabilities closer to the expected values, thereby reducing the effect size. But because of the nature of the computational formula for the row chi-square, this reduction in effect size is more than offset by the increase in n.

Under these circumstances, the power of the chi-square test increases con-siderably as the total number of observations increases, an effect demonstrated when we generated two additional equal MST signals—in this case extensions of S1 to 3840 and 5120 units. Basic statistics for these signals fell between the S1 and S2 values in Table 1. Representative values showing the increase in power appear in Table 3. Subjecting these longer signals to the analyses already de-scribed produces a narrower range of adequate resolution: from 5 to 7 units for the shorter of the two signals, and only 5 and 6 units for the longer. (Results for the likelihood ratio tests are parallel.) The range of adequate resolution therefore depends in part on the total number of observations. In addition, it is clear that once information on a signal is lost through under resolution, neither increasing the length of the signal nor averaging the results of several similar signals will regain that information (Arundale, 1977).

TABLE 3

REPRESENTATIVE POWER VALUES FOR CHI-SQUARE
TEST FOR SAMPLES OF DIFFERENT LENGTH[a]

		Total length of signal N		
		2560	*3840*	*5120*
Sampling	1	.995	.995	.995
Interval	3	.995	.995	.995
(In Time	5	.96	.99	.995
Units)	7	.86	.97	.99
	10	.67	.88	.96
	12	.57	.79	.91
	15	.46	.67	.83
	20	.35	.51	.67

a: From Cohen (1969). The values given are for df = 10, p = .05, and effect size = .05, the
smallest effect size for which Cohen provides values. Signals with higher df (see Figures 1
and 2) will have lower power values than the table, while lower df signals will have higher
values.

DIFFERENT MST SIGNALS

The chi-square values for comparing the transition probabilities for each
sample from the different MST signals with those in its respective standard information matrix appear in Figure 2. In this case, sampling intervals from 4 to 7
units adequately resolve signals S1 and S2, while intervals from 3 to 11 resolve
signal J. To assess these results in view of the guideline, one must also consider
degree of resolution and power, but with an emphasis on the individual states
in the signal.

An analysis of the effects of sampling on resolution based on absolute differences in transition frequencies produces exactly the same pattern of results for
the different MST signals as for the equal MST signals. That is, despite the fact
that in these signals only state 4 has an MST of 5 units, the pattern of over,
exact, and under resolution remains the same, and only sampling intevals from
1 through 5 units completely resolve the signal. The analysis based on transition
probabilities presented in Figure 2 adds a criterion of significance, and in this
case the results for the different MST signals diverge slightly from those for the
equal MST signals. The overall pattern of resolution remains the same, however,
as does the explanation for it. Specifically, the range of adequate resolution
shifts slightly toward shorter sampling intervals for signals S1 and S2 and ex-
pands considerably for signal J. Both effects can be explained by examining the
ranges of adequate resolution for the individual states (or rows).

For the different MST transforms of signals S1 and S2, the lower end of the
adequate resolution range is an interval of 4 units, as opposed to 5 units for the
equal MST version. Closer examination shows that with two exceptions the indi-

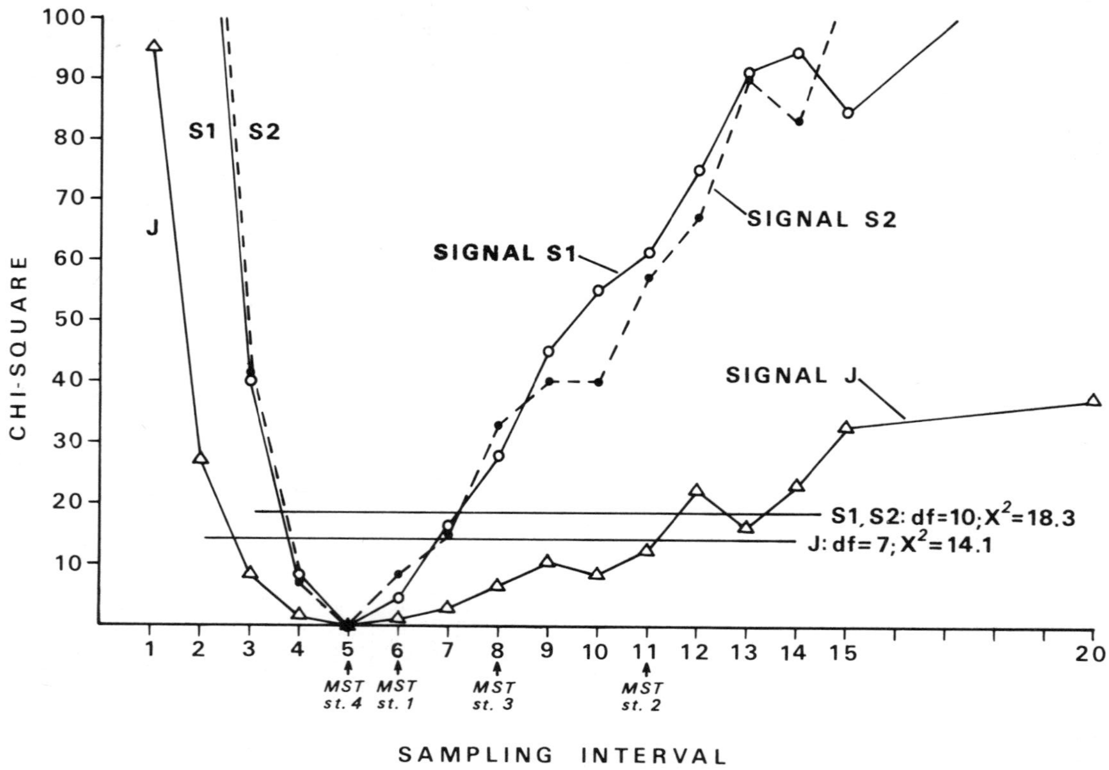

Figure 2: GOODNESS-OF-FIT (RESOLUTION) versus SAMPLING INTERVAL FOR DIFFERENT MST SIGNALS

vidual states in all signals reach adequate resolution at the 4 unit sampling interval. The two exceptions appear in state 1 in the equal MST version of S1 and S2, where over 50% of the signal time is spent in this state (Table 1), resulting in a high n and a high row chi-square at the 4 unit sampling interval. At the upper end of the range, the different MST versions S1 and S2 adequately resolve only through a sampling interval of 7 units, instead of 8 units as in the equal MST version. A study of the individual states in both S1 and S2 shows that two of them are adequately resolved through 8 units, while the two with 30% or more of the signal time resolve only through 7 units, raising the sum of the four individual row chi-squares at 8 units above the criterion. In short, the upper and lower limits of the range of adequate resolution vary slightly from signal to signal depending on the distribution of the signal time or row n among the individual states, even though the total number of observations remains constant. In general, however, the range of adequate resolution extends from just below to slightly above the shortest MST value.

Why then does the different MST version of signal J have a range of adequate resolution extending from 3 through 11 units? Table 1 suggests three reasons: First, state 4 occurs only twice in the different MST signal, for 0.4% of the total time. Consequently, it makes only a negligible contribution to the total chi-square and is therefore excluded from consideration. Second, states 1 and 3 each account for just over 14% of the total signal time, and like other states with a low n, these two have moderately broad ranges of adequate resolution. Third, and most significantly, state 2 comprises 70.4% of the total signal time. This value is not greatly different from the 60.7% for the equal MST signal, where the high n results in a narrow range of resolution for state 2 and, in turn, restricts the range for the entire signal. However, the different MST version of signal J contains a single continuous sojourn in state 2 of 609 units (23.8% of the signal), as well as two others of over 300 units (together totaling 26.9%). No comparable sojourn lengths appear in the equal MST version (see Table 1).

These extremely long sojourns result in a very high frequency for the same state transition in state 2, even when the signal is exactly resolved. Consequently a sampling interval of 3 units does not produce enough over resolution to generate a significant chi-square for this state, despite the high power. Similarly, sampling at an interval as high as 11 units does not under resolve the signal enough to result in a high chi-square. These extremely long sojourns thus produce a broad range of adequate resolution for state 2, and when combined with both the broad range of resolution in states 1 and 3 and the virtual absence of state 4, the result is the broad range of adequate resolution observed for signal J. In addition to the effects of differences in power among the different states in a signal, then, the range of adequate resolution is affected by extremes both of very long sojourns (from 20 to 30% of the signal and above) and of virtual absence of a state or states (near 1% of the signal).

These analyses of the different MST signals must also be considered in light of the total number of observations in the signal. To demonstrate the effect of increased power, another two additional different MST signals were generated, again by extending S1 to 3840 and 5120 units. The basic statistics fell between the S1 and S2 values in Table 1. Subjecting these longer signals to the same analyses as above, but at the higher power levels indicated in Table 3, results in a range of adequate resolution of from 4 through 6 units for both signals. This finding compares with the range of 4 through 7 units reported above, and confirms that the extent of the range of adequate resolution depends in part on the total number of observations. Analytic techniques other than the Markov chain model can be expected to show similar effects as the number of observations varies, whether for a particular state or for the entire signal.

DISCUSSION

These results clearly illustrate how the interval one employs in taking a time sequence sample affects the sample's ability to resolve the information contained in the the original signal. Again, the guideline notes that for *complete resolution,* "the sampling interval must be equal to (or shorter than) the shortest time interval for which the variable under study can remain in any one of its states." The analyses based on transition frequencies confirm that sampling at an interval within the guideline results in no loss of information, though it may add "unnecessary" information. Sampling at intervals longer than the shortest MST results in a loss of information that cannot be regained, and the magnitude of the loss increases with the sampling interval. For many studies, this complete or exact resolution is not required, though it remains essential that a given sample *adequately resolve* the signal. The analyses based on transition probabilities not only indicate the presence of a range of sampling intervals for which the resolution is not statistically different from exact resolution, but also confirm that this range centers on a sampling interval equal to the shortest MST, and extends from intervals just below it ot slightly above it.

The "unnecessary" information present in samples taken at intervals less than the shortest MST results from the over resolution of transitions to the same state. But because the frequencies of transitions to different states remain constant for all sampling intervals within the guideline, a straightforward procedure exists for "filtering out" the extra information. For analyses based on frequencies of transitions (and not on their order), first multiply each row total in the TFM by a fraction whose numerator is the interval at which the sample was taken and whose denominator is the value of the shortest MST. Second, subtract from each of the resulting values the sum of all transitions to *different* states in the respective row. The remainder will be a highly accurate estimate of the *same* state transition frequency for that row, were the sample taken at an interval equal to the shortest MST. This procedure cannot be used to regain information lost by under resolution because the different state transitions are also under resolved.[10] For analyses that use information on the order of the transitions, the procedure for obtaining "exact" resolution involves reducing the length of each successive sojourn by the fraction just described.

The results of this study also clarify an important aspect of the guideline: Of the possible values that might be selected for the criterion sampling interval, only the *shortest* of the MSTs among the states is appropriate. The point would not deserve emphasis were there not faulty guidance present in the literature. Both Abelson (1967:46) and Hayes et al. (1970:268n) suggest that in sampling from a continuous time Markov chain, the sampling interval is "arbitrary." This study clearly shows it is not. Darwin (1959:414) is more helpful than either Abelson or Hayes et al.: "If [the sampling interval] is smaller than the average amount of time spent in the state in which the chain stays for the shortest time it is unlikely that any change of state has been missed." Yet the results discussed here, together with a study of Table 1, reveal that many of the sampling intervals that fall within Darwin's criterion are nevertheless highly likely to miss changes in state. Cane's (1959:47) advice on an appropriate sampling interval is accurate: "If the sampling interval is not very different from the minimum [sojourn] length the effect [of sampling] will not be important." Unfortunately this comment, made casually in an article on continuous time semi-Markov chains, receives neither mathematical nor empirical support.

Two empirical studies in which the researchers took steps to assure adequate resolution combine to support the pattern of results in this study. In his research on speaker switching in informal conversations, Scheidel (personal communications, 1976) tape recorded his subjects, then sampled the interactions with an automatic coding system at intervals of 0.1, 0.2, 0.3, to 1.0 seconds. He compared the transition matrices produced by the different sampling intervals and found that intervals of 0.2 and 0.3 seconds gave him the "best picture" of the phenomenon, neither over representing transitions to the same state nor under representing transitions to different states. On this basis, he chose an interval of 0.25 seconds for his subsequent studies (1974). Although Scheidel's criteria for adequate resolution were informal, they are clearly consistent with this study's findings regarding significant over or under resolution.

Scheidel's choice of sampling interval is further supported by Jaffe and Feldstein's (1970) work on speaker switching. Following earlier empirical evidence on speech durations, they chose a sampling interval of 0.3 seconds. In addition, they provide means and standard deviations for the sojourn times observed in each state. Of the three experiments they describe, the third most resembles Scheidel's conversations, and among the means reported, the smallest is 0.413 seconds (SD = .055) for state 4, or simultaneous speech. Subtracting two SDs from each of the means in order to encompass most of the cases shows that the shortest of the "MSTs" among the four states is 0.303 seconds for state 4.[11] Jaffe and Feldstein's research thus suggests that a value of approximately 0.3

seconds has validity as the shortest sojourn time for speaker switching states in informal dyadic communication. This value appears consistent with Scheidel's results, and together the studies confirm both the guideline and the concept of a range of adequate resolution.

PROSPECTIVE USE OF THE GUIDELINE

The guideline is most useful in an a priori or prospective sense in designing studies of change over time in discrete state variables. Three steps are important in creating a design which assures representative sampling:

(1) *Determine whether data can be obtained which will provide complete resolution.* This key step requires information on the length of the shortest MST among those states that hold theoretical interest. The means of obtaining this information varies with the particular research problem, but in general it may involve (a) theoretical considerations (for example, the shortest time required to utter a "complete sentence"); (b) pilot studies designed in part to yield sojourn time distributions; or (c) the results of previous research.

Once this information is available, the primary concern becomes whether reliable data can be gathered at this sampling interval, given the measurement procedures and the time and monetary constraints involved. For example, if the shortest MST is a nonverbal behavior two seconds long, and trained coders can perform the required scoring in no less than four seconds, one must film or videotape the event under study and code on repeated passes. But clearly any step of this procedure may be impractical, too unreliable, too time consuming, or too expensive. If one cannot sample at an interval that provides complete resolution, the investigation should be directed toward other ends. There is no point in proceeding if the resulting data fail to resolve the information needed for the theoretical conclusions one wishes to draw.

(2) *Determine whether a sufficient number of observations can be obtained, in view of the required sampling interval.* This step requires information on the number of observations needed to provide the desired level of power in the chosen analytic technique. Where the required sampling interval is fairly short, the concern is to insure that enough data can be gathered to encompass long term changes in the phenomenon (as in the phases of a group discussion). As the sampling interval grows longer, the concern increasingly becomes one of modifying the projected design to increase the available N. For example, in cases where the goal is to study a unique interaction event, increasing the number of observations involves extending that interaction. In other situations, where the events of interest are of limited length, increasing N involves combining the results of several separate events. Finally, in a cross-sectional study where the number of time points is strictly limited, increasing the number of observations centers primarily on obtaining more subjects. But increasing the number of observations

in any of these ways will increase the effort, time, and expense involved in obtaining and processing the observations. It may also increase the possibility of violating such statistical assumptions as stationarity or homogeneity. As with step 1, if one cannot gather enough data, there is little point in proceeding, for too few observations will result in questionable resolution and low power in any statistical test.

(3) *Examine sojourn time distributions and correct for over resolution in the data gathered.* If steps 1 and 2 are satisfied, the data gathered will completely resolve the signal under study, though they may over resolve it as well. Step 3 involves examining the distributions of sojourn times for each state for three important types of information: First, the presence of such extreme cases as very long single sojourns or the virtual absence of a state may indicate the need for special treatment of the data. Second, the presence of a larger number of sojourns than expected with values very close to the sampling interval may suggest that the original signal contains some sojourns shorter than the sampling interval, indicating a need to reconsider step 1. Third, the virtual absence of sojourns with lengths close to the sampling interval may indicate the presence of over resolution, requiring correction with the procedure outlined in the Discussion.

These three steps in design all focus on *complete* resolution, since it is premature to consider *adequate* resolution without having the information required in step 3. That is, choosing a sampling interval that will produce adequate (as opposed to complete) resolution requires considerable knowledge of the MSTs involved. Such knowledge could come only from previous closely related studies that provide information on distributions and resolution. As a consequence, a pilot study is highly desirable when choosing a sampling interval longer than the shortest MST but still capable of providing adequate resolution.

RETROSPECTIVE USE OF THE GUIDELINE

Because many existing studies overlook the problems associated with sampling across time, the guideline is also useful in evaluating the extent to which such studies have resolved key variables and drawn warranted conclusions. An examination of two studies should illustrate this post hoc or retrospective use.

Over resolution of a signal occurs less often than under resolution because it stems from sampling more frequently than necessary. Over resolution may be suggested by either means or distributions of sojourn times with values well above the sampling interval, or by transition matrices with relatively high values on the diagonal. But in the absence of such data, over resolution can be confirmed only if one has independent information on the MSTs of the states under study.

Scheidel (1974) and Jaffe and Feldstein (1970) provide just such information for studies of speaker switching. They show that a sampling interval between 0.25 and 0.30 seconds is appropriate to the conversational tasks they studied. Hayes et al. (1970), for reasons they do not explain, chose to sample similar conversations at an interval of 0.16 seconds and concluded from the high frequency of transitions to the same state that the behaviors of the two speakers were independent of each other. Hayes et al. acknowledged the influence of the sampling interval on the results, but provided no basis for favoring their findings over Jaffe and Feldstein's. In view of the guideline and this independent information, an interval of 0.16 seconds will certainly over resolve this type of speaker switching, and will probably fail to provide adequate resolution, as well. The evidence on which Hayes et al. base their conclusion is clearly an artifact of their sampling interval, and one is inclined to prefer Jaffe and Feldstein's conclusion of speaker interdependence.

Over resolution can be corrected if the sample data remain available. But because no such remedy exists for under resolution, its presence in a study has more serious implications. Unfortunately, under resolution is also more likely to occur, because both reduced effort and lower cost encourage longer sampling intervals. Under resolution may be suggested by means or distributions of sojourn times with values quite close to the sampling interval, but transition matrices are of little help. Independent empirical or theoretical information on the shortest MSTs likely to occur is thus the key to detecting and confirming under resolution.

In their well known study of interview communication, Hawes and Foley (1973) sampled the verbal interaction of physicians and patients during the first interview of a physical examination. They used a 13-state category system to code the interaction at least once every five seconds, and they analyzed the results with a discrete state Markov chain technique. In their independent study of initial interviews in which "factual biographical information" was obtained from interviewees, Jaffe and Feldstein (1970:29 and 137) found a mean vocalization time of 1.683 seconds (SD = .316), and they suggest (p. 77) that a typical range of vocalizations in dialogue is from 0.3 to 7.5 seconds. In addition, they provide linguistic evidence indicating that this mean value corresponds closely to the mean length of phonemic clauses in speech, which average five words and generally range from 2 to 20 words (p. 22).

Hawes and Foley provide no information on the distributions of sojourn times or utterance lengths for their category system. But given the nature of an interview for a physical examination, one would expect to find many utterances equal to or shorter than Jaffe and Feldstein's mean vocalization or clause length. For example, the category "objective questions" could include, "Have you had the measles?" An "objective clarification" would cover "I had rubella last year." And a positive reinforcement could include "Yes." The guideline indicates that sampling at an interval of five seconds will not completely resolve events shorter than five seconds, so that utterances at or near the mean vocalization or clause length would be under resolved in Hawes and Foley's study, perhaps to the extent that the sample falls short of adequately resolving the dialogues.

The high likelihood of MSTs shorter than their sampling interval does not automatically invalidate Hawes and Foley's conclusions, but it does suggest the need for considerable care in their use. Three different evaluations of Hawes and Foley's results appear possible, but one cannot choose among them without more information. First, if the shortest MSTs for the states in these particular interviews are close to five seconds, despite the Jaffe and Feldstein data, or if there are so few sojourns below five seconds that they are virtually absent, then it is likely that Hawes and Foley adequately resolved the verbal behavior in these interviews and that their conclusions can be accepted. Second, if only some states in the category system have MSTs less than five seconds, it may be possible to restrict the conclusions to statements regarding the states with longer MSTs. This step would be difficult in Hawes and Foley's work, but it may be possible in other cases.

Third, it is entirely possible that Hawes and Foley's coding procedure did produce a representative sample in that they allowed more than one category of behavior to be coded in each five second interval. Unfortunately, they fail to indicate how many of the sampling intervals received more than one code. If the number were small, then one of the two evaluations just described would apply. But if the number were even moderately large compared to the total number of intervals, one would be forced to question why Hawes and Foley chose the basic pattern of a time sequence sample as opposed to an event sequence sample. If the rationale for a time sequence sample were to utilize a discrete time Markov chain to model a continuous time analysis, the presence of added codes within the five second intervals would be inappropriate. Such extra codes create the equivalent of unequal time intervals and call for the use of a continuous time Markov chain analysis. On the other hand, if the intent were to use a discrete time Markov chain in the context of a conceptualization of time as fully discrete, then an event sequence sample based on "utterances" would be most viable. In this case, however, the overlay of the time sequence sampling scheme would be inappropriate, since it would add considerable "noise" to the data. The Hawes and Foley study is *only one example* of research whose conclusions may require re-examination because of under resolution. Indeed, one should carefully examine the sampling interval chosen in any study employing a time sequence sample, regardless of whether it is an interaction analysis of one situation over an extended time (as in the three second interval used by Flanders, 1967, for classroom interaction), or at the other extreme, a cross-sectional study of many subjects at only a few time points (as in the two day interval used by Hewes and Evans-Hewes, 1974, in studying attitudes).[12]

CONCLUSION

The guideline developed here provides a formal criterion for choosing a sampling interval in studies of change over time in discrete state variables. The associated study "extends" the guideline to encompass the concept of adequate resolution of a signal. Sampling across time within the guideline assures that the data will contain information fully representative of the change in the variable under study—data essential both to meaningful analyses and to valid theoretical interpretations concerning change over time. Whether the guideline is applied prospectively or retrospectively, its very use points to the fact that studies which sample across time encounter an unusually strong interaction between theoretical concerns involving the nature of the variables and their states, and design concerns involving the choice of an appropriate sampling interval.

A research design becomes, in effect, an instrument that must be carefully tuned to the signal under study in order to resolve the information most relevant to the research goals. Sampling across time is not as simple as it may seem. In commenting recently on the complexities of studying how communication variables change over time, Scheidel (1974:9) noted "a temptation because of the frustrations when confronting human communication behavior as a process, to give up the quest and spend time speculating about the abstract merits of process research. I believe our field will make more of a contribution if we spend somewhat less time extolling the advantages of the systems and process view, and somewhat more time attempting to learn how better to apply it." This article is addressed directly to Scheidel's concern.

NOTES

1. The concept of *"information* contained in the data" employed in this article reflects Krippendorff's (1970) discussion of the treatment of data in research: (1) the researcher decides which observations are to be made; (2) the observations are "formalized," or translated into "data"; (3) analytic techniques are employed to produce "evidence" for inferences; and (4) the researcher makes a semantic or theoretical interpretation of the evidence. The decisions made in steps (1) and (2) determine the information available in the data, and limit the operations possible in steps (3) and (4).

2. Processes like diffusion, growth, and decay are described by referring to the time dimension, but are not *explained* by it. Other events like media contact, cell division, and cell breakdown constitute the explanatory factors. "Time" may become a variable with explanatory force, as in "length of study" and "test success." But note the transformation required: Points on the time dimension (the beginning and end of study) are first converted to a distance, which is then arrayed in a *new* state space whose dimension involves "length" or "amount," not "clock time." The sampling problems addressed in this article do not apply to these transformed cases.

3. Analog treatment of time (measuring the variable at every instant) avoids the problem of choosing an appropriate sampling interval but is not a satisfactory solution. Aside

from the need for analog computation in analysis, many communication variables (e.g., attitude, knowledge of content, self concept) are difficult or impossible to operationalize in a form that permits such measurement.

4. Continuous state-discrete time variables are rare in communications engineering where time is typically measured as continuous. The phrase "discrete time" appears throughout this literature (for example in Freeman, 1965), but always with reference to "digital but continuous" measurement and analysis of time. Among the very few sources of guidance for sampling from continuous state variables are Blackman and Tukey (1958:54-55) and Enochson and Otnes (1968:18). Even this guidance may need further development to be directly applicable to communication research (see Arundale, 1971:144-154).

5. Adequate sampling of change over time requires one to meet other conditions, as well, like those regarding the minimum number of time points and the length of the overall time period considered (see Arundale, 1971:151-164). The condition regarding the sampling interval has the most direct influence on research results, yet is the most often overlooked. Note that the restrictions imposed by the guideline may be relaxed only if one has a priori information on the nature of the variation—for example, if one knows that it is monotonically increasing or decreasing.

6. A time constant of 0.05 seconds would mean a total signal length just under two minutes, in keeping with Scheidel's (1974) studies. The results reported would be no different were the time constant five seconds and the total length nearly 43 minutes.

7. A set of highly general computer programs to perform all the analyses discussed in this article is available from the author.

8. Hewes (1975b:272) statement that "A 'discrete' model is one based on data gathered at fixed intervals" is incorrect. Bhat (1972:7-10) provides examples of truly discrete time Markov chains. Note that unlike other authors, Bhat uses the term "chain" (p. 13) to refer to the discrete time aspect, as opposed to its common usage to refer to the discrete state space.

9. The likelihood ratio statistics produced an identical pattern of results and will not be reported. Because chi-square is used as a measure of similarity rather than difference, the p = .05 level is actually a more stringent criterion, since chi-square values are smaller here than for p = .01. The p = .05 level is therefore not a criterion for significance in the normal sense, but a standard for comparison that compensates for different degrees of freedom.

10. This technique may facilitate two other types of studies, if the data they use were originally collected with a time sequence sample. One such type analyzes each state separately, rather than as a set as in Markov analyses; the second is based on a discrete time conceptualization and uses a discrete time analytic technique. In these cases, each state (or row in the TFM) should be analyzed on the basis of its unique MST, hence one must be able to exactly resolve each state at a sampling interval equal to its MST. A separate study of these cases shows that the procedure described provides an accurate estimate of exact resolution if the denominator is replaced by the MST for the particular state. Predictions and analyses based on such a TFM are restricted to the discrete time case (case 2 in the discussion of sample types and analytic techniques).

11. This procedure for determining MSTs from means and standard deviations may be useful if more specific information on the distribution of sojourn times is not available. Means and standard deviations may be somewhat misleading, however, in that the distribution may be exponential, not normal.

12. Adequate resolution is essential in studies that seek to predict to future points in time using Markov chain techniques (Arundale, 1977). It is also essential in cross-sectional studies with only a few time points.

REFERENCES

ABELSON, R.P. (1967). "Mathematical models in social psychology." Pp. 1-54 in L. Berkowitz (ed.), Advances in experimental social psychology (vol. 3). New York: Academic Press.

ANDERSON, T.W., and GOODMAN, L.A. (1959). "Statistical inference about Markov chains." Annals of Mathematical Statistics, 28:89-110.

ARUNDALE, R.B. (1971). "The concept of process in human communication research." Unpublished Ph.D. dissertation, Michigan State University (University Microfilms no. 71-23157).

——— (1977). "Sampling across time: Effect on meeting the assumptions of Markov chain analysis." Unpublished manuscript. Speech Communication Research Center, University of Washington, Seattle.

ASHBY, W.R. (1958). An introduction to cybernetics. New York: John Wiley.

BARTHOLOMEW, D.J. (1967). Stochastic models for social processes. New York: John Wiley.

BHAT, U.N. (1972). Elements of applied stochastic processes. New York: John Wiley.

BLACKMAN, R.B., and TUKEY, J.W. (1958). The measurement of power spectra. New York: Dover.

CANE, V.R. (1959). "Behavior sequences as semi-Markov chains." Journal of the Royal Statistical Society, 21(Series B):36-58.

CAPPELLA, J.N. (1976). "Modeling interpersonal communication systems as a pair of machines coupled through feedback." Pp. 59-85 in G.R. Miller (ed.), Explorations in interpersonal communication. Beverly Hills, Calif.: Sage.

CHERRY, C. (1957). On human communication. New York: John Wiley.

COHEN, J. (1969). Statistical power analysis for the behavioral sciences. New York: Academic Press.

COLEMAN, J.S. (1964). Introduction to mathematical sociology. New York: Free Press.

DARWIN, J.H. (1959). "Note on the comparison of several realizations of a Markov chain." Biometrika, 46:412-419.

ENOCHSON, L.D., and OTNES, R.K. (1968). Programming and analysis for digital time series analysis. Washington, D.C.: Naval Research Laboratory.

FLANDERS, N.A. (1967). "Teacher influence in the classroom." Pp. 103-116 in E.J. Amidon and J.B. Hough (eds.), Interaction analysis: Theory, research, and application. Reading, Mass.: Addison-Wesley.

FREEMAN, H. (1965). Discrete-time systems. New York: John Wiley.

GABOR, D. (1946). "Theory of communication." Journal of the Institution of Electrical Engineers (London), 93(pt. 3):429-441.

HALPERIN, S., and LISSITZ, R.W. (1971). "Statistical properties of Markov chains: A computer program." Behavioral Science, 16:244-247.

HAWES, L.C., and FOLEY, J.M. (1973). "A Markov analysis of interview communication." Speech Monographs, 40:208-219.

——— (1974). "The stability of decisioning systems." Paper presented at the convention of the International Communication Association, New Orleans.

HAYES, D.P., MELTZER, L., and WOLF, G. (1970). "Substantive conclusions are dependent upon techniques of measurement." Behavioral Science, 15:265-268.

HEWES, D.E. (1975a). "A stochastic model of the relationship between attitudes and behaviors." Paper presented at the convention of the International Communication Association, Chicago.

——— (1975b). "Finite stochastic modeling of communication processes: An introduction and some basic readings." Human Communication Research, 1:271-283.

HEWES, D.E., and EVANS-HEWES, D. (1974). "Toward a Markov chain model of attitude change." Paper presented at the convention of the Speech Communication Association, Chicago.

JAECKEL, M. (1971). "Coleman's process approach." Pp. 236-275 in H.L. Costner (ed.), Sociological methodology: 1971. San Francisco: Jossey-Bass.

JAFFE, J., and FELDSTEIN, S. (1970). Rhythms of dialogue. New York: Academic Press.

KRIPPENDORFF, K. (1970). "On generating data in communication research." Journal of Communication, 20:241-269.

——— (1971). "A calculus for diagreements: A categorical equivalence to variance analysis. General Systems, 16:187-203.

LEWIS, G.H. (1970). "The assumption of stationary parameters in theories of group discussion." Behavioral Science, 15:269-273.

McCOMBS, M.E., BECKER, L.B., and WEAVER, D.H. (1975). "Measuring the cumulative agenda-setting influence of mass media." Paper presented at the convention of the Speech Communication Association, Houston, Texas.

SCHEIDEL, T.M. (1974). "A systems analysis of two-person conversations." Paper presented to the Speech Communication Association Doctoral Honors Seminar on Modern Systems Theory in Human Communication, University of Utah, Salt Lake City.

SINGER, B., and SPILERMAN, S. (1974). "Social mobility models for heterogeneous populations." Pp. 356-401 in H.L. Costner (ed.), Sociological methodology: 1973-1974. San Francisco: Jossey-Bass.

STECH, E.L., and GOLDBERG, A.A. (1972). "Sampling discussion group interaction." Speech Monographs, 39:312-314.

SUPPES, P., and ATKINSON, R.C. (1960). Markov learning models for multiperson interactions. Stanford, Calif.: Stanford University Press.

TICK, L.J., and SHAMAN, P. (1966). "Sampling rates and the appearance of stationary Gaussian processes." Technometrics, 8:91-106.

WIEMANN, J.M., and KNAPP, J.L. (1975). "Turn-taking in conversations." Journal of Communication, 25:75-92.

ABOUT THE CONTRIBUTORS

ROBERT B. ARUNDALE received his Ph.D. from Michigan State University and is an Assistant Professor of Speech Communication at the University of Washington. His research interests include communication theory, theoretical and methodological issues in the study of change over time, and the use and functions of language in interpersonal communication.

CHARLES CANNELL is a Program Director in the Institute for Social Research and Professor of Psychology in Journalism at the University of Michigan. He is just completing a program of research of several years duration into problems of response bias in surveys and field experiments on techniques for improving reporting accuracy.

NEAL E. CUTLER is Associate Professor of Political Science and Laboratory Chief of Social Policy at the Andrus Gerontology Center at the University of Southern California. He has contributed extensively to both substantive and methodological aspects of social research.

JAMES DANOWSKI is Assistant Professor in the Annenberg School of Communications at the University of California. He received his Ph.D. in Communications from Michigan State University.

ERIC S. FREDIN is a Ph.D. student in the Interdepartmental Doctoral Program in Mass Communication Research at the University of Michigan. He has worked as a newspaper reporter. His research interests include theory development and methodology.

SUSAN C. GREENDALE is a student in the Interdepartmental Doctoral Program in Mass Communication Research at the University of Michigan. She has been an Assistant Study Director in the Center for Political Studies of the Institute for Social Research and has served as an analyst in the Political Research Division of Market Opinion Research.

PAUL M. HIRSCH is a sociologist on the faculty of the University of Chicago Graduate School of Business. He has also taught at Stanford and Indiana Universities, and served as consultant to the Social Science Research Council's Committee on Television and Social Behavior, and Assistant Program Director of the University of Chicago's National Humanities Institute. His articles on complex organization and mass communication have appeared in *American Journal of Sociology, School Review, Journal of Communication, American Sociologist, Administrative Science Quarterly, Psychology Today, The Wall Street Journal,* and elsewhere. In 1975 he was awarded a Rockefeller Foundation Humanities Fellowship to study the television industry.

F. GERALD KLINE is Director of the Doctoral Program in Mass Communication Research at the University of Michigan. His interests center on theory and methods as they relate to communication behavior. He is editor of *Communication Research,* coeditor, with Peter Clarke, of this annual series, the series *People and Communication,* and editor of a new textbook series by SAGE, *CommTexts.*

ROBERT KRULL is Assistant Professor of Communication and Coordinator of the Communication Research Laboratory at Rensselaer Polytechnic Institute. His interests center on development of communication theory with a strong interest in methodological applications.

WILLIAM N. McPHEE is Professor of Sociology and Computing Science at the University of Colorado. He is interested in sociological theory and mathematical modeling, and author of *Formal Models of Mass Behavior.* He also conducted and participated in many of the innovative studies in mass communication undertaken at Columbia University's Bureau of Applied Social Research through the early 1960s.

PETER V. MILLER is Research Assistant Professor in the Institute of Communications Research and Assistant Professor of Journalism, University of Illinois, Urbana-Champaign. A Michigan Ph.D. in mass communication, his research interests include measurement in communication, survey research methods, public opinion and mass media organizations.

ALBERT S. PAULSON is Associate Professor of Operations Research and Statistics and an affiliated faculty member of the Communication Research Laboratory at Rensselaer Polytechnic Institute.

E. BARBARA PHILLIPS received an interdisciplinary Ph.D. from the Maxwell School, Syracuse University, and is currently Assistant Professor of Sociology and member of the Urban Studies Program at San Francisco State University. Her research interests include mass communication theory and practice, the development of visual literacy, and the political, social, and economic implications of alternative life-styles.

GAYE TUCHMAN received her Ph.D. from Brandeis University and is Associate Professor of Sociology at Queens College and the Graduate Center, CUNY. She has edited *The TV Establishment* and coedited the forthcoming *Hearth and Home: Images of Women in the Mass Media.* She is also author of articles on news and culture and of the forthcoming *Making News: A Study in the Construction of Reality.*

JOSEPH TUROW is an Assistant Professor of Communication at Purdue University. He received his M.A. and Ph.D. from the Annenberg School of Communications, University of Pennsylvania. His published research has dealt with mass media organizations and mass media content as well as with people's uses for and gratifications from the mass media.